Gustav Mahler

Titles in the series Critical Lives present the work of leading cultural figures of the modern period. Each book explores the life of the artist, writer, philosopher or architect in question and relates it to their major works.

In the same series

Hannah Arendt *Samantha Rose Hill*
Antonin Artaud *David A. Shafer*
John Ashbery *Jess Cotton*
Roland Barthes *Andy Stafford*
Georges Bataille *Stuart Kendall*
Charles Baudelaire *Rosemary Lloyd*
Simone de Beauvoir *Ursula Tidd*
Samuel Beckett *Andrew Gibson*
Walter Benjamin *Esther Leslie*
John Berger *Andy Merrifield*
Leonard Bernstein *Paul R. Laird*
Joseph Beuys *Claudia Mesch*
Jorge Luis Borges *Jason Wilson*
Constantin Brancusi *Sanda Miller*
Bertolt Brecht *Philip Glahn*
Charles Bukowski *David Stephen Calonne*
Mikhail Bulgakov *J.A.E. Curtis*
William S. Burroughs *Phil Baker*
Byron *David Ellis*
John Cage *Rob Haskins*
Albert Camus *Edward J. Hughes*
Fidel Castro *Nick Caistor*
Paul Cézanne *Jon Kear*
Coco Chanel *Linda Simon*
Noam Chomsky *Wolfgang B. Sperlich*
Jean Cocteau *James S. Williams*
Joseph Conrad *Robert Hampson*
H.D. (Hilda Doolittle) *Lara Vetter*
Salvador Dalí *Mary Ann Caws*
Charles Darwin *J. David Archibald*
Guy Debord *Andy Merrifield*
Claude Debussy *David J. Code*
Gilles Deleuze *Frida Beckman*
Fyodor Dostoevsky *Robert Bird*
Marcel Duchamp *Caroline Cros*
Sergei Eisenstein *Mike O'Mahony*
Frantz Fanon *James Williams*
William Faulkner *Kirk Curnutt*
Gustave Flaubert *Anne Green*
Ford Madox Ford *Max Saunders*
Michel Foucault *David Macey*
Benjamin Franklin *Kevin J. Hayes*
Sigmund Freud *Matthew ffytche*
Mahatma Gandhi *Douglas Allen*
Antoni Gaudí *Michael Eaude*
Jean Genet *Stephen Barber*
Allen Ginsberg *Steve Finbow*
Johann Wolfgang von Goethe *Jeremy Adler*
Günter Grass *Julian Preece*
Ernest Hemingway *Verna Kale*
Langston Hughes *W. Jason Miller*
Victor Hugo *Bradley Stephens*
Zora Neale Hurston *Cheryl R. Hopson*
Aldous Huxley *Jake Poller*
J.-K. Huysmans *Ruth Antosh*
Christopher Isherwood *Jake Poller*
Derek Jarman *Michael Charlesworth*
Alfred Jarry *Jill Fell*
James Joyce *Andrew Gibson*
Carl Jung *Paul Bishop*
Franz Kafka *Sander L. Gilman*
Frida Kahlo *Gannit Ankori*
Søren Kierkegaard *Alastair Hannay*
Yves Klein *Nuit Banai*
Arthur Koestler *Edward Saunders*
Akira Kurosawa *Peter Wild*
D. H. Lawrence *David Ellis*
Lenin *Lars T. Lih*
Jack London *Kenneth K. Brandt*
Pierre Loti *Richard M. Berrong*
Rosa Luxemburg *Dana Mills*
Jean-François Lyotard *Kiff Bamford*
René Magritte *Patricia Allmer*
Gustav Mahler *Stephen Downes*
Stéphane Mallarmé *Roger Pearson*
Thomas Mann *Herbert Lehnert and Eva Wessell*
Gabriel García Márquez *Stephen M. Hart*
Karl Marx *Paul Thomas*
Henri Matisse *Kathryn Brown*
Guy de Maupassant *Christopher Lloyd*
Herman Melville *Kevin J. Hayes*
Henry Miller *David Stephen Calonne*
Yukio Mishima *Damian Flanagan*
Eadweard Muybridge *Marta Braun*
Vladimir Nabokov *Barbara Wyllie*
Pablo Neruda *Dominic Moran*
Friedrich Nietzsche *Ritchie Robertson*
Georgia O'Keeffe *Nancy J. Scott*
Richard Owen *Patrick Armstrong*
Octavio Paz *Nick Caistor*
Fernando Pessoa *Bartholomew Ryan*
Pablo Picasso *Mary Ann Caws*
Edgar Allan Poe *Kevin J. Hayes*
Ezra Pound *Alec Marsh*
Sergei Prokofiev *Christina Guillaumier*
Marcel Proust *Adam Watt*
Sergei Rachmaninoff *Rebecca Mitchell*
Arthur Rimbaud *Seth Whidden*
John Ruskin *Andrew Ballantyne*
Jean-Paul Sartre *Andrew Leak*
Erik Satie *Mary E. Davis*
Arnold Schoenberg *Mark Berry*
Arthur Schopenhauer *Peter B. Lewis*
Dmitry Shostakovich *Pauline Fairclough*
Adam Smith *Jonathan Conlin*
Susan Sontag *Jerome Boyd Maunsell*
Gertrude Stein *Lucy Daniel*
Stendhal *Francesco Manzini*
Igor Stravinsky *Jonathan Cross*
Rabindranath Tagore *Bashabi Fraser*
Pyotr Tchaikovsky *Philip Ross Bullock*
Dylan Thomas *John Goodby and Chris Wigginton*
Leo Tolstoy *Andrei Zorin*
Leon Trotsky *Paul Le Blanc*
Mark Twain *Kevin J. Hayes*
Richard Wagner *Raymond Furness*
Alfred Russel Wallace *Patrick Armstrong*
Simone Weil *Palle Yourgrau*
Tennessee Williams *Paul Ibell*
Ludwig Wittgenstein *Edward Kanterian*
Virginia Woolf *Ira Nadel*
Frank Lloyd Wright *Robert McCarter*

Gustav Mahler

Stephen Downes

REAKTION BOOKS

Published by Reaktion Books Ltd
Unit 32 Waterside
44–48 Wharf Road
London N1 7UX, UK

www.reaktionbooks.co.uk

First published 2025

EU GPSR Authorised Representative
LOGOS EUROPE, 9 rue Nicolas Poussin, 17000, LA ROCHELLE, France
email: contact@logoseurope.eu

Printed and bound in Great Britain by Bell & Bain, Glasgow

A catalogue record for this book is available from the British Library

ISBN 978 1 83639 030 5

Contents

Gustav Mahler, 1905, photograph by Friedrich Viktor von Spitzer.

Prologue: Mahler's Deaths/ Mahler's Lives

Mahler's Deaths

'Gustav Mahler' has died: again and again. Perhaps no other composer's posthumous reputation has been so repeatedly and remorselessly shadowed by their own death. Mozart, Tchaikovsky and Chopin may come close, but in the last the myth focuses on the sickness rather than the death, and in the first two death only really haunts the 'last' work (the incomplete Requiem and the Sixth Symphony, the *Pathétique*, respectively). The symbolic burden placed on an artist's death, particularly when it is perceived as tragically early, is oppressive. Suffering and fear of death, and the great questions of belief and afterlife, are mythologized as keys to both the life and work. In a relation of sorrow and sympathy, the compulsion is forever to repeat the dying moment in a sentimentalized necrophilia. The revered artist's death scene is not only spooled in endless imaginary reruns but perceived as darkly foreshadowed in their most precious works. Such deathly premonitions are relentlessly pursued, constructed and imagined because they are deemed to grant these works superior value. The artworks become runic relics of a life cut short. Like a death mask, they are scrutinized for secrets as a sphinx-like image of the lost artist.

'Last' works, such as Chopin's Mazurka in F minor (not his last work but mythologized as such because of its lamenting tone, harmonic complexity and endlessness), or those left cruelly unfinished (Mozart's Requiem, Mahler's Tenth Symphony), may be the prime exhibits in such memorialization. But funeral marches, laments and elegies proliferate in Mahler's output. Devotees of the death myth have therefore had copious encouragement. Even where these tones are absent, the reception of Mahler's music has filled in the gaps, perhaps most notoriously in the identification of (Gustav) Mahler with Thomas Mann's (Gustav) von Aschenbach in Luchino Visconti's film *Death in Venice* (1971), in which what was originally a wordless love song (the Adagietto of the Fifth Symphony) is cinematically projected as a seemingly endless dirge (and so the most famous aspect of Mahler's private life, his relationship with Alma Schindler, is morbidly displaced). The trope was repeated in Philip Roth's novel *The Human Stain* (2000) when the finale of the Third Symphony is played at the funeral of Coleman Silk: 'we were, at Mahler's mounting insistence, inside the coffin with Coleman, attuned to all the terror of endlessness and to the passionate desire to escape death . . . By the end of it, we were all crying.'[1] Works that were once affirmative expressions of the amorous (whether personal or celestial) become subsumed into a lexicon of human infirmity, heard as euphonious euphemisms for fatality. With his music ubiquitously interpreted (and valued) in this way, Mahler is perpetually confined to his deathbed; 18 May 1911 becomes Groundhog Day.

Perhaps Mahler only has himself to blame. 'I will die, in order to live.' So declares the first line of the final strophe of the Second Symphony, a line Mahler added to Friedrich Gottlieb Klopstock's 'Auferstehung' ('Resurrection'), which he had heard sung at a memorial service for the conductor Hans von Bülow in Hamburg (29 March 1894) and inspired him to overcome a creative hiatus and complete his symphony. Concerning the symphony's finale, Mahler wrote in urgent tones to the composer and critic Max Marschalk: '*What do you live for*? Why did you suffer? Is it all only a vast, terrifying joke? – We *have* to answer these questions somehow if we are to go on living – indeed, even if we are only to go on dying!'[2] The compulsion to 'go on dying' sounds unrestrainable.

Perhaps Mahler had no choice. His life was shadowed by death from childhood: of his thirteen brothers and sisters, seven died in infancy. He felt the loss of brother Ernst in 1875 particularly deeply. His adult life was punctuated by a brush with death due to serious illness in February 1901, the loss of his first daughter Maria (the beloved 'Putzi') in 1907 when she was just four years old, and the diagnosis of his heart disease. The psychoanalyst and Mahler biographer Stuart Feder wrote not only of Mahler's morbid fear of death but of his 'lifelong romance with death'.[3] In these terms Mahler's relationship with death is a necessary, unavoidable one of ambivalent psychological obsession.

Up to the debilitating effects of his final illness, however, Mahler was an energetic man of small, taut and muscular build who enjoyed vigorous physical activity. He was not beholden to continuous ailing, mewling or unremittingly despondent resignation. In the introduction to the first edition of her first husband's letters (1924) Alma Mahler wrote: 'the current popularity of sentimental biographies has led to attempts to portray Gustav Mahler as a very unhappy man. This is a fallacy. He was cheerful, active, energetic.'[4] Her caution against caricaturing Mahler as a habitual pessimist is worth heeding. This nuanced characterization is also suggested by his music. In his symphonies only the end of the Sixth is unremittingly bleak. Even the *Kindertotenlieder* (Songs on the Death of Children) end with tones of gentle comfort.

It is, nonetheless, apparent that Mahler experienced in his life and sought to express in his music, time and again, the pain of death's sting. In the legacy of Romanticism which Mahler inherited and transformed, art was widely understood as a form of self-expression and therefore also as a form of self-creation. Expressing the relationship of that 'self' to death therefore loomed as a crucial artistic challenge. In 'Our Attitude towards Death' (1915) Sigmund Freud wrote that it is 'impossible to imagine our own death'. In any attempt to do so we are present at a fantasy death scene as a spectator contemplating our own doomed stunt double. It is ultimately a futile attempt to understand – or perhaps to perform or give meaning to – our own mortality. However, in art, Freud notes, subjects can be created 'who know how to die'; art can form characters and expressions allowing a reconciliation with death, for 'in the realm of fiction we find the plurality of lives which we need. We die with the hero with whom we have identified ourselves; yet we survive him, and are ready to die again just as safely with another hero.'[5] An artist's self-created demise through the subject of an artwork (be it symphony, song, poem or painting) is one which can be fashioned to perform death better, to offer closure through a farewell more profound than the painful insignificance that, with dread, we fear will characterize our own 'real-life' death.

Mahler created multiple musical figurations of both death and the dying hero. In the first movement of the Second Symphony, originally titled 'Todtenfeier' ('Death Rites'), he carries the hero of his First Symphony to the grave.[6] In the scherzo of the Fourth Symphony 'Freund Hein' (friend death) 'strikes up the dance; death bows the fiddle quite strangely and fiddles us up to heaven'. This figure has been associated with Mahler's enthusiasms for the *Bilder des Todes* (Dance of Death) woodcuts of Hans Holbein the Younger (first published as a book in 1538) and Arnold Böcklin's self-portrait, *Selbstbildnis mit fiedelndem Tod* (Self Portrait with Death Playing the Fiddle, 1872), in which Death fiddles into the ear of an artist who tilts his head so as to better hear the music. The artist's brush is poised to respond with renewed creativity. Death may reap, but he also sows inspirational seeds. The brush with death brings new artistic life.

An important stimulus for the 'Todtenfeier' movement was Adam Mickiewicz's *Dziady* (Forefathers' Eve, 1832), a major text of Polish Romanticism which had been translated by Mahler's friend Siegfried Lipiner. Its hero, yet another 'Gustav', commits suicide when his beloved Maria marries another. During the period of writing the movement Mahler reported to his confidante, Natalie Bauer-Lechner, that he had a disturbing dream in which 'he saw himself lying dead on a bier under heaps of wreaths and flowers.' (The bouquets were from the 1888 performance of Mahler's completion of Carl Maria von Weber's opera *Die drei Pintos* (The Three Pintos): Mahler had fallen in love with, and planned at one moment to elope with, Marion, the wife of Weber's grandson.) Natalie cites the dream alongside an account of Mahler seeing

Hans Holbein the Younger, *Dance of Death: The Old Woman*, *c.* 1526, woodcut.

himself as a dark doppelgänger during the composition of *Das klagende Lied* (The Song of Lamentation, 1878–80) as an example of the 'agonies of creation'.[7]

It is striking that in both visions Mahler is observing a deathly double of himself. A draft programme for the Second Symphony, written in 1901 and surviving in Mahler's own hand, says of the first movement: 'We stand by the coffin of a well-loved person. His life, struggles, passions and aspirations once more, for the last time, pass before our mind's eye' – a moment which demands the questions 'What now? What is this life – and this death?'[8] Is this corpse an ersatz 'Mahler'? In the finale's use of the first person, who is the 'I' in Mahler's line, 'I will die so to live'? If the work of art is the death and resurrection of the author's double then the sympathetic listener is invited to die and rise with him. When Maureen Lipman's cameo character in the film of Willy Russell's *Educating Rita* (dir. Lewis

Arnold Böcklin, *Self-Portrait with Death Playing the Fiddle*, 1872, oil on canvas.

Gilbert, 1983) famously exclaimed 'Wouldn't you just die without Mahler?', she asks (rhetorically) the wrong question. We die *with* him. Again and again. In the words of Mahler's beloved Goethe: 'Stirb und werde!' ('Die and Become!').

From the Second Symphony onwards, for Charles Youmans, Mahler's 'mortality would condition everything he created.' Whatever the topic or mood, 'they all served in some way to help him come to terms with death.' Youmans somewhat uncharitably characterizes Mahler as a 'seething introvert' who 'crouched behind nameless heroic protagonists who nonetheless voiced authorial confessions'. These heroes function as stand-ins for a timorous composer: 'tragedies are at the centre of gravity in Mahler's creative work, and all the tragedies are his own,' writes Youmans. The life's musical project begins with the story of the six-year-old Gustav composing a 'Polka with Introductory Funeral March', a piece already revealing a divided personality, an aspect later manifested in the third movement of the First Symphony, where in a crucial creative decision the 'presence of death' is incorporated within the work's 'collage of autobiographical fragments'.[9]

Youmans adopts a rather extreme position. True, Mahler is reported by Bauer-Lechner to have said that 'to understand these works properly would be to see my life transparently revealed in them.' But contrary, if flowery, words come from Lipiner, who was intellectually very close to Mahler. In the introduction to his 'Todtenfeier' translation Lipiner argues that the personal experience of the artist may present an 'opportune cause' for creating, but the flames of a life's passion are not directly turned to art, for there is a move from the heart's heat to the 'warm sun' of the spirit, which would be 'always conquered by truth, never tyrannized by reality' and so 'convey what is unexpressed of life'.[10] Mahler similarly explained to Marschalk: 'The fact that the impulse toward a musical creation is an experience of the composer does not change anything, even if it were an event so concrete as to be able to be clothed in words.' Of his First Symphony, Mahler wrote: 'real life experience was the reason for the work, not its content.'[11]

In 1878 Lipiner argued (in terms which partly pre-empt Freud while also echoing Friedrich Nietzsche) that death is projected and overcome through tragic art, as the 'real' self is transcended.[12] Transcendent art evokes the absolute, the radical separation of life and art which was contentiously prominent in the cultural polemics of Mahler's life and times. Two tropes were sustained by those who held to the separation. First, the romantic image of the genius who is driven (for Wagnerians such as Mahler) by the deep-seated, deindividualizing force that the philosopher

Arthur Schopenhauer called the 'Will' and which music alone, as the only artistic medium not reliant on forms of representation, fully reveals. Second, and in part consequently, the idea of the autonomous artwork, of 'absolute' music. Guido Adler, the pioneering Vienna musicologist, insisted in his study of his long-time friend Mahler that the composer's everyday life was not significant for the interpretation and importance of his work. However, though Mahler, unlike Richard Strauss, wrote no *Sinfonia Domestica*, his position with regard to the then rather old but still contentious dispute between the claims of programmatic and absolute music was ambiguous. This is a crucial aspect of Mahler's relationship with Romanticism. Mahler's musical 'Heldenleben' ('Hero's Life', to use the title of Strauss's eighth tone poem, 1898) resounds with the legacy of Robert Schumann's distinction between the pictorial and poetic, with the latter entering the inner world of the soul. Mahler's symphonies also sustain aspects of the modern hero that Liszt proposed in an 1855 essay on Berlioz's *Harold in Italy*, where he contrasts the ancient epic (for example, Homer) with its modern counterpart (for example, Goethe's *Faust*); in the former the hero acts in the foreground of the artwork; in the latter there is internalization, as external events lose their importance and the number of characters generally meld into one. The primary subject is no longer deeds but deep feelings.

However, when that modernist martinet Pierre Boulez asked 'Gustav Mahler: Why Biography?' he remained convinced that Mahler's music 'does not exclude the biographical'. Mahler's works therefore often broke the seal (or dispelled the myth) of the autonomous artwork and sometimes dismantled the expectations of symphonic form. Lapsing into a 'disconnected string of uninvited confidences' would lead to potential incomprehension for the listener, argued Boulez, but there always remains a gap between life and creation, 'this shifting and elusive slide that operates between the incidents of an artist's life and their elaboration in . . . art'. Mahler's music offers an 'other' biography, one often richer and more attractive than the 'real' biography and 'which sends us rebounding with vexation back to the "imaginary" biography contained in his work'.[13] But the rebounds between these two 'lives' perpetuate. The challenge for a Mahler biographer lies in how to articulate the particularities and peculiarities of that relationship.

Mahler's Lives

On Mahler's insistence, nothing was inscribed on his tombstone other than his name. Contemplating Mahler's inscrutable grave, how might his life be effectively told? In our time, when biographical information can seem ubiquitous, super-abundant ('we swim in biography; we are sick with biography'[14]), how might another Mahler 'resurrection' be narrated in a critically illuminating form, one avoiding the trappings of eulogy, superfluity or hagiography?

Freud again offered cautionary words. A biography, he pointed out, can too easily be a parodic monument to our wishful relationship to the dead (Boris Johnson's *The Churchill Factor* (2014) springs to mind). Wishful because a biographer is insurmountably challenged by the task of describing an ultimately unknowable subject (the 'real' person, especially if they are dead, will always be elusive and chimerical). In the face of this predicament, the response can be either to accumulate the anecdotal, mundane and incidental or, in the search for significance, pursue deceptive fabrications, indulging in flattering flights of fancy that tell nothing of what is most valued, which is the life's work. In the first approach, the exhaustive collection of facts that make for a monumental biography is driven by the conviction that truth can emerge from the sum of all known information. But the character of the subject always transcends factual accumulation. In the second type of response, a biography constructs connections, patterns and motives. But its narratives are not neutral, slipping into the illusions of chronology and direct cause and effect. Freud argued that truth always eludes the biographer. A biographer's hopes of finding coherence, motive and causality are forlorn: the story of a life is authored by unpredictable instinctual impulse and shaped by the caprice and vicissitudes of circumstance.[15] Whatever the method,

Mahler's gravestone, Grinzing cemetery.

the 'Mahler' constructed as a biographical subject will always partially reflect the biographer, and only be a partially reliable substitute for the real man.

It is nothing new to argue that biography is best understood as a critical and interpretative act. But the case of Mahler, or 'Mahler' (the constructed, enigmatic image of our hero), makes that reflectiveness rather urgent.[16] He wrote no autobiography.

(When he supplied a very abbreviated life history in a letter to Marschalk in December 1896 he declared, perhaps to the despair of aspiring biographers, that 'a music-maker's life, after all, offers nothing in the way of external events – he lives *inwardly*.'[17]) However, two of his greatest heroes, Goethe and Richard Wagner, did write famous versions of their life stories. They can both help to develop a 'Mahlerian' understanding of the artist's life and how it relates to creative work. Wagner's *Mein Leben* (1870) tells more of how he wished to have lived than his actual life. His art, he declared, was ahead of life experience: indeed, life may retrospectively be rewritten to manifest what art already revealed.[18] (It is a position close to Oscar Wilde's famous aphorism from his *The Decay of Lying* (1891): 'Life imitates art far more than art imitates life.') The modern biographer might be inclined to scoff at Wagner's pretentions. But Mahler would have read and nodded in assent. A critical biography may seek to demythologize, but the significance of the cultural roles performed by such myths should not be underestimated, for they can greatly help in understanding the biographical subject and the aims of their work.

Another important biographical model for Mahler was Goethe. Late one warm summer evening in 1904, friend Erica Conrat joined Mahler on the terrace of his house overlooking the Wörthersee at Maiernigg. From their convivial discussion Erica recalled Mahler proceeding to

> quote the lines from the *West-östlicher Divan*, 'Das Lebendige will ich singen . . .', and then he spoke of Goethe's life, that it is really fragmentary, since he is a beginner, a beginner in a higher sense, a beginner in a sphere which we can never come to understand.[19]

Goethe's poem is misquoted. The couplet, from 'Selige Sehnsucht' ('Blessed Longing'), reads:

> *Das Lebendige will ich preisen,*
> *Das nach Flammentod sich sehnet*

> I will praise the living,
> That longs for death in flames

The error may be more likely to be Erica's than Gustav's, since Mahler's capacity for committing passages of Goethe to memory was widely reported. But the misquotation nonetheless seems appropriate (and therefore may be Mahler's), for it turns Goethe's exaltation into singing, into music: perhaps Mahler was purposefully rewriting, as he did with Klopstock's Resurrection poem when he composed the Second Symphony. The lines become a song of life and death, of a joyful yearning for a self-immolation which, rather than being suicidal, is the source of life's meaning and vitality, of how the heavenly life might be glimpsed in the earthly.

It is hard to overestimate the importance of Goethe for Mahler. Goethe's works held precious shelf space in Mahler's tiny composing huts, alongside those of Kant and Bach. On rereading, 'as I usually do in summer', the conversations with Goethe famously collected and published by Johann Peter Eckermann, Mahler wrote in 1908: 'I have been reading bits of it here and there, again and again, for decades, and I can say it is one of my dearest possessions ... At every stage of one's life one comes to this book as a different person.'[20] One Dr Richard Horn recalled of Mahler while they were staying with the Conrats in September 1906:

> when he found his apples for breakfast, lunch and dinner and the first volume of Bielschowsky's biography of Goethe at Dornbach and the second in Walfischgasse, he was in heaven; Goethe and apples are two things he can't live without.[21]

On an earlier occasion, in the summer of 1893, when describing the relationship of his life and work, Mahler overtly alluded to Goethe's autobiography. Bauer-Lechner, the faithful, doting companion of these years, reports him declaring:

> My two symphonies contain the inner aspect of my whole life: I have written into them, in my own blood, everything that I

> have experienced and endured – Truth and Poetry in music. To understand these works properly would be to see my life transparently revealed in them.[22]

'Poetry and Truth' (*Dichtung und Wahrheit*) is the subtitle of Goethe's *Aus meinem leben* (1811–33), in which Mahler, an avid reader of biographies, considered Goethe to have raised the level of the autobiographical genre to great heights. There is little doubt he aspired towards living a Goethean life, one that might be most effectively told after Goethe's literary example.

For Goethe, the self was something cultivated and developed through effort, will, learning and experience. He was also convinced of the vital role of historical circumstance in self-formation, its impact on a life's potential for achieving ambitions and how in turn this self can then have impact on history. That, for Goethe, was the mark of an artist of significance. Famously, he modelled this image of the self in literary form as *Bildungsroman*, a life story best told through recourse to myriad styles – the lyrical, epic, ironic, picaresque, tragic. The literary critic Eugene Stelzig comments that Goethe's *Leben* emphasizes the 'creative, the sensitive, the morbid, and even the pathological'; 'psychological truths' are 'dramatically enacted or poetically enunciated', with the result that the Utopian unity of self 'breaks down into fragment, doubt, irony'. Goethe tells his life story in 'distinctive imaginative forms', in stylized fantasies of eschatology and closure. These aspects of the artfulness which Mahler admired in Goethe's autobiography encourage a hearing of comparable techniques and meanings in Mahler's work. On Goethe, Stelzig concludes: 'Poetry facilitates telling the truth of the *bios*.'[23] Might Mahler's music do the same?

By contrast with Mahler's well-known veneration of Goethe, it has been less widely recognized that Mahler was also particularly taken by Laurence Sterne's *The Life and Opinions of Tristram Shandy, Gentleman* (1759–67). Sterne was highly valued by several of Mahler's favourite thinkers. Goethe called Sterne the 'freest spirit of the century'; Nietzsche upped the ante further, calling Sterne 'the freest writer of all time'. In *Shandy* Sterne famously presented a fictionalized life story through a narrative which is by turns digressive, ironic and comic. The reader is thereby exposed to the constant, irresolvable (but stimulating) problem of organizing and writing the content of a life. Peter Conrad heard 'Shandyism' in the way Mahler's music switches between the comic and tragic and subverts formal cohesion and narrative connection. Conrad points out that Mahler was torn between two romantic transformations of Sterne, one characterized by a renewed appeal of the redemptive and the other by an aspiration to universalism, the urge to embrace or speak to the world.[24] Both are vital aspects of his music. Can Mahler's life be understood in similar fashion, through the way precarious connections, dispiriting conflicts, cosmic ambitions and comic misunderstandings inflect his personal, creative and professional aspirations? Mahler certainly seems to have seen it as a model for coping: on noting the position of Sterne's *Shandy* among Mahler's 'favourite books' Bruno Walter continues that 'Mahler often said that without humour, the antidote for the poisons of life, he would have been unable to bear up under the tragedy of human existence.' Walter noted that conversational allusions to Sterne, alongside other literary heroes of humour light and dark, such as Jean Paul and Dostoyevsky, 'never failed to elicit his loud and hearty laughter'.[25]

A Shandyan life story is appealing, but perhaps the best literary model for a Mahlerian 'life' is that constructed in E.T.A. Hoffmann's none-too-pithily titled *The Life and Opinions of the Tomcat Murr Together with a Fragmentary Biography of Kapellmeister Johannes Kreisler on Random Sheets of Waste Paper* (1820–22). In this famous text a cat's biography is written on the back of the proofs of a 'Life of Kreisler', a fictional musician who is to some degree a doppelgänger for Hoffmann himself (who as well as a writer was an opera director and composer). Two 'lives' textually coexist, one ridiculous the other portentous. Hoffmann's satire on the biographical method, in which authenticity and unity are challenged by borrowings, quotation and digression, was greatly indebted to Sterne (the opening of the book's long title is an allusion to *Tristram Shandy*). Multiple narrative strands and fragmentations break down the cohesion sought in chronological succession. In the accounts of these 'lives', authorial and editorial intrusions abound; everyday distractions and mishaps proliferate. The mundane coexists with the sacred, the ludic with the tragic. Kreisler is an anguished alter ego, an artist swinging between the sublime and the ridiculous, a persona which itself can split into self and doppelgänger. A fictional biography of a musician is presented in counterpoint with a 'real' autobiography (of a cat), one which is a feline parody of the Goethean *Bildungsroman*, the journey to deeper wisdom and self-understanding. As narrative parallelisms break in and out of each strand, Kreisler's biographer is unable to sustain a coherently connected, chronological life story.[26]

Guido Adler noted not only that the young Mahler was especially fond of E.T.A. Hoffmann's work, but that the figure of 'Kapellmeister Kreisler left many traces in Mahler or, more accurately, provided many analogies, such as his over-excitement and lack of composure'.[27] Adler's comment is one of many examples where Mahler is identified with Hoffmann's Kreisler. Max Steinitzer, professor of music at the University of Freiburg, when recalling Mahler during his days as a young conductor in Leipzig (1886–8), said he was 'uncannily like' Kreisler as described in *Tomcat Murr* because of his deceptive wit and shifting manner.[28] Paul Stefan declared, in his pioneering life and work study of Mahler: 'Kreisler's resurrection on the plane of earthly life is Gustav Mahler.'[29] For Ernst Křenek, Mahler's youthful letters show debts to the 'rampant, tortuous and often ornate prose of Hoffmann'.[30] Bruno Walter, later to become Mahler's most trusted conducting disciple, wrote of his first meeting with Mahler in Hamburg in 1894:

> His appearance, his blazing, indeed fanatical artistic zeal, his intensity, his grotesque humour, all struck me as the incarnation of one of E.T.A. Hoffmann's fantasy figures. His incomparably passionate concentration while rehearsing and conducting, forever reminding me of his fantastical forerunner, Kreisler.[31]

The impression was clearly important because Walter repeated and elaborated the comparison in the account of this meeting in his later, longer study of Mahler:

> pale, thin, small of stature, with longish features, the steep forehead framed by intensely black hair, remarkable eyes behind the spectacles, lines of sorrow and humour in the face which, when he spoke, would show the most astonishing change of expression – the very incarnation of that Kapellmeister Kreisler – interesting, demoniac, intimidating.[32]

In his reflection on Mahler's personality Walter wrote:

> It is natural that, especially in his younger years, his heart went out to E.T.A. Hoffmann whose mind was so congenial to his. The poet's glowing imagination, his buoyancy, his humour, and, not the least, the nocturnal side of his nature, strongly attracted him.[33]

The comparison continues with Mahler in later life. Polish pianist Sigismund Stojowski, describing Mahler when he was in the final part of his conducting career in New York, wrote:

> He seemed a fantastic figure cut out from some tale of E.T.A. Hoffmann, the Romantic poet-musician: the pale, emaciated face, the ascetic look behind the spectacles, a supremely nervous demeanour – though his manner was appealing in its directness and simplicity – bespoke a soul of ardour and unrest, the noble and uncompromising spirit of an artist-apostle.[34]

But for Walter there was another, more austere side to Mahler. In his 1912 essay, he recalls entering Mahler's office for their first meeting and being drawn to the reproduction of Giorgione's *Pastoral Concert* painting (now attributed to Titian, *c.* 1509) hanging on the wall. The monk at the keyboard, Walter writes, is 'lost to the world' while making music and 'appeared to me to throw new light on the essence of Mahler. Kapellmeister Kreisler faded into insignificance' as Mahler is identified with the monk's asceticism, 'a man drawn towards deepest suffering'; 'Romantic or ascetic, demon-artist or moral genius, my first impressions of the essence of Mahler swung between these contradictions' – a character Walter also heard in his works, for example the finale of the Second Symphony offering resolution in which 'the iridescent Kreisler had finally resolved the savagely beautiful, if painful, dissonances of his inner being.'[35]

If Mahler had written an autobiography, Hoffmann's 'Kreisler', Sterne's 'Shandy', Goethe's 'Goethe' and Wagner's 'Wagner' would surely have been his great models because each, in their different ways, presents a self-fashioning formed through multiple styles and strands of sometimes contradictory narration. For some, of course, Mahler wrote multiple autobiographies in his music. In 1905 his early advocate, Richard Specht, described the Third Symphony as a piece of 'musical autobiography, a diary in notes'.[36] The image persists. In his widely read 'Master Musicians' biography, Michael Kennedy calls Mahler's works 'among the most autobiographical music ever written': 'each of his symphonies is an extension of personality, an exploration of himself'; 'it is wrong', Kennedy concludes, 'to separate the music from the life.'[37] But his book *is* separated into life, then works. A more productive approach, one pursued in the chapters which follow, is to adopt a multi-stranded

Titian (previously attrib. Giorgione), *Pastoral Concert*, *c*. 1509, oil on canvas.

mode and topically organized way of telling Mahler's life, and weave it with complementary elaborations on his comparably multi-stranded compositions.

Kennedy's words may seem to sink into simplistic biographism. But the key words here are 'extension' and 'exploration'. In his music Mahler expanded and reflected critically upon the Romantic idea of artistic self-expression and the ironies of Sterne and Hoffmann, presenting the construction and deconstruction (the lives, loves and deaths) of authorial personae, the multiple voices of 'Mahler' in sometimes-dissonant counterpoint.[38] The result is a musical self-consciousness in which he sometimes punctures his work's fictional illusion and exposes its process of composition. This can be a protective or anxiously revelatory self-mockery (Youmans is not completely off the mark) involving a playful attitude towards the conventions of musical genre and the tensions between the humorous (dark, ironic or playful) and the catastrophic, with the prospect that profundity or deception may lie in both these things.

The domination of Mahler's output by nine (completed, numbered) symphonies has led to comparisons with the way Beethoven's Third, Fifth and Ninth, in particular, have become tied to the composer's supposed, mythologized, life and character.[39] On one level these symphonies were heard as autobiographical, but on another as Universal: in Beethoven's Fifth, A. B. Marx influentially argued, 'Beethoven's life experience becomes . . . the decisive fate of all mankind.' In the private, inward experience of Romanticism the listener identifies with this heroic life. But by the late nineteenth century this was a 'fiction of self-representation' that was readily exposed, leading to a tension, an anxiety, and a level of irony written into Mahler's post-Beethovenian symphonic narratives.[40] Hoffmann again provides an influential precedent. In his famous 1810 review of Beethoven's Fifth, Hoffmann in effect proposes a double self at play in the symphony's composition. He heralded the composer's 'controlling self', the 'rational awareness', his capacity for self-reflection in order to rule over the 'inner realm' – his 'I' which is the master of the inward expression.[41] In the creative process the initial enthusiastic inspiration is succeeded, or accompanied, by a critically reflective process which can lead to ruptures and oppositions. This is Hoffmann's irony, not as the Classical mode of the saying of one thing but meaning another, but a specific romantic form of irony, an attitude to life and art, summarized by Friedrich Schlegel as shifting between 'self-creation and self-destruction'.[42]

Gustav wrote to Alma describing Hoffmann's style as 'a source of light and inspiration for musicians'. 'If you will turn a sympathetic eye on Hoffmann's works,' he continued,

> you will find a new light on the relation of music to reality; for music, mysterious as it is, often illumines our souls with a flash of lightning, and you will feel that the only true reality on earth is our soul. For anyone who has once grasped this, what we call reality is no more than a formula, a shadow with no substance.[43]

These lines reveal Mahler following Hoffmann's double-sided idealism. First, a 'negative idealism' in which the 'sensory world is a shadow of a higher, ideal world', the 'unknown realm' which Hoffmann heard unlocked by music and has 'nothing in common with the external world'; second, a 'positive idealism', in which the artist aspires to a transformation or intensification of the external world, especially 'nature'.[44] The musical results may be only partly decipherable, allowing freedom to bring new meanings. Writing to Marschalk of his Second Symphony Mahler explained:

> the parallelism between life and music may go deeper and further than one is at present capable of realizing. – However, I am far from requiring everyone to follow me in this. I gladly leave the interpretation of details to each listener's imagination.[45]

Perhaps the most imaginative, controversial, even notorious interpretation of Mahler's life remains Ken Russell's *Mahler* (1974), a biopic presented as a series of flashbacks, fantasy scenes, memories and dreams. The film is wilfully tasteless, *faux* Freudian, wayward, even chaotic, but has been viewed as organized in a manner comparable with the musical form of the rondo, in which a recurring main 'A' section is Love (the love of Gustav and Alma) and the interleaving episodes are a series of deaths, including the death of Love.[46] Russell's shifts between reality and fantasy are as much interpretations of the music as commentary or exposition of the life. Within its set-pieces and fragments there are parodies of other films (including Visconti's *Death in Venice*, so that Russell's 'Mahler', portrayed by Robert Powell, sees an impersonation of Dirk Bogarde's 'Gustav') and (reflecting Mahler's practice of self-quotation) borrowings from Russell's own earlier works. Mahler and Russell therefore share comparable aesthetic sensibilities in the deployment of a range of stylistic strategies: the use of exaggeration, a pushing of the boundaries of taste and willingness to rewrite sources, including their own work (and also in their personal lives; for example both converted to Catholicism, if for very different reasons).[47]

One memorably provocative scene has Mahler seeing his own cremation, looking out from his coffin as his cortège passes a bust of Beethoven, first to the opening funeral march of his own Fifth (with its rhythmic allusion to Beethoven's Fifth, but now the 'heroic' mode of death is mocked), then to the juxtaposition of the lugubrious version of 'Frère Jacques' and klezmer-style music from the third movement of his First Symphony (death figured through darkly humorous distortions of the sounds of childhood memories). His coffin enters the crematorium's furnace (a literal Goethean 'flaming death') to what Leonard Bernstein (contentiously) identified as the rhythm of Mahler's faltering heartbeat in the first movement of the Ninth. The parallels are striking with the dream Mahler recalled from when he was composing his 'Todtenfeier', of seeing 'himself lying dead on a bier under heaps of wreaths and flowers'. Russell projects a fantasy death of Mahler which seeks to be more 'Mahlerian' than the composer's 'real' death. The freedom of imaginative interpretation which Mahler 'gladly' left to his listeners gives Russell a licence to kill. 'Gustav Mahler' has died again.

Russell's film asks how the content and character of Mahler's music might inform the ways of telling his life; how the music's own provocations can facilitate play with both the claims and the disclaimers of the biographer's art. And so, if the reader is inclined, the following chapters of this biography are like a Mahlerian symphony. The opening funeral march has now closed (but with 'Mahler' still alive in his burning coffin); a scherzo follows (the precocious, playful child, shadowed again by death); then two intermezzi (Mahler as reader and conductor); a pastoral slow movement (the composer in the countryside); an anguished amoroso (his love for Alma); and a cyclic Adagio finale (the end which takes us back to the beginning).

1

Mahler's Childhood

In creative work the only impressions that later bear fruit and prove decisive are those that one receives between the ages of four and eleven.

Mahler, 1905[1]

Men must again become like simple children if they want to open their eyes to what is to be seen in the full light.

E.T.A. Hoffmann, 1814[2]

The Lord God has many children
In his flowering pastures,
They play a strange game indeed,
It's life and often also sorrow.

Mahler, poem, mid-1880s[3]

Many of Mahler's close associates ascribed a childlike aspect to his adult character. Guido Adler, for example, when trying to identify those aspects of personality most important for the appreciation of Mahler's musical creations and interpretations, wrote, 'like a child he let himself be carried away by the moment' and described his 'feeling for fellow creatures' as 'childlike'.[4] Childishness was considered attractive, valued and crucial for understanding Mahler the man.

Mahler would have recognized the cultural legacies lying behind this characterization.[5] Childhood had long fascinated the Romantics. It became the idealized source of subjective development, the key initial aspect of biography told as *Bildungsroman*. The inevitable passing of childhood meant, for those who wrote on it, that it was interiorized, thereby occupying a central place within *Innigkeit*, a concept of self-reflective inwardness which was so important in German Romanticism. In the adult imagination the child becomes a fantasy, a figurative, fictional, and often sentimentalized, projection. In art and biography an upbringing became characterized as a site of both conflict and formation, a powerful conjunction of innocence and suffering, depicted in imagined scenes from childhood that blur fact and fiction, myth and memory. The autobiography of Mahler's beloved Goethe, *Aus meinem Leben*, was seminal in its emphasis on the formation of self through the experiences of childhood. Life is drawn as a development informed by crucial aspects of infancy and moving from poetized accounts of family life, its comforts and distresses, to self-reflective and self-constructing adulthood. This way of telling a life story was an inspirational example for later nineteenth-century analyses emphasizing the sustained significance of childhood. In 1893 Bauer-Lechner recalled Mahler declaring 'I am becoming more and more aware that it was the mental impressions and experiences I went through at that time . . . which gave form and content to all of my subsequent life and achievement.'[6]

Symbolic investment in the experiences of childhood (and perhaps the most important musical precursor for Mahler in this regard is Robert Schumann) not only inflected Mahler's adult self-analysis, it profoundly informed the characterizations of him as a man and artist by his close contemporaries. Richard Specht, for example, wrote in 1905 that 'it is impossible to understand his works' without taking into account his boyhood experiences. Specht here echoes Mahler, who himself once declared that

> Composing is like playing with bricks, continually making new buildings from the same old stones. But the stones have lain there since one's youth, which is the only time for gathering and hoarding them. They are all ready and shaped for use from that time.[7]

The relationship of an artist's childhood to their later work is, nonetheless, a controversial one. The impact of Freud on life writing is perhaps never so strong, or as contentious, as where analysis of the impact of experiences in an artist's early years is concerned. (Freud's essay 'Leonardo da Vinci and a Memory of His Childhood' (1910) is perhaps the most famous example.) Of special resonance with Mahler is Freud's 'A Childhood Recollection from *Dichtung und Wahrheit*' (1917), an analysis of the way Goethe writes in his autobiography about the impact of the death of siblings during his childhood. Mahler's life as a child was similarly shadowed by the pain of a series of childhood deaths.

Born on 7 July 1860, in the Bohemian village of Kalischt (now Kaliště), northwest of the Moravian town of Iglau (now Jihlava), in the predominantly German-speaking Bohemian-Moravian borders, Gustav was the second of fourteen children born to Bernhard and Marie Mahler between 1858 and 1879.[8] Their firstborn, Isidor, was lost in an unidentified fatal accident in her first year. Mother Marie was to see a further seven of her children die (two, Arnold and Friedrich, fell victim to scarlet fever on the same dark day, 14 December 1871). Even when they didn't die, it seems the children

Mahler's birthplace, Kalischt (now Kaliště), Bohemia; postcard issued in the year of Mahler's death.

might stage their own death as a pretence: once, as a six-year-old, sister Justine (the eighth-born, 15 December 1868, who lived to be nearly seventy) 'stuck candles all round the edge of her cot. Then she lay down and lit the candles and firmly believed that she was dead.'[9] Acting out one's deathbed is a particularly macabre form of play.

Mahler's experience of multiple sibling death was, of course, far from unusual. Infant mortality rates were still tragically high in late nineteenth-century Europe. Death therefore loomed not only as the inevitable end of life but as a permanently present memory of childhood. The autobiographical telling of a life story is initiated by the voice of the enduring inner child, and its refrain is the ambivalent memory of an irretrievable home in which love and belonging coexist with loss and suffering. Mahler's music has often therefore been heard as incorporating expressions of the child figured as inhabiting a world of both innocent play and emotional vulnerability, as an immanent component of an adult self that, 'exiled' from the world of the child, is always pursuing meaning, belonging and closure through its evocation. Mahler did not shirk from expressing the bleakest aspects of this pursuit. The third movement of the First Symphony (partially inspired, perhaps, by Moritz von Schwind's image of *The Hunter's Funeral Procession* of 1850) is especially overt and dark in this regard, as the children's rhyme most widely known as 'Frère Jacques' is played in minor key and with a slow, deathly tread.

No biography of Mahler fails to mention a series of symbolically charged events from his early childhood years. The array of significant stories begins with the image of the family home in Kalischt into which Gustav was born, the 'lowly birth' which 'the composer himself was occasionally led to exaggerate', the 'mythical poverty of his own childhood'.[10] Mahler told Bauer-Lechner that he was born in a 'wretched little house', with no glass in the windows and a stagnant puddle in front.[11] Alma, however, was dismissive: Gustav, she insisted, 'did not come of a poor home, merely one of soul-destroying narrowness'.[12] The major biographers diverge on this issue. Henry-Louis de La Grange says Mahler's description of the Kalischt house is 'obviously romanticised',[13] but

Iglau (now Jihlava) town square, late 19th century.

Donald Mitchell believes 'there is no need to imagine that Mahler romanticized the poverty of his early days. All the evidence indicates that his home conditions, from every angle, were exceptionally depressing.'[14] Whatever the truth of the conditions of his birth, it was clearly important to Mahler. Humble nativities can easily be told as symbolic stories.

With their first son still a babe in arms, the Mahler family moved to the nearby town of Iglau in October 1860. Recent extensions of Jewish freedoms concerning residential mobility and property ownership allowed father Bernhard to move his liquor business to larger premises with better prospects. Bernhard possessed a strong business acumen and harboured ambitions of greater prosperity. Their first Iglau house was rented, but being very close to the large and bustling town square it was in a favourable location, and the business developed profitably so that in 1872 Bernhard was able to buy the larger property next door on Pirnitzergasse. The family budget improved to allow for a small number of servants. Despite spats with the local authorities over regulations on selling liquor, Bernhard became a prominent and respectable person in both town society and the synagogue.

It was a proud moment when, in 1873, Bernhard was made a citizen of the town (*Bürgerrecht*). Gustav's childhood friend Theodor Fischer recalled the certificate being prominently hung on the wall of the family home. Fischer also described a glass case full of ornaments and knick-knacks, a well-stocked bookcase and a Vopaterny grand piano.[15] Embourgeoised and assimilated, Bernhard embraced the values of *Bildung*, of improvement through (a German) education. He was always concerned for the completeness of Gustav's education, but when their young son began to show remarkable musical ability money was always found for his music lessons. Parental pride is reflected in the portrait of Gustav, aged about five, holding a musical score, an image which, due to his fear of the photographic equipment, shows a visage of childish trepidation.

But Bernhard could be a short-tempered taskmaster. Following his reluctance to be photographed, Gustav told Bauer-Lechner that his father 'had to take strong measures with me'.[16] Alma, in particular, promulgated an unpleasant image of Bernhard as a violent husband and father, claiming that the boorish Bernhard, lacking inhibition and concern for the feelings of his wife, was openly flirtatious with servant girls. Mahler insisted that his parents had been an unhappy match: Bauer-Lechner recalled Mahler saying his father and mother were 'like fire and water. He was all stubbornness, she gentleness itself.' Mitchell put Gustav's unhappy circumstances in strong terms, describing the young years as 'flawed by conflicts at every level; and nowhere did conflicts rage more fiercely than in his home, the very centre of his fractured universe'. There was, in Mitchell's words, an 'almost grotesquely contorted background to Mahler's youth . . . not even a Strindberg, Ibsen or Dostoyevsky could have contrived a family charged with a greater variety of high-voltage psychic tensions.'[17]

Mitchell paints a chilling domestic portrait. But there was also warmth. Gustav was certainly much closer emotionally to his mother. Marie, ten years younger than her husband and the most observant Jew in the family, had a character which charmed many. Adolf Fidelly (Marie's step-great nephew) described her as 'angelic',

Gustav, aged five.

with a charisma like 'a transfiguration that miraculously drew you to her'.[18] Gustav was devoted. When she was in poor health he suffered intensely. If Marie had a bad headache he would (as a three- or four-year-old) hide under her bed and pray. Mahler told Bauer-Lechner of a polka with introductory funeral march composed when he was six to please mother Marie, giving a long account of his attempts (undertook with entreaties for God's help) to avoid ink blobs on his manuscript in order to gain a small treat from her in return.[19] A spotless musical offering was required for a spotless rose.

Much has been made of child-Mahler's lost polka funeral march for Mummy. For commentators with psychoanalytical enthusiasms the striking duality of dirge and dance is irresistibly evocative. Its title suggests extreme contrast between sorrow and joy, horror and humour, mortality and vitality. It was offered as a creative attempt to express his torment when father mistreated her, as consolation to her for suffering bad health, marital strife and bereavement, and in particular (to move to more controversial psychoanalytic territory) in his role as replacement for her lost firstborn.[20]

Perhaps the most famous, indeed notorious, example of Mahler recollecting childhood domestic trauma emerged during a tantalizing and fleeting meeting of great minds, when Mahler consulted Freud in emotional turmoil concerning the state of his marriage to Alma. In what Freud's biographer, Ernest Jones, called a 'sort of psychoanalysis' during a 'four-hour stroll' in the Dutch city of Leiden on 26 August 1910, Freud was apparently impressed by the acuity of Mahler's psychoanalytical understanding.[21] Jones offered a gloss on comments recorded in a personal communication between Freud and his patient Marie Bonaparte in 1925. Bonaparte's unpublished text recounts Freud reporting:

> he [Mahler] told me the following story: His father was a peculiar person who harassed his mother with irrational, pathological jealousy. Young Mahler had often to witness such scenes. One day, while sitting in his room, he heard his father in the next room engaged in a violent scene with his mother. He eavesdropped by the door until he could bear it no longer,

Mahler's mother, Marie, *c*. 1870.

> and then ran out into the street. There was a barrel-organ playing a well-known tune: 'Ach, du lieber Augustin, Augustin', an old Viennese melody.[22]

In a 1935 letter to his former pupil and Mahler enthusiast, Theodor Reik, Freud confirmed his diagnosis of Mahler's Holy Mary complex and mother fixation (*Marienkomplex-Mutterbindung*), with the trauma of mother Marie's suffering and death (both Marie and Bernhard died in 1889) driving profound anxieties over loss and the seeking of worthy substitutes for her in all other love relationships with women. (Jones's account includes Freud saying to Mahler: 'I take it that your mother was called Marie. I should surmise it from various hints in your conversation' and that 'your mother evidently played a dominating part in your life.')

The interpretative usefulness of partially recalled and indirectly reported results of an ambulant and singular psychoanalytical consultation has been disputed. For Feder, there is sufficient in these recollections to demonstrate that Freud uncovered the 'child in the man', and that the traumatic experiences of Mahler's early years left him fearful of being abandoned, needful of maternal love.[23] By contrast, for Jonathan Carr, the outcome of Mahler's conversation with Freud was 'predictable' and the 'Ach, du lieber' recollection is 'absorbing but dangerous', readily leading to interpretations that tend to be either overcooked or reductive.[24] Dika Newlin is especially dismissive: Mahler is couched as a 'favourite victim of the necropsychiatrists' – in the 'psychobiography of the deceased, the subject is mute, they cannot talk back' and so, in the absence of dialogue, there is a dependence on conjecture.[25] Mitchell, who was always far more convinced by the validity of psychoanalytical insights, suggested that Gustav's 'jerking foot', which was observed by many in later years, may be a psychosomatic echo of his mother's lameness (a disability only noted by Alma, however), and that Mahler's recollections of childhood experiences were 'motivated by the most powerful of psychic tensions'.[26] There is little doubt, however, that the particular timbres of the barrel-organ were of especially powerful and sustained psychological resonance: in 1908, when Mahler heard the sound of 'such a lovely barrel organ' from the street below their New York apartment, he told Alma that it 'took me straight back to my childhood'.[27]

In later life Mahler clearly delighted in telling tales which emphasized his precocious musical talent. To the ever-attentive Bauer-Lechner he recounted:

> Apparently I was still a babe in arms when I copied little songs and sang them back. Then, when I must have been about three, I was given an accordion and by working out the notes of the things I had heard I was soon able to play them perfectly.

And on a visit to the maternal grandparents in Ledeč the very young boy discovered an old piano in the attic:

> I was still so small that I could only reach the keys with my hand held high above my head, but in this uncomfortable position and with my tiny fingers I plonked out all sorts of things I had heard, so recognizably that my parents and grandparents . . . were absolutely astonished.

The 'monstrosity', the 'jangling hulk', as Gustav called the neglected instrument in his recollection, was duly transported to Iglau on an oxcart.[28]

The results of his assiduous piano practice, 'to please my mother', were quickly impressive. Mahler recalled his public debut aged six, when his legs were still too short to reach the pedals (no documentary evidence of this event has been found). Musical tuition in the town was quickly sought. Especially influential among his early teachers was Heinrich Fischer (whose son was boyhood friend Theodor; in November 1872 Bernhard bought the house next door from Heinrich's widowed mother). Fischer was a prominent local musician, serving as music director of the Stadttheater and choirmaster of the Catholic Jakobskirche, where Mahler sang. Fischer opened up the riches of the concert musical repertory to his star student, and Mahler devoured the local library's collection of scores.

Gustav's progress was such that by the age of eight he was himself teaching piano to local children, though with very little patience and showing a short, sharp temper when dealing with untalented pupils (inherited shades, perhaps, of his father's flawed character).

In boyhood concerts he immediately established a dazzling local reputation. Following an appearance in October 1870, the ten-year-old Gustav was described by the Iglau press as a 'virtuoso'. It is not known what music he played on that occasion, but in a concert of 1872 it is recorded that he played Sigismond Thalberg's *Grand Fantasia and Variations on Themes from Bellini's 'Norma'*, and in November of that year, at a concert to mark the birthday anniversary of Friedrich Schiller, Liszt's Variations on the 'Wedding March' and 'Dance of the Fairies' from Mendelssohn's *A Midsummer Night's Dream*. Both are fiendishly difficult warhorses from the two leading piano virtuosos of the mid-nineteenth century (they had a celebrated keyboard 'duel' in Paris in 1837), teeming with fistfuls of notes and fierce technical challenges.

Mahler's performance as a school pupil was far less stellar. He first attended, from autumn 1866, the Imperial and Royal Primary School in the Brünnergasse, moving on to the Iglau German Grammar School three years later. He generally made poor progress. In one of his school reports from 1870, only in Mosaic Religion and Gymnastics does he rise above the satisfactory (a glimpse, perhaps, of his dual enthusiasm for both physical and metaphysical exertions in later life).[29] In the autumn of 1871, frustrated by his son's scholarly failings, Bernhard sent Gustav to the Neustadter Gymnasium in Prague. This meant his son leaving home, and accommodation was arranged with the Grünfelds. It was a very unhappy time. Gustav felt neglected, even abused. In one especially disturbing event he witnessed one of the older Grünfeld boys having boisterous sex with one of the maids. Gustav made the mistake of trying to rescue her from what he perceived as an attack. He was to recall this incident to Alma as the witnessing of the 'brutal love-scene'. His stay, nonetheless, allowed further opportunity to impress with his musical talents; he amazed his 'fellow inmates' with the ability to transcribe at first hearing anything they played on the piano.[30]

Bernhard soon released his son from his unhappy sojourn with the Grünfelds, but the completion of schooling proved to be a protracted affair. In September 1875 Gustav was still continuing his school education at the Iglau Gymnasium while already studying at the Vienna Conservatoire. In the summer of 1877 he failed to pass all his school-leaving examinations, being required to retake four subjects.

Outside the confines and conflicts of school and home Mahler's childhood provided happier recollections. His early musical encounters in Iglau's streets and surrounding countryside have become central to the image of child Gustav as possessing an inquisitive, sensitive and remarkably retentive ear. With his young playmates he delighted in watching local folk festivities and hearing popular songs and dances. Pinning down the precise musical character of the activities he witnessed is challenging: what is heard in Mahler's compositions are imaginative recollections and transformations which often enhance a supposed (and attractive) primitivism. Mahler pointed out to Bauer-Lechner how, in his song setting of 'Des Antonius von Padua Fischpredigt' (1893), the 'Bohemian music of my childhood home' is heard 'in its most crude and basic form, in the tootling of the Bohemian pipes'.[31]

The story is often told of Mahler following a military band to the town square and neighbours offering to take him home if he played what he had just heard on his toy accordion; so, perched on a fruit stall, he duly entertained the gathered folk.[32] Recalling another occasion, Mahler tells of being so protractedly transfixed in listening to the band music he encountered in town that he soiled himself. Debate continues regarding the extent to which he would have heard klezmer music in Iglau and its environs. There may have been fewer opportunities than in more eastern territories, but it seems probable that some Jewish music outside the rituals of the synagogue would have been part of his childhood soundscape. Serendipitous aural juxtapositions particularly delighted him. In the summer of 1900, while on a woodland walk, Bauer-Lechner reports Mahler being 'much disturbed by a barrel-organ' and then listening with 'delight' at the subsequent clashes with the sounds of a second barrel-organ and a nearby military band. On the next day, an even more cacophonous combination, an 'incredible musical pandemonium', was heard. Mahler declared: 'that's polyphony . . . even when I was quite a small child, in the woods at Iglau, this sort of thing used to move me strangely.' Of this kind of musical mélange, he told his companion, 'if you like my symphonies, you must like that too!'[33]

The idyllic noises of nature play a role in the final mythologized image of child Gustav, that of a chronic daydreamer. Alma wrote in her memoirs that 'indoors and outdoors he lived in a dream; he dreamed his way through family life and childhood.'[34] Bauer-Lechner noted that Mahler's

> absent-mindedness went so far that people had to seize him with both hands and shake him . . . This distractedness and dreaminess were held against him as major defects. Throughout his youth he was tormented by the constant demand that he should be like other children.[35]

This widely reported aspect of Mahler's childhood behaviour has been identified with two impulses: first, to escape the travails of parental squabbles and tragedies of sibling loss, and second, to 'concentrate and develop his inner potentialities'.[36] The former is unsurprising, and while the latter might be considered a somewhat romanticized interpretation, it is a characterization put even more strongly by Mitchell: 'in Mahler's dreaminess', he argued,

> we can see that genius, in the most adverse circumstances, will find means of self-protection, of subterranean development and nourishment – as an artist, we may say that he owed something positive and valuable to being thrown back, however roughly, on his own resources.[37]

As a young boy, in another frequently recounted incident, when once carelessly left alone in the woods by his father, Gustav remained there obliviously lost in his own thoughts until, as night was falling, Bernhard finally remembered and returned to collect his son. In her introduction to the 1924 edition of Mahler's letters, Alma wrote a rather poetic description of this episode, one which La Grange considered notably well balanced:

> This image of the lonely child waiting in the forest is both magnificently heartrending, and also wonderfully touching. Gustav Mahler always remained that child . . . always to wrestle with his dangerous mystical dreaminess. But with wonderful consistency his inner life always returns to the visionary childhood scene in the forest. Isn't his farewell, the *Lied von der Erde*, the mature fruit of this wistful withdrawal, the seed of which might have germinated in the waiting boy?[38]

Alma was convinced that the child-dreamer lies behind the symbolic, interiorized evocations of nature in one of Mahler's late masterpieces.

While it is sensible to be cautious about overplaying the interpretative significance of the characterization of young Gustav as daydreamer,[39] both Alma's poetic picture and Mitchell's tying of Mahler's behaviour to a 'subterranean development' in the child-genius, which was crucial for Mahler the mature artist, sustain a prominent trope. Freud again provides a controversial but resonant example in his conjunction of children's games, daydreaming and artistic creation in an essay of 1907, 'Creative Writers and Day-Dreaming'.[40] Freud begins with a relatively uncontentious identification of the first traces of creative activity in early child's play (*Kinderspiel*). More provocatively, he sees these games substituted by ludic and tragic fantasies central to adult artistic creativity, an 'as if' allowing deep-seated, distressing and traumatic childhood memories to inform the content of aesthetically pleasurable and emotionally moving artworks. The suggestive parallels with Mahler's work intensify when Freud speaks of 'psychological' novels in which the hero is 'described from within' as 'the author sits inside his mind'. Freud noted the 'inclination of the modern writer to split up his ego, by self-observation, into many part-egos, and, in consequence, to personify the conflicting currents of his own mental life in several heroes'. Recall how, as described in the Prologue, the symphonic 'subject' was often heard as a projection of multiple, self-reflective 'Mahlers'.

It is probably unlikely that Mahler read Freud's essay (though it was published in Vienna in March 1908), but Mahler's description of composition as being like 'playing with blocks [that] have all been lying about since childhood' suggests he would have found it at least intriguing. Feder's psychoanalytically enriched biography unsurprisingly pins its colours to the Freudian mast. Feder notes that Bonaparte and Freud shared the view that geniuses tended to be neurotic. Neuroses, therefore, determine the character of Mahler's creative process, with specific, highly charged childhood memories playing a crucial unconscious role: 'The boy Mahler heard this ['Ach, du lieber'] and for the rest of his life he reproduced in his music the strange contrast of a common hurdy-gurdy tune alongside one reminiscent of the violence of his father in the scene between his parents.' Bonaparte's recollection of Mahler's meeting with Freud reports that after the recounting of the memory of that traumatic incident, 'Suddenly Mahler cried out: "Now I understand something about my music. I have often been criticized for crude changes from the noblest melody to one that is banal."'[41]

Perhaps the juvenile juxtaposition in the polka-funeral march mentioned above already sounded something like that. The story Mahler made up, around the same time, for Beethoven's Op. 121a, ten variations on 'Ich bin der Schneider Kakadu', from Wenzel Müller's now forgotten singspiel, *Die Schwestern von Prag* (The Sisters of Prague, 1794), is also indicative. He constructed an imaginary biography of the titular tailor and his struggles, death and burial, complete with a parody of a funeral march. The young Gustav's interpretation was undoubtedly encouraged by the slow, melancholic, minor-key introduction and penultimate variation that Beethoven generated from Müller's otherwise sprightly, even comically couched, theme.

After telling Bauer-Lechner the story of how he wrote his funeral march and polka, Mahler listed a series of other pieces and fragments from his early youth: a sonata for violin and piano; a nocturne for cello; numerous piano pieces. None survive. There is no extant music by Mahler until his mid–late teens. Especially fascinating among the reported lost juvenilia is an incomplete opera with a libretto by school friend Josef Steiner. This work is widely assumed to be based on Ludwig Uhland's 'trauerspiel' *Herzog Ernst von Schwaben* (1818). Mahler may have played it in 1875 to Gustav Schwarz, the manager of a country estate whose musical manuscripts he had asked the young Mahler to examine. Composition of the opera might in part have been an attempt to come to terms with the tragic loss, on 13 April 1875, of his brother, Ernst.[42] The relationship with Ernst was particularly close, and his death is widely identified as having momentous significance as Gustav grew out of childhood into adolescence.

Four years later, in some especially heartfelt correspondence with Steiner, the depth and persistence of this death's psychological impact is revealed. With shades once again of polkas and funeral marches, Mahler wrote on 17 June 1879: 'The greatest intensity of the most joyful vitality and the most consuming yearning for death dominate my heart in turn, very often alternate hour by hour.' And a day later, on contemplating the Hungarian landscape in 'holy stillness' (a sanctified moment of daydreaming), the identification of the two Ernsts is made explicit, once again through an unsettling evocation of the tones of a hurdy-gurdy:

> Then the pallid shapes that people my life pass by me like shadows of long-lost happiness. – And once again we roam familiar pastures together, and yonder stands the hurdy-gurdy man, holding out his hat in his skinny hand. And in the tuneless melody I recognize Ernst of Schwabia's salutation, and he himself steps forth, opening his arms to me, and when I look closer, it is my poor brother; veils come floating down, the images, the notes, grow dim.[43]

In the recollections of childhood friend Theodor Fischer, we read: 'Mahler himself often stressed that, above all else, childhood impressions determine the nature of artistically gifted men.'[44] The relationship of Mahler's mature music to his experience during childhood has always been a major critical trope, right from Adler's claim that it is the 'scarlet thread', the continuous line of secret meaning, running through all his work.[45] Mahler's own reading in later life (to pre-empt the next chapter) offered distinguished support for this view. For Nietzsche, *Kinderspiel* is the highest form of play, a source of Dionysian energetics. A child's play is free because there are, as yet, no burdens of the past. In adulthood, while there is always the wish of rebirth into childhood, to momentarily recover or return to a first home, the games are not so uninhibited, they are always drawn from fragile memories. The loss of childhood is once more and repeatedly experienced. But the cycle continues with a revitalized childish spirit offering another new beginning. In *Thus Spoke Zarathustra* (1883–5) Nietzsche called this rejuvenation a new 'first movement'. When Mahler set Zarathustra's 'Midnight Song' in his Third Symphony, a poem in which mankind is told to pay heed to the depth of the world's sorrows, it is answered at the opening of the following movement by a choir of boys singing chirpy, childish onomatopoeia of heavenly bells, 'Bimm, bamm!' (the performance instruction is '*Lustig*', which is cheerful, almost funny). One can easily imagine a child-like glint in maestro Mahler's eyes as he summons the boys to sing. Their playful sounds can open the celestial gates.

Feder considers Mahler to be an artist who 'seem[s] to retain psychological access to childhood modes and meanings throughout life'. Recurring in life and work as a kind of leitmotif, reconfigurations of childishness confirm the psychological truth that 'the human phase of childhood in general is never completed in a terminal sense,' it is 'latent' and 'consistently revivable' in adulthood. Mahler's music demonstrates this when the 'auditory sensitivity' to multifarious sounds and musics, a potent trope in his own recollections of childhood, is manifest in the broken surfaces of his mature works, with interjections drawn from the sounds of childhood breaking through as if from another (deeper) source.[46] Some of the darkest and most potent of these configurations evoke the marches the young Mahler heard played by the soldiers from

Iglau's garrison, established after the 1866 Austro-Prussian War, whose most brutal conflict happened just over 110 kilometres (70 mi.) north of Iglau in the Battle of Königgrätz (Sadowa). The Prussian defeat of the Austrians would have dominated the local press and tavern conversations, with defeated soldiers a regular sight in town. The image resounds in the funereal marches of the doomed drummer boys in his last two settings of poems from Achim von Arnim and Clemens Brentano's early nineteenth-century 'folk' collection, *Des Knaben Wunderhorn* (The Boy's Magic Horn, 1805–8), 'Revelge' ('Reveille', 1899) and 'Der Tambourg'sell' ('The Drummer Boy', 1901).

Sweeter effects combine with dark shadows in the deceptively complicated constructions of childishness in the Fourth Symphony (1899–1900). Of the symphony Mahler once said to Bauer-Lechner: 'the voice of the child explains it all.' Childhood is here associated with a heavenly world. But all is not simple. The finale offers a lullaby, but it is one of adult artifice, during which no child is meant to nod off. The paradise evoked is that of the union of mother and child, but it is one which is forever lost in adulthood. Worldly noises intrude in the instrumental interludes, and the symphony's opening sleigh bells return in less innocent, more uncanny fashion.[47] The idealizing tendencies of nostalgia are resisted: tenderness is tempered with trepidation. Concerning the theme of the slow third movement's set of variations, which Mahler called 'divinely serene, yet profoundly sad', he told Bauer-Lechner that the melody carries 'St Ursula's smile', for 'in it, his mother's face, recalled from childhood, had hovered before his mind's eye: sad and yet laughing, as if through tears. For she, too, had suffered endlessly, but had always resolved everything in love and forgiveness.'[48] The struggles of the mother–child relationship are evoked in bleaker tones in his setting of the *Wunderhorn* poem 'Das irdische Leben' ('The Earthly Life'), of which Mahler commented darkly that:

> In life, everything that one most needs for the growth of spirit and body is withheld – as with the dead child – until it is too late. And I believe that this is characteristically and frighteningly

> expressed in the uncanny notes of the accompaniment, which bluster past as in a storm; in the child's anguished cry of fear, and the slow, monotonous responses of the mother.[49]

Finally, the public debut of Mahler's own childish voice may have been heard when, as a three- or four-year-old, he stood up to interrupt the solemn rituals of the Iglau synagogue by shouting and singing 'At se pinkl házi' ('Let the knapsack rock'), a Czech folk song about a wayfarer.[50] It would no doubt have caused considerable commotion and sharp parental rebuke. Toddler Gustav may have heard the tune lustily sung in his father's drinking establishment; it is now recalled in another example of his precocious ear picking up and retaining the musical sounds around him. The disruptive dissonance between a Czech country ditty and the sacred tones of the cantor strikingly resounds the complexity of Mahler's childhood 'Heimat' – a hybrid home reflected not only in his famous statements in adulthood around being Bohemian or German or Austrian or Jew, or all, or forever exiled as none of the above,[51] but in the fractured musical language of, for example, his Fifth Symphony (1901–2). Here Mahler begins by evoking (in the guise of another funeral march) Beethoven's own Fifth (the opening rhythmic motif sounds as synecdoche for German high art culture). But the symphony soon evokes disruptive voices, with intrusions of 'low' Bohemian rural naivety threatening to break the dominance of the 'high' German musical tradition.[52] The functional power of the 'German' symphony as the controlling host, in which representations of others from Mahler's childhood world (Bohemian folk, Jewish musicians, military bands) might be subsumed, stylized or assimilated, is severely challenged. The resulting potential for destabilizing inherited hierarchies is magnified in the interpretation by Uri Caine's jazz ensemble on *Urlicht/Primal Light* (1997), in which the opening post-Beethovenian funeral music becomes more evocative of a street marching band, and the second theme breaks into the klezmer melodic tones of a Yiddish fiddler.

Mahler never doubted the significance of childhood experiences for later creativity. In fact, as he grew older the conviction seems to have become stronger. This was perhaps driven by his experiences of love and loss as a father, and by intensified nostalgia for his own increasingly distant childhood. In a letter to Alma from Vienna on 6 June 1910 he wrote: 'The bells were ringing, and in the distance was a confused din of Sunday trouble-makers – harmonicas, hurdy-gurdies etc. It was as if my whole childhood was welling up within me! I can't tell you how much I adore it.'[53] And in an interview conducted sometime during the last weeks of his life for the Philadelphia magazine *The Etude* he is reported as saying:

> the musical influences which surround the child are those which have the greatest influence upon his afterlife [later life] . . . the melodies which composers evolve in their maturity are but the flowers which bloom from . . . the seeds of the folk-song in their childhood.

Or, more succinctly, as he continued: '"As the child is, so will the man be". So it is in music, that the songs which a child assimilates in his youth will determine his musical manhood.'[54]

2

Mahler the Reader

> Heavens, if I had no books!
>
> Mahler, 1894[1]

During the summer of 1875 Mahler was invited to the Moravian country estate managed by Gustav Schwarz (who knew one of Mahler's tutors) to sift through a dusty pile of scores. Greatly impressed with Mahler's abilities to play the virtuosic Thalberg pieces he found, Schwarz persuaded Mahler's hesitant father to arrange a meeting with Julius Epstein, professor of piano at the Vienna Conservatoire (the Conservatorium of the Gesellschaft der Musikfreunde). The audition went sufficiently well (Epstein also scrutinized some of young Mahler's compositions) that on 10 September Mahler was enrolled on Epstein's advanced piano class. (Epstein was to be a crucial influence and supporter; at the beginning of Mahler's second year at the conservatoire he successfully argued that the gifted but cash-poor student should be allowed to be on half fees.) Mahler thereby entered an institution whose prevailingly conservative ethos was led by the directorship of Joseph Hellmesberger Sr, who had been in charge since 1851 (and would remain so until 1893). Alongside his piano studies, Mahler took composition classes with Franz Krenn and harmony with Robert Fuchs. Both were resolute traditionalists. At the end of his first year, in June 1876, Mahler was awarded first prize in piano, performing one of Schubert's A minor sonatas (it is unclear which one), and he also won a composition prize. It was an auspicious start.

The new Musikverein building in Karlsplatz, *c.* 1870: prestigious home of the Vienna Philharmonic Orchestra.

Hugo Wolf also enrolled at the conservatoire in September 1875, and thus began a friendship with Mahler which would last several years. Along with their close student associate Rudolf Krzyzanowski, Wolf and Mahler moved rapidly around Vienna's cheap digs. Mahler was always short of money and needed to give piano lessons (and receive occasional food parcels from home) to keep the wolf from the door. It is not clear how many of Vienna's concerts and operatic performances he and his friends could afford to attend – the new Musikverein concert hall would not be cheap – and petitions were made to gain access to rehearsals taken by the newly appointed conductor at the Opera House, Hans Richter. After graduating, Krzyzanowski, who died the same year as Mahler, pursued a conducting career in Prague and Weimar. Wolf, a disruptive student, was dismissed from the conservatoire in his second year. Subsequently a prolific and highly innovative song composer, the final six years of his life were blighted by severe mental illness. He died in an asylum in 1903 at the age of 42.

Hans Rott, also within Mahler's circle of conservatoire associates though not a close friend, was a composer of great promise, but he too succumbed to mental illness while tragically young, dying in 1884 when only 25 years old. Some years later (in the summer of 1900), Bauer-Lechner recalled Mahler saying: 'What music has lost in him cannot be estimated. Such is the height to which his genius already soars in [his] First Symphony.' Mahler then hailed Rott as the 'founder of the new symphony'.[2] Rott began this work, the Symphony in E, while at the conservatoire during the spring of 1878 and completed it in 1880, only for it to gather dust for a hundred years. Long forgotten, the symphony attracted much interest after it was finally premiered in 1989, with several scholars observing striking similarities with materials in Mahler's symphonies.[3] Mahler seems to have known Rott's symphony soon after its completion: a recently discovered transcription of an 1882 conversation with Rott in the asylum mentions an event at which Mahler played the symphony 'beautifully' at the piano.[4] He returned to the score and studied it closely in 1890 and 1900. The extent of Rott's influence on Mahler's own symphonies has, however, been disputed. La Grange, for example, considered Rott's importance for Mahler's compositions to have been exaggerated.

At the end of his first summer holiday from the conservatoire Mahler was back in Iglau, and on 12 September 1876 he performed Schubert's technically and interpretatively demanding 'Wanderer' *Fantasy* D. 760 (teacher Epstein was a Schubert expert) along with two of his own compositions, including a piano quartet movement. On returning to Vienna, however, enthusiasm for his conservatoire studies seems to decline. Frustratingly, he also still needed to prepare to retake his remaining school examinations. Two school essay fragments from 1877 survive: in one, titled 'The Influence of the Orient on German Literature', Mahler observes that in German writers 'we find an attraction in what is strange,' and that 'the German mind . . . aspires to a comprehensive outlook.' It is a fascinatingly prophetic insight, given Mahler's soon to be developed eclectic reading and compositional outlook.[5]

In the autumn of 1877, having finally matriculated from the Iglau Gymnasium, Mahler enrolled at Vienna's university. He took courses in German literary history and ancient Greek art. Mahler attended lectures on music history by the influential critic Eduard Hanslick and classes given by the philosopher and priest Franz Brentano, whose efforts to reconcile Catholicism with modern science opened up intellectual syntheses of the kind which long fascinated Mahler. He also attended Anton Bruckner's university lectures, but without formally enrolling. On 16 December 1877 he heard the disastrous premiere of Bruckner's Third Symphony under the unskilled baton of the composer. But Mahler was very impressed. He worked diligently, with Krzyzanowski, to produce the 1880 piano reduction of the symphony. Bruckner tellingly dedicated his work to Wagner; for Mahler it represented a model for the symphony of the future, even if his own symphonies were to be quite different in style. (Surviving passages from Bauer-Lechner's unpublished diaries make it clear that Mahler's later opinion of Bruckner, for example of the Fourth and Fifth Symphonies, was highly critical.)

In his final conservatoire year (1877–8), composition took over from the piano as Mahler's main specialism. He had heard performances by Franz Liszt and Anton Rubinstein during the spring of 1877, an experience which may have convinced him that he was unlikely to make the highest level as a virtuoso. He did, however, play the first movement of Xawer Scharwenka's newly composed (and technically very demanding) Piano Concerto in B♭ minor, Op. 32, in an October 1877 conservatoire concert. Mahler graduated in 1878, winning first prizes in piano and composition (though his attempts to win the prestigious Beethoven composition prize, with music for the now lost operatic project *Die Argonauten*, was unsuccessful). The conservatoire offered no opportunities for Mahler to take formal conducting lessons, but plenty of occasions to conduct student ensembles were likely to arise. Mahler had been an ambitious, assertive but sometimes ill-disciplined and quixotic student at the conservatoire. But he was beginning to draw especially important intellectual sustenance from his university connections.

Mahler returned to Iglau for the summer of 1878, but Vienna held more opportunities to scrape a living and, of course, a far richer cultural, intellectual and social environment. So, he was

Mahler as a student, 1878.

back in the capital during the following academic term and once again attended some lectures at the university. He did not, however, formally re-register for the 1878–9 year, only enrolling, for the last time, at the start of the winter term of 1879–80. This is a period of Mahler's life for which the surviving documentary evidence is scant, but it was one of fundamental importance for his intellectual development. The university opened up to Mahler a vibrant world of debates in philosophy, the arts, politics and science, led by some of Vienna's most brilliant young minds. In such a stimulating milieu he read voraciously.

Mahler was a bookworm from early childhood. He told Bauer-Lechner: 'my most ardent desire was to read day and night without stopping,' climbing onto the roof to find the required solitude.[6] Later in life he declared to Friedrich Löhr that books are 'the only friends I keep by me! And what friends! . . . They become ever more intimate and consoling to me, my true brothers and fathers and lovers.'[7] His early literary tastes were strongly influenced by the books in the Iglau family home, the well-stocked bookcase that his friend Fischer confirms Gustav read at an early age,[8] as well as the collection held in the local library. Bernhard's aspirations of self-improvement and Iglau's character as a German cultural enclave both strongly inflected his available reading material. As a student in Vienna, Mahler may have been counting the pennies, but his own library would be taking shape under the influence of his student friends. (Mahler's library was lost when Alma fled Vienna in 1938.) According to both Richard Specht and Guido Adler, biographers who knew Mahler personally, such was the strength of Mahler's literary enthusiasm as a student that, fleetingly, a career as a poet held great attraction.[9] German Romantic poets – Eichendorff, Heine and Hölderlin – were, along with everything by Goethe and the philosophy of Kant, favourites among the literature he eagerly absorbed during his youthful years. This German canon was supplemented by Shakespeare and the Greek classics, both of which he held in the highest esteem throughout his life.

University intellectual circles offered opportunities for Mahler to deepen and widen his understanding of literature and philosophy. From 1878 an informal association with the Leseverein der deutschen Studenten Wiens (The Reading Society of German Students in Vienna, formed in 1871) brought Mahler into contact with several charismatic and influential figures, especially Engelbert Pernerstorfer, Victor Adler and Siegfried Lipiner. The political motivations of the Leseverein (Adler was founder of the Austrian Social Democratic movement) led to government censure and its enforced dissolution in December 1878. While it is unclear to what extent Mahler shared the group's enthusiasm for political activism, which had the causes of socialism and pan-German nationalism at its core, the society's passion for German Idealism, literature and myth was one he shared deeply. In these circles Wagner's new music and selections from his voluminous writings were discussed with unbridled enthusiasm. Wagner's notorious *Judaism in Music* had been recently reprinted (1869), but it is important to note that Adler and Pernerstorfer sought distance from antisemitism, and that Mahler would have been part of an assimilated Jewish cultural community. In the 1880s, however, the climate in Vienna was to change, as the political discourse became overtly racial and antisemitism more prominently pronounced.

Along with friends Wolf and Krzyzanowski, Mahler joined the Academic Wagner Society in 1877 (Guido Adler, slightly older than Gustav and of fellow Iglau upbringing, was a founding member). When Wagner was in Vienna during the 1875–6 season for performances of *Lohengrin* and *Tannhäuser*, the teenage Mahler was too shy to help his idol with his coat when they bumped into each other in the opera house lobby. Among Wagner's writings the recently published centennial essay on *Beethoven* (1870) and, later, *Religion and Art* (1880), were especially influential, the latter famously advocating vegetarianism. Mitchell notes with wry culinary reference: 'the thought that the salvation of the world might be accomplished, so to speak, by nibbling at a carrot, formed part of the lunatic fringe of Wagnerianism.'[10] At one gathering of these committed Wagner disciples a meat-free feast accompanied a concert during which Mahler performed at the piano.[11]

Considerable sections of Wagner's *Beethoven* present glosses and extensions of Schopenhauer, whose philosophy of music in *The World as Will and Representation* (1819) was a game-changer for Wagner when he read it in 1854, demanding a rethink of the function of music in his idea of the *Gesamtkunstwerk*, the total work of art. Schopenhauer distinguished the world of sensory cognition (the world of appearance in ideas and representations that form the basis of daily individual experience) from what he called the 'Will' – a universal and fundamental inner force beyond reason or representation, beyond the multiplicity of individual, material objectifications. The suffering of everyday life can only be assuaged by a negation of individual desires. Glimpses of, or an approach toward, this state of rest can be achieved through ascetic retreat (Buddhism was attractive in this regard) or inward aesthetic contemplation of art. For Schopenhauer, music held the highest place among the arts (and this is what excited Wagner, Mahler and much of the late nineteenth century, the French as well as the Germans) since music alone is a direct copy of the Will, because it is not based on forms of worldly representation. Of the worldly life, Schopenhauer was profoundly pessimistic. Walter recalls Mahler posing a series of fundamental questions inspired by his reading of Schopenhauer: 'How dark is the foundation upon which our life rests . . . What is the object of toil and sorrow? . . . Will the meaning of life be finally revealed by death?'[12] These questions seem deeply pessimistic (and famously it was the judgement of – the enduringly pessimistic – Theodor Adorno that Mahler was 'a poor yea-sayer'[13]), but Mahler found counters to such a gloomy world view in literature endorsed by Schopenhauer himself.

In one of his essays collected in 1851 Schopenhauer identifies examples of novels that approach the inner world, where literary art, in other words, moves closer to the condition of music. Here Mahler (who surely read it) would find affirmations of his wider literary tastes:

> A novel will be of a loftier and nobler nature, the more of the *inner* and the less of the *outer* it portrays . . . [Sterne's] *Tristram Shandy* has, in fact, practically no action at all; but how little there is in [Rousseau's] *La Nouvelle Héloïse* and [Goethe's] *Wilhelm Meister*! Even [Cervantes's] *Don Quixote* has relatively little; it is very insignificant and tends to be comical; and these four novels are at the top of their class. Consider further the wonderful novels of Jean Paul and see how much inner life they set in motion on the narrowest foundation of the outer.[14]

The paragraph name-checks many of Mahler's favourites. The value of comedy is especially interesting. Walter noted the importance of Sterne's *Tristram* for Mahler as a counter to Schopenhauerian pessimism: 'without humour, the antidote for the poisons of life, he would have been unable to bear up under the tragedy of human existence.'[15] Sterne widely influenced the fusions and juxtapositions of tragedy and comedy deployed in the work of several Romantic writers, for example in Jean Paul's *Siebenkäs* (1796–7), a psychologically double-plotted story of a hero which Mahler deeply admired. As Peter Conrad notes, in this novel Sterne's physical comedy is allegorized and ironized: Mahler's musical amalgamations of humour and pathos can be heard as intense sonic parallelisms of the procedures he read in *Tristram*'s romantic progeny such as Jean Paul.[16]

Rousseau's influence on Jean Paul was profound (born Johann Richter, he took his pen-name in the Frenchman's honour). Rousseau's famous notion of *rêverie*, a visionary moment of reflective inwardness that reveals a more complete self than is possible in the constant flux of existence, is an experience which inevitably brings to mind the young Mahler's propensity for protracted daydreaming. A more potent parallel for Mahler's mature music lies in the way the outer world and the inner, blissful dream are mediated in novels like Rousseau's *La Nouvelle Héloïse*, which are more or less autobiographical works in which art is informed by a life as revealed through inward visionary states and the outward contemplation of nature. Mahler also greatly enjoyed Cervantes's humour as a means of assuaging life's pain. An anecdote from Mahler's childhood recounted by Bauer-Lechner makes the point with appropriate amusement:

> One day, when he had hurt his finger very badly and cried for hours, refusing to be comforted, his father brought him *Don Quixote* to read. Suddenly his parents heard little Gustav roaring with such loud laughter that they thought he must have gone out of his mind.[17]

The pleasures of Cervantes's light literary touch were to remain important when Mahler was challenged by more adult sufferings.

Goethe would have held a privileged place on bookshelves in both the Iglau public library and the Mahler family home. Eckermann's *Conversations with Goethe* (1837, 1848) was regular summer reading for Mahler throughout his life. The *Conversations* were crucial for his understanding of Goethe's play *Faust,* whose closing scene he famously set in the second part of the Eighth Symphony. Mahler was also fascinated by Goethe's interests in natural science. The philosophical conflict between materialism and idealism was a perennial question for Mahler. He was especially taken with Friedrich Albert Lange's *Die Geschichte des Materialismus* (The History of Materialism, 1866), which argued that scientific method was not on its own completely sufficient in the pursuit of knowledge, for the key aspiration was to understand the relationship of matter and spirit.

Mahler's beloved Kant argued that great artists can establish connections from the natural world, that of sensory perception and understanding, to the transcendent, thereby moving between the physical and the metaphysical, from the phenomenal to the noumenal. Idealist philosophy proposed that behind the world of outer appearance lies a deeper, transcendent, other-worldly domain. E.T.A. Hoffmann, who was sceptical concerning traditional religious doctrines and more persuaded by an Idealist claim that the experience of the world must be transformed, heard this transport to the ineffable in Beethoven's symphonies. He believed that such music 'reveals to man an unknown realm, a world quite separate from the outer sensual world surrounding him, a world in which he leaves behind all precise feelings in order to embrace an inexpressible longing'.[18] It is a view rather movingly encapsulated in the final scene of Jim Jarmusch's film *Coffee and Cigarettes* (2003), in which two workmen on a routine coffee break discuss Mahler's setting of Friedrich Rückert's 'Ich bin der Welt abhanden gekommen' (1901) and, cupping a hand to their ears, hear it (or imagine it) as distant sounds: 'I am lost to the world . . . I live alone in my heaven, in my love, in my song!' The coffee is terrible; the music ethereal, transfiguring, other-worldly.

After Mahler had conducted Offenbach's *Tales of Hoffmann* (1881) in December 1901 he wrote to Alma despairing that the opera, lacking Hoffmann's 'spirit', offers only 'dregs'. Offenbach's failure was especially apparent to him in the third act, based on Hoffmann's *Rath Krespel* (1819). Gustav told Alma: 'Antonia does *not* die of consumption' (a disease which in the performance the singer Madame Shoder displayed through affecting 'that cursed cough so beloved of the stage'). Rather,

> It is the demonic principle of art, which pushes anybody who is possessed by it to relinquish his own personality; and in this case so penetrates a nature peculiarly disposed to give up the ghost that it snatches her out of life. One might say it is not the ghost she gives up but the body. Or – in one of those images you love so much – she takes her way into the realm of night, from which there is no return.[19]

In Mahler's purple prose there are echoes both of Goethe's 'daemonic' (the inner creative force) and Schopenhauer's image of life as suffering, relief from which is only possible through a withdrawal from the world, into Hoffmann's 'unknown realm'.

When, in his review of Beethoven's Fifth, Hoffmann clarified that Beethoven's music 'sets in motion the machinery of awe, of fear, of terror, of pain, and awakens that infinite yearning which is the essence of romanticism', he is identifying it with the aesthetic concept of the sublime.[20] It was Kant who offered one of the most influential definitions of the sublime, an experience of overwhelming force or magnitude which can be exhilarating but also shocking and deeply alarming. It is enjoyment conjoining with horror, with the present threat of chaos or annihilation. In the late eighteenth century (in both Kant and Edmund Burke) the sublime was counterpoised with the beautiful, a category identified with restraint, reason, formal cohesion and more pleasurable feeling. Mahler's reading of Jean Paul and Friedrich Nietzsche offered enticing alternative prospects for imagining the sublime in art.

Jean Paul analyses humour as the 'inverse' sublime in his *Preschool of Aesthetics* (1804). He argues that 'laughing matter' is 'derived from' but annihilates the sublime and takes the place granted to reason in the Kantian model. Jean Paul proposes an ironic position of 'humoristic subjectivity' in which juxtaposition of details of the finite world with the idea of the infinite provokes not a position claiming superiority over the world but a sympathetic response to the revelation of the whole world's folly. It contains a serious, darker element, 'bearing the tragic mask, at least in its hand' as Jean Paul puts it. For the greatest humourists, he said, 'we have to thank a melancholy people.' Jean Paul writes that 'after each pathetic strain . . . a comic relaxing' is desired and that this is achieved by a 'reductive seriousness' as the grand pathetic sensation is scaled down, into sensuous, individualized particles which 'cannot be gaudy enough in humour' and which might be pursued 'into trivial details'.[21] There are strong resonances between Jean Paul's description and Mahler's predilection for musical juxtapositions of profundity and triviality, and shifts between the gargantuan and the miniature. The importance of Jean Paul's writings goes far beyond the widely discussed relationship between Mahler's First Symphony and Jean Paul's *Titan* (1800–1803). Mahler's pilgrimage to Bayreuth in 1883 was to honour Jean Paul as well as Wagner, for that was where the writer lived his last years and was buried.

Nietzsche was revered by members of the Leseverein. His *The Birth of Tragedy* (1872), indelibly linked with its initial dedicatee, Wagner, and especially with *Tristan and Isolde* (1859), was of especial importance. In this book Nietzsche proposed a theory of art based on a dualism inspired by the Greek gods Apollo (sun god of perfect beauty) and Dionysus (god of the wildly licentious). In the Apollonian there is measured restraint, calmness and formal order. The Dionysian (the greatest expression of which he identifies with the music of Beethoven and Wagner) is an intoxicated state of unbridled ecstasy but also holds dangers of chaos and disintegration. Nietzsche argued that an Apollonian 'beautiful illusion' is necessary, for unrestrained Dionysianism would destroy us; it would be unbearable. In the third act of Wagner's *Tristan*,

Nietzsche heard beautiful illusion existing in a mutually intensifying dialectic with pain and contradiction. Intense erotic yearning coexists with an awareness of the horror and absurdity of existence.

The student Mahler was enraptured. In later years Mahler's enthusiasm for Nietzsche became more selective. By the early 1890s Walter reports that though Mahler (still enthralled with Schopenhauer) was impressed by the 'poetic fire' of Nietzsche's style in *Thus Spoke Zarathustra* (1883–5) he was 'repelled' by aspects of its thought.[22] Mahler became unsympathetic with the turn away from Wagner, nihilism (the notorious declaration of the 'death of god') and rejection of metaphysics in Nietzsche's late work. While the Third Symphony (completed in 1896) is Mahler's most overtly Nietzschean symphony (in the summer of 1895 he planned to call the whole symphony 'Die fröhliche Wissenschaft', the title of Nietzsche's book of 1882), it also reveals that Nietzsche is a stage, a step towards other messages. The symphony's first movement has been interpreted as a symbolic Greek tragedy drawing inspiration from *The Birth of Tragedy*, with the god Pan (who Mahler declared was 'awoken' at the opening) identified with Dionysus.[23] The fourth movement is a setting of Zarathustra's 'Midnight Song' – 'O Mensch! Gib acht!' ('O man, take heed'). But the symphony's message is subsequently delivered by angels. Ultimately this becomes a symphony *contra* Nietzsche as its trajectory is an approach towards a Godhead. In one of their early romantic meetings (in late 1901) Gustav urged Alma Schindler to burn her Nietzsche. He may either have been trying to protect her sensibilities (in *Zarathustra* Nietzsche infamously wrote that if a man visits a woman he should not forget to bring a whip) or to make clear that a Nietzschean wife would not suit his needs. But Mahler surely underestimated an intellectually inquisitive young woman. And this was not an outright dismissal of Nietzsche. Aspects of Nietzsche remain crucial in Mahler's later music, if less overtly than in the early symphonies.

Adler recalled that while Mahler 'read Schopenhauer and Nietzsche with partiality', he 'buried himself in Dostoyevsky's works'.[24] Dostoyevsky is a possible influence on the programme of the Third Symphony: Mahler's 'eternal love' in the final movement can be compared with the 'love sermon' of Father Zossima in *The Brothers Karamazov* (1879–80).[25] This was a favourite novel of Mahler's (it was published in German in 1884) because of its profound elucidation of the struggle between disbelief and a spiritual quest. Walter reports:

> A passionate spiritual relationship connected [Mahler] with the works of Dostoyevsky, who had greatly influenced his general view of the world. In the conversation between [the atheist] Ivan and [the believer] Aliosha from the *Brothers Karamazov* we find a fundamental expression of all that I have called Mahler's world-sorrow.[26]

The themes of Dostoyevsky's fiction were powerfully resonant and timely for Mahler: the problem of faith in an age of scepticism; the justification of the existence of God and hopes of redemption in the face of the world's seemingly endless suffering (the latter chiming with what he read in Schopenhauer).

Another attractive Dostoyevskian idea was entelechy, the force which drives the development from potential to fulsome being, the move to realization through ever more advanced, more nearly perfect forms.[27] That, in summary, is the narrative of the Third Symphony. Indeed, Adorno (who noted Mahler's 'impassioned relation to Dostoyevsky') argued that Mahler's symphonic forms are 'modelled on the novel'. Adorno continues: 'it is not only that Mahler's music so often sounds as if it were trying to tell something . . . the curve it describes is novelistic, rising to great situations, collapsing into itself,' after which he makes a specific comparison with Dostoyevsky's *The Idiot*.[28] Dostoyevsky's work was of sustained importance for Mahler. In the summer of 1909, while back in Vienna after his second season conducting in New York, Mahler said to Schoenberg: 'Make your pupils read Dostoevsky. That's more important than counterpoint.'[29]

Alma, who described Mahler as a Dostoyevsky 'disciple', used the same description for Gustav's talented but dissolute brother,

Otto (b. 1873). Gustav repeatedly attempted, with exasperating results, to support Otto in his studies and musical aspirations. Otto was a 'fanatic' for Dostoyevsky, Alma recalls, who 'philosophized about his approaching death, in the manner of the great Russian in the presence of an old woman acquaintance of Gustav'.[30] On 6 February 1895 Otto shot himself in the apartment of that family friend, Nina Hoffmann-Matscheko, Siegfried Lipiner's first wife (they had married in 1881). Matscheko published a German biography of Dostoyevsky in 1899. Mahler's sister Justine implicitly blamed her for not talking Otto, who had previously harboured suicidal thoughts, out of the terrible deed. No record of Gustav's reaction to this family tragedy is extant.

The exalted place Dostoyevsky held in Mahler's estimation contrasts with the low regard he had for much contemporary literature (Ibsen's *Peer Gynt* (1876) sits with Dostoyevsky as an exception). He forbade Alma to read Oscar Wilde's *Picture of Dorian Gray* (1891).[31] The eroticism which was a prominent literary preoccupation of *fin-de-siècle* artists was not to his taste. He did, however, come to recognize the achievement of Richard Strauss's operatic setting (first prod. 1905) of Wilde's play *Salomé* (first perf. 1896) and rated Frank Wedekind's *Frühlings Erwachen* (Spring Awakening, 1891; first perf. 1906) highly when he saw the play in 1907. But most recent artistic trends – naturalism, realism, symbolism, decadence – were allowed no space on Mahler's crowded bookshelves, and he set no poetry in these styles to music. Richard Dehmel (1863–1920), for example, who so widely inspired song settings by Schoenberg and others (including Alma), could not compare with his beloved Romantic poets.

Alma dismissed Lipiner, Mahler's intellectual confidant during his student years, as both a person and writer. In letters to Lipiner of 1898–1900, the years immediately before the fateful meeting with Alma, Mahler enthusiastically discusses *Adam* (1898), which Lipiner wrote as a prelude to a proposed trilogy, *Christus*. Mahler particularly hailed the work's Nietzschean quality – 'a truly Dionysian work!' – and for that reason considers Lipiner's poetry to be 'music'.[32] The young Lipiner was lauded by Wagner and declared by Nietzsche to be a genius. In 1878 the *Verein* published his *On the Elements of a Renewal of Religious Ideas in the Present*. Greatly influenced by Schopenhauer and Nietzsche, Lipiner posed the question of the relationship between human feeling and metaphysics, with tragic art (after Nietzsche) exalted, but also a place held in the work of the artist for religion, as manifest in the longing for something lying beyond the earthly experience. It is easy to see how much Mahler would have approved. The programmatic basis of the Third Symphony may have gained impetus from two of Lipiner's poems of 1880: 'Genesis', which relates to the first movement, and 'Hymne', to the finale.[33] (Previously, Lipiner's translation of Mickiewicz, the 'Todtenfeier', was crucial for the first movement of the Second Symphony.) But Alma's dislike of Lipiner, which seems to have been mutual, led to estrangement between the two men. This was clearly to Mahler's lingering regret: in early 1909 he wrote to Walter:

> I can't help thinking very often of Lipiner . . . I should like to know whether he still thinks the same way about death as he did eight years ago, when he told me about his very peculiar views (at my somewhat importunate – I was convalescent after my haemorrhage [*sic*]).[34]

On Walter's mediation (probably), a reconciliation was to follow.

Lipiner also held great interest in the work of Gustav Fechner. (Before meeting Mahler in Vienna he had attended Fechner's philosophy lectures in Leipzig.) Fechner was an expansively eclectic thinker, and in retrospect he can therefore seem eccentric. But his work shares many of the intellectual ambitions held by the writers Mahler most admired. Early medical and scientific training forms part of the multifarious foundation of his *Elements of Psychophysics* (1860), which proposed a 'psychophysical parallelism', a relation between mind and body, and between idealist philosophy and empiricism. Mahler read Fechner widely and enthusiastically. Walter wrote that 'Fechner's *Zend-Avesta* made a lasting impression upon him, and the same author's *Nana, or the Soul-Life of the Plants* [1848], was a source of real joy.'[35] Fechner developed an idiosyncratic view of the relationship of natural and metaphysical realms. All parts of the natural world are related to the body of God. Flora as well as fauna has feeling; but humankind needs to be told of this, for we are alienated from this natural unity. All this resonates in the second movement of Mahler's Third Symphony, 'What the flowers in the meadow tell me'. The 'learned satire' of Fechner's earlier work was also important for Mahler. It shared characteristics with Jean Paul. It could be serious, elevated and self-reflective, but also ludicrous, as logical and formal processes are undermined, and outlandish, as arguments are pursued, for example, concerning the shape of angels.[36] In the third movement of the Third, 'What the animals in the forest tell me', Mahler turns towards the absurd, incongruous and exaggerated in both naive and complex musical effects. Five of the symphony's six movements are to some extent humorous. Mahler spoke of his Third as 'pure humour . . . a great laugh at the whole world!'[37] Nietzsche's notions of a 'gay' or 'joyous' science (*fröhliche Wissenschaft*) also seem once more relevant.

The Third Symphony's finale, however, is dominated by an instrumental chorale, carrying echoes of Wagner's *Parsifal* (and, perhaps, also of the slow movement of Rott's Symphony in E major[38]). If this offers a kind of redemption, has Mahler, as Nietzsche famously condemned Wagner in *Parsifal,* prostrated himself at the foot of the cross? Given the Fechnerian inspiration, hardly. For Fechner, solutions proposed by traditional religion were of declining relevance. And the equally persuasive reading that the Third Symphony moves towards the goal of Dostoyevskean entelechy, the highest most perfect form, the moment when the human ascends to become Godlike, suggests the heretically *in potentia* unorthodox.

The Third Symphony also confirms that this end lies in the origin, in the awakening of life. Mahler shared with Lipiner (who was born in Polish lands), as well as others of his close intellectual associates from student years, a notably plural identity. Mahler's experiences during those years can give new light to his oft-quoted grumble (as reported by Alma): 'I am thrice homeless . . . as a native of Bohemia in Austria, as an Austrian among Germans, and as a

Jew throughout the world.'[39] Mahler's Viennese cultural milieu in the second half of the 1870s was founded on young intellectuals and artists whose complex ethnic identity was formed from belonging to German-speaking Jewish families whose origins lay in Slavic outposts of the Austro-Hungarian Empire. In this respect, the conglomeration of Jewish, Bohemian and German is what identifies Mahler as a late nineteenth-century 'Austrian'.[40] It is perhaps too simplistic to find in that multiple origin an overriding explanation for Mahler's breadth of literary, philosophical and scientific enthusiasms. But it must have strongly driven his desire to be both 'lost to this world' and to negotiate a complex and unique place within it, a double ambition which was one of his fundamental challenges to express as a composer.

Unfortunately, nearly all of Mahler's compositions from his conservatoire years are lost. The precise number of these works will probably never be known, but because the conservatoire kept records of its prize competitions we know of some of Mahler's class compositions, including a couple of prize-winning quintets and a Violin Sonata performed in Iglau in the summer of 1876, even if the scores will probably never be discovered. Paul Banks has made a case for the student Mahler being the composer of a Symphonic Prelude in C minor, which survives only as the manuscript of a piano arrangement made by a relative of Krzyzanowski, who themselves identified the music as being a copy Krzyzanowski made of someone else's work.[41] But all we confidently have left is a single movement from a Piano Quartet in A minor, and fragments – the opening of a scherzo for piano quartet (on which Alfred Schnittke elaborated in his *Klavierquartett* of 1988) and two incomplete song settings, including one of Heine's 'Im wunderschönen Monat Mai', a poem famously set by Schumann as the opening to *Dichterliebe*.

The surviving complete Piano Quartet movement (probably composed in 1877) has received mixed critical reaction. Given the lack of extant and extensive music from Mahler's student years it inevitably arouses much, sometimes disproportionate, interest. There are some hints of things to come: its dramatic oppositions, the play with generic and formal expectations and harmonic adventure, and it might be that this was the student work with which Mahler was most pleased and therefore did not destroy with other pieces of that period. In its adherence to Austro-German traditional features, however, the movement betrays that it was written in large part to gain his conservative composition teacher's approval.

The earliest completed songs that survive date from 1880 and are settings of his own poems inspired by his infatuation with Josephine Poisl, daughter of the Iglau postmaster. She first appears on the scene in spring 1879 and studied piano with Mahler during that summer. Letters written when Mahler was back in Vienna in September reveal that the feeling was increasingly ardent (at least on Gustav's side). In the early spring of 1880 Mahler turned to writing poetry on the suffering of the lover and the joys of nature, in a folkish tone foreshadowing the *Lieder eines fahrenden Gesellen* (1884). He set three of these poems ('Im Lenz', 'Winterlied' and 'Maitanz im Grünen') as part of a projected collection of five songs, and inevitably dedicated them to Josephine. The music adumbrates many mature Mahlerian traits: the use of stylized folk-like materials, striking emotional contrasts, the ambiguous image of nature and expressions of amorous yearning. In June 1880, however, Josephine's father wrote to his daughter's suitor warning Mahler off.

The major work of these years is *Das klagende Lied*. Mahler worked on its poetic text from early 1878 (at first under the title 'Ballade'). The music was composed in 1879–80. Three times, however, he substantially revised the score, including removal of the original first movement, 'Waldmärchen'. The resulting two-part form is the one most widely valued. But publication of the critical edition of the original three-movement version in 1997 led to more 'complete' performances, often of a hybrid, with the first movement combined with the later, revised versions of the second and third. One solution is to think of them as two different works. The three-movement version displays the grand, perhaps overstretched scope of youthful ambition and a struggle to accommodate diverse aims and influences. The later two-movement version shows more experience, even if many of the decisions were driven by the need to get it published and premiered (which wasn't to be until 1901).

The publisher Schott turned it down in 1891 and Mahler embarked on several further revisions from 1893.

The poet-composer Mahler modelled his text after the fashion of Ludwig Bechstein's *Das klagende Lied* and the story of *Der singende Knochen* (The Singing Bone) by the Brothers Grimm. Mahler pursued his favoured poetic style, combining folksiness with stylistic and formal borrowings from the texts of Wagner's music dramas. The story takes place in a mythic, ancient world of knights, virgin queens and minstrels. Part One reveals that whoever can find a certain red flower in the forest will gain the hand of the young queen; the younger of two brothers finds it first, but he is robbed of it and killed by the older one. In Part Two a minstrel picks up a bone from the buried body of the murdered youth and fashions from it a flute, which when played tells the story of fratricide. Part Three is the queen's wedding day; the minstrel plays the fateful flute; the guilty older brother takes the instrument but cannot prevent it singing of his crime; the queen collapses, as do the walls of the castle.

The work is generically ambiguous. Though the title denotes 'lied', it is most often called a cantata. But the appropriateness of this title is weakened by the strong dramatic narrative and theatricality, which combines with through-composed symphonic writing for large orchestral forces. The resulting generic hybridity is prophetic of works such as the Eighth Symphony. Leitmotifs are deployed in the Wagnerian manner, and there are some echoes of the later Wagner idiom. (Mahler heard *Götterdämmerung* in 1879; he, Wolf and Krzyzanowski were to drive their landlady to distraction by singing the work loudly and lustily in their tiny lodgings.) The strongest Wagner influence, however, is from the earlier operas (*Lohengrin, Tannhäuser*).

Mahler unsuccessfully submitted the score for the Beethoven Prize and, in summer 1881, for a scholarship from the ministry of culture and education, to be awarded to 'promising artists who do not have the means to continue their education'. Mahler's personal statement for the latter bid describes the breadth of his interests at the university as forming the education 'necessary for a modern artist'. If successful he would, he proposes, alongside undertaking further studies, complete his operatic project, *Rübezahl*.[42] During the winter of 1879–80, while immersed in composing *Das klagende Lied*, Mahler had discussed the idea of an operatic *Rübezahl* with Wolf and, rather jumping the gun on his friend, quickly drafted a libretto. Mahler's enthusiasm for *Rübezahl* was sustained and, after completing *Das klagende Lied*, he attempted to write music for it during 1881–2. Paul Stefan tells of Mahler composing music in winter 1882 that was 'bright humour, and the dark, biting, perverse style à la Callot'.[43] But progress stuttered in 1883. When expressing his frustration to Friedrich Löhr in October Mahler wrote: 'If you can send me something to read, some time, you will satisfy an urgent need of mine.'[44] His thoughts may have returned to the project in 1885, and he contemplated it again in 1890, when he asked Justine to send him the libretto.

No music survives, though Stephen Hefling thinks large stretches of Act One must have been sketched.[45] However, a copy of the libretto, in Mahler's hand, was discovered among Alma's papers after her death. Its title figure is a capricious mountain spirit found in the folklore of Silesia, Bohemia, and with more distant variants. The fairy-tale character appears in works by Clemens Brentano and Hoffmann, but Mahler's principal source was probably J.K.A. Musäus's *Volksmärchen der Deutschen* (1782–7). The story was also well-known in various versions for children, and in turning to it Mahler reflects the enthusiasm for folk culture he shared with those in the Pernerstorfer circle, particularly the interests in myth and legend pursued by a spin-off group, The Saga Society, of which Mahler was a founder member in 1881.

When Mahler showed his libretto to friends (including Lipiner) it met with a lukewarm reception. The text has been closely analysed by Hefling. Its themes are comparable with *Das klagende Lied* but the treatment is more humorous, even frivolous and farcical, a tone not really found in Mahler's later work. Of the two texts, Hefling considers that of the cantata to be more successful. Mahler seems to have come to the same conclusion. In 1896 he offered the *Rübezahl* libretto to Marschalk, whom he held in only modest regard as a composer, so he was obviously by then convinced that the opera wouldn't work for him. Indeed, operatic composition *en tout*. To Marschalk he expressed his view that the post-Beethovenian symphony and the post-Wagnerian opera were on 'divergent paths', even if they may to some degree cross-fertilize.[46] Mahler's destiny was to be a composer of symphonies and songs, while also becoming the leading operatic conductor of his time.

'Maitanz im Grünen', the last of the three songs composed in 1880 for sweetheart Josephine (it was published as 'Hans und Grethe' in 1892) may relate to the lost music for *Rübezahl*, while material from 'Im Lenz', the first song, is drawn upon in *Das klagende Lied*. The Poisl poems set in these songs were probably written before he had studied *Des Knaben Wunderhorn* (1805–8), the 'alte deutsche Lieder' compiled (perhaps, better, constructed, as the folk poems are freely modified and, in some cases, newly invented) by Ludwig Achim von Arnim and Clemens Brentano. It is not clear when Mahler first read this collection, which was dedicated to his hero Goethe. It may have been during these early student years. Whenever he first became familiar with them, he was greatly attracted by their 'folk' qualities, the juxtapositions of dances, love-songs and laments, and their expressive diversity – from pastoral idylls to dirges tinged with humour by turns bucolic and dark. Their poetic style is often very close to his own *fahrenden*. Mahler would no doubt have agreed with Nietzsche's verdict in *The Birth of Tragedy* that the *Wunderhorn* collection showed how folk song is a 'musical mirror to the world' which can be 'most intensely stimulated by Dionysiac currents', drawing its power from 'emitting sparks of images . . . their brilliance, their sudden transitions, their headlong rush'.[47]

From the late 1880s *Wunderhorn* was a major source of Mahler's compositional inspiration. In the years up to 1901 he set more than twenty *Wunderhorn* texts. They were also crucial for the first four symphonies. Their diversity is exemplified by the role played in the Second Symphony, in the striking contrast between 'Urlicht' and the Scherzo, which reinvents, in symphonically extended and voiceless form, his song setting of the *Wunderhorn* poem 'St Anthony of Padua's Sermon to the Fishes'. The holy man's desperation at his failed attempt to spread the truth is the subject of parody and

Des Knaben Wunderhorn, vol. III (1808), frontispiece and title page.

humorous mockery (his church is empty, so he turns to preach to the fish in the river). It was a predicament of rejection with which Mahler identified when, in October 1893, he conducted his First Symphony in Hamburg to decidedly mixed reception:

> I prepare my performances in the minutest detail, and with the utmost exertion of all my powers, until everything really works and is all of a piece. And for whom do I take all this trouble? For this flock of sheep who listen mindlessly and pointlessly – everything going in one ear and out of the other, just like the sermon of St Anthony of Padua to the fishes![48]

But less than four years later Mahler was to ascend to become director of what could claim to be the most prestigious opera house in Europe. Mahler would become the maestro.

3

Mahler the Maestro

> Looking back, I've often felt sorry for the poor fellows who were my first victims, and whose last breath and last energies I mercilessly extorted in my rehearsals.
>
> Mahler to Natalie Bauer-Lechner, 1893[1]

> Mahler was a great conductor, but he was also one of the most hated conductors.
>
> Ernestine Schumann-Heink, 1928[2]

It was a conducting career which began in humble circumstances. In 1880 Julius Epstein recommended Mahler to the impresario and agent Gustav Lewy. Having signed a contract with Lewy, Mahler gained the conducting position at a small theatre in Bad Hall for the May–August summer season. Unpretentious musical entertainment was served up for visitors to the health spa town in Upper Austria. Mahler would have about twenty musicians and young singers with which to work. While the precise repertory is unknown, he would have conducted a light selection of operetta and musical comedy. High art it was not, but starts must be made somewhere, and Mahler also needed the money. When the contract ended in mid-August he returned to Vienna, with no employment lined up for the coming season.

After a frustrating hiatus Lewy was eventually able to help Mahler find his next post. In September 1881 he went to the Landschaftlichen Theater in Laibach (now Ljubljana) for his first full season as a conductor. Compared with Bad Hall the repertory was a major step up, with music by Donizetti, Gounod, Mozart, Rossini, Verdi and Weber. But there was also a considerable amount of music of less substance. At his first performance, on 24 September 1881, Mahler conducted Beethoven's *Egmont* Overture followed by the now forgotten *Bürgerlich und Romantisch* (Bourgeois and Romantic, 1835), a comedy by Eduard von Bauernfeld. Performances of *Il trovatore* and *The Magic Flute*, which notably stretched the capabilities of the musicians under his direction, were critically well received. Gounod's *Faust* and Weber's *Der Freischütz* were also programmed, but the lighter end of opera and operetta still prevailed. The available instrumental forces were limited, and at times Mahler needed to resort to using bespoke simplified arrangements.

When his one-season contract at Laibach ended in April 1882 Mahler was once more at a loose end. In the middle of the 1882–3 season Lewy found his client another employment opportunity, as a vacancy suddenly arose at the Royal Municipal Theatre in the Moravian town of Olmütz. Mahler arrived in January 1883 and his first task was to conduct Meyerbeer's grand opera *Les Huguenots*. But with Mahler's appointment being made at such short notice the scheduled first performance was postponed, and some misgivings were expressed in the local press: was the young and inexperienced Mahler a good appointment? Just two days later Mahler took his place on the podium, with press notices highlighting his vitality during the performance. Two months into his contract, with the local premiere of Bizet's *Carmen* (March 1883), Mahler was hailed for overcoming the limitations of the theatre and singers at his disposal and for coaxing new levels of excellence from the orchestra. A performance of *Rigoletto* was similarly praised. But his demanding rehearsals were unpopular: the baritone Jacques Manheit recalled singers emerging 'in despair, declaring they were hoarse and could not work with the new conductor . . . we regarded him with total antipathy.'[3] Mahler was quickly learning both the skills and the challenges of opera conducting. A propensity for driving his musicians hard to meet his high, perhaps exorbitant, expectations was quickly emerging. He was becoming much admired by critics, but he felt restricted by the levels of musicianship in the pit and on the stage; he could not see them coping with Mozart or Wagner, both of which he removed from the repertory. The quality of the results that were achieved, however, led to Mahler being recommended (again with thanks to Lewy) for the post of second conductor at the Hoftheater in Kassel, where resources would be much stronger.

Having passed an audition in May, Mahler gained a contract for two seasons from August 1883. In July, before taking up the Kassel position, Mahler made his first visit to the Bayreuth Wagner festival. He described emerging out of the Festspielhaus (built to Wagner's specifications for the inaugural festival in 1876) feeling dazed and enthused: 'incapable of uttering a word, I knew I had come to understand all that is greatest and most painful and that I would bear it within me, inviolate, for the rest of my life.'[4] It was the first festival since Wagner's death in Venice on 13 February. Manheit recalled Mahler's despair at hearing news of his idol's demise: 'on my way to the theatre I saw a man running demented, weeping loudly, through the streets. With some difficulty, I recognised Mahler.' Having heard the previous day from Mahler that his father was ill, he continues '"In heaven's name, has something happened to your father?" "Worse, worse, much worse", howled Mahler, "The worst has happened. The Master has died!"'[5]

Mahler's first Kassel production was Meyerbeer's *Robert le diable*. Critics noted a combination of energy, communication and calmness. His schedule quickly proved to be hectic. Alongside the opera productions he was required to perform many additional duties, both trivial (including many dozens of nights of theatrical incidental music: he composed a suite of music, now lost, for a stage adaptation of Joseph von Scheffel's popular *Der Trompeter von Säckingen*) and more elevating, as with the parallel directorship of Münden Choral Society he gained his first opportunities at concert hall conducting. In February 1885, for example, he directed Haydn's *The Seasons*, and a performance of Mendelssohn's *St Paul* in June was a particular triumph. As in Olmütz, however, he worked his musicians to the brink of mutiny. To Bauer-Lechner in 1893, describing himself now as 'quite gentle today compared with what I used to be', he recalled:

In the first few years of my career as a conductor, when I didn't yet quite know how to go about things and made people rehearse eight hours and more a day, matters once deteriorated in Kassel to such extent that a real revolution threatened to break out in my orchestra . . . Looking back, I've often felt sorry for the poor fellows who were my first victims, and whose last breath and last energies I mercilessly extorted in my rehearsals.[6]

Mahler recognized that his busy combination of responsibilities in Kassel represented a good apprenticeship, but he was quickly frustrated as, holding the position of second conductor, he did not get first pick of repertory. He was allocated more Meyerbeer, Italian opera and Weber's *Der Freischütz*, but also works by composers of decidedly lesser importance (if Heinrich Marschner is marginal, then Louis-Aimé Maillart is long forgotten). Mahler's relationship with the principal conductor, Wilhelm Treiber, quickly became fraught, with Mahler retaining little respect for his boss. In a letter to Friedrich Löhr (19 September 1883), in which he already described his post as 'bondage', Mahler gripes that Treiber 'has an option on all the classics; he is the cheerfullest 4/4-beat man ever to come my way. I, of course, am the 'most stiff-necked young man in the world', who refuses to be initiated into the mysteries of art by him.'[7] When Hans von Bülow performed in Kassel in January 1884, Mahler was greatly impressed and sought escape from his 'bondage' by asking him for an apprentice position. The approach was fruitless; unsympathetically, von Bülow showed Mahler's letter to Treiber. In March 1885, however, having successfully applied for a post at the Leipzig Stadttheater, Mahler was finally released from the shackles of his Kassel contract.

With the Leipzig job not starting until the summer of 1886 Mahler was invited to take a short-term position from August 1885 as second conductor at the Deutsches Landestheater in Prague. It proved to be a highly valuable and successful step forward, if one with a keen political edge. (In one sense Mahler was hired as 'representative of an embattled official German culture' in the face of a 'flourishing' Czech National Theatre.[8]) Mahler finally got his conducting hands on the great repertory, including *Don Giovanni, Das Rheingold, Die Walküre, Fidelio* and Beethoven's Ninth. Angelo Neumann, a highly respected Wagner associate, had been newly appointed in early 1885 and had rapidly raised the game at the previously struggling theatre. (His colleague and fellow Wagner expert Anton Seidl had, however, handed in his notice and subsequently left to take up a post with the New York Metropolitan Opera.) The foundations were established for Mahler to direct performances of Mozart and Wagner that were critical sensations. On 21 February 1886 Mahler gave the concert hall premiere of *Parsifal* excerpts, as Cosima Wagner had granted Neumann special dispensation in gratitude for his work at Bayreuth. (During his first visit to the Bayreuth Festival in 1883 Mahler had heard Hermann Levi's *Parsifal*.) In a gargantuan concert Mahler conducted sections from Act One, followed by Beethoven's Ninth (from memory). Exhilarated by his reception, Mahler would have preferred to have stayed in Prague – a deteriorating relationship with Neumann notwithstanding – rather than move on to Leipzig that summer, where the roost was ruled by a supremely talented rising star, Arthur Nikisch.

Neumann had previously worked at the Leipzig Stadttheater, assisted by Seidl, before moving to Prague, but when Mahler arrived in the summer of 1886 Nikisch was clearly Leipzig's top dog. Mahler conducted operatic repertory in which he was by now becoming strongly assured (Meyerbeer, Weber, Gluck, and on his first night Wagner – *Lohengrin*), but probably the greatest public success came with his completion and performance of Weber's *Die drei Pintos*. Before the premiere, Mahler played the first act on the piano to Richard Strauss, who initially told von Bülow that it 'seems to me a masterpiece'. But von Bülow loathed it (he was never to like any of Mahler's compositions), and when Strauss heard the full versions of the second and third acts he quickly (and self-servingly?) changed his mind, citing 'terrible blunders'.[9] The first performance on 20 January 1888 (with Hanslick and Levi among the VIPs in the audience) was, however, widely greeted as a triumph, and news of Mahler's success with *Pintos* spread rapidly beyond Leipzig.

In the Leipzig theatre Mahler soon began to display a characteristic 'ruthlessness' in seeking control, sometimes beyond his then capabilities,[10] and once more working himself and his company to the bone. Nikisch, who was to go on to great things with the Leipzig Gewandhaus Orchestra and Berlin Philharmonic, quickly became a bitter rival. At the beginning all seemed rosy. Mahler wrote to Justine in late August 1886: 'So far, my position is very agreeable, which bodes very well. We will probably perform the Nibelungen [Wagner's *Ring* cycle] next year. If so, it will be divided between Nikisch and me. My orchestra is really one of the best in the world.' But within months Mahler's tone had changed. In early 1887 Nikisch succumbed to illness lasting three months, which meant he could not conduct the *Ring*. Mahler seized the opportunity. In a letter to his parents of 13 May he wrote:

> Tonight is the premiere of *Siegfried*. Before the dress rehearsal, the director, [Max] Staegemann, made a very flattering speech about me in front of the entire cast and orchestra . . . Nikisch, who ought to have come two weeks ago, then asked for another short extension of his leave since it is so painful for him to be at the Leipzig premiere of *Siegfried* and see someone else conducting it.

Ten days later, again to his parents, Mahler writes not only of how he is on the cusp of usurping Nikisch, but how his cosy relationship with Staegemann was a marked contrast with the one Nikisch had with the director:

> You will know from the newspaper that Nikisch has already returned. [The previous night he had conducted *Die Meistersinger*.] I am really now his equal . . . My relationship with Staegemann is still as close as it always has been. I eat there almost every Sunday and holiday, and overall I have a standing invitation there. They do not get along with Nikisch, and would be happy if he rather submitted his resignation.

By early June he declares,

> my position is a very dominant one. Even if Nikisch still gets to conduct the majority of the so-called 'significant operas' because of his seniority (which, by the way, will soon have an end too), it is still evident that my influence on things is stronger than his.

Mahler anticipates, with somewhat unappealing relish, his 'triumph over Nikisch'.[11]

One wonders if Bernhard and Marie would rather have had their son Gustav play his own trumpet a little less loudly. Mahler was acutely aware of Nikisch's abilities on the podium and wanted to better him. (Mahler's conniving actions and words did not, however, stop Nikisch promoting Mahler's compositions in later years, conducting the second movement of the Third Symphony with the Berlin Philharmonic in November 1896 and again with his Leipzig band in January 1897.) The relationship with Staegemann deteriorated, however, and in May 1888 Mahler resigned. He was once again unemployed. But his reputational stock had substantially risen following the successes in both Leipzig and Prague, where he was invited to return that summer to conduct his *Pintos*. During this brief return to Prague he met David Popper, cellist at the Budapest Conservatoire, who had been greatly impressed by Mahler's Weber completion. In cahoots with Guido Adler, Popper had hopes of enticing Mahler to the Royal Hungarian Opera in Budapest. As events transpired, Mahler was selected for the vacant position by the Opera's chief administrator, Ferenc Beniczky. Spurning speculative approaches from the New York Met, Mahler agreed a contract for two and a half years.

When Mahler arrived in Budapest at the end of September 1888, the Royal Opera, though established only four years previously, was already in artistic decline and in dire financial straits (the expensive policy of hiring star singers from abroad, though it pleased audiences, placed productions in deficit, and cuts to staffing were imposed just before Mahler started work). Mahler delivered a rousing inaugural speech to the company on 10 October. Beniczky proudly declared that all productions were to be in Hungarian, explicitly espousing a national responsibility for the opera house. It was a challenge that Mahler duly accepted, as he declared that performing operas in multiple languages (which had become common practice) was artistically unacceptable and that the talents of native singers should be developed. (Mahler could not speak Hungarian, however, and learned very little during his time there.) The simultaneous appointment of Ede Ujházy, an actor of high standing, as playmaster, and very soon afterwards of Kálmán Alszeghy as stage director, made clear the ambitions of developing the opera house's theatrical (and explicitly 'Hungarian') excellence.[12] A semi-*Ring* (*Das Rheingold* and *Die Walküre*) was performed, to wide acclaim, for the first time in Hungarian under Mahler's baton on 26 and 27 January 1889. Characteristically, Mahler had rehearsed the musicians very hard, an experience in marked contrast to the more casual culture he had inherited (inevitably, there were grumbles from sections of the orchestra).

Repertory in Budapest was dominated by French and Italian opera, but Mahler received his best critical reviews for the two Wagners and for Mozart's *Don Giovanni* (as was customary, titled *Don Juan*) and *Figaro*. Of Mahler's production of the latter in April 1889 (in Hungarian, of course) the *Nemzet* critic wrote 'Hardly anyone in the theatre could have recognized in today's impressive opera the old, shabby piece which had usually been listened to only out of reverence.' The critic was especially impressed with Mahler's remarkable attention to detail and ability to shift the focus of his direction seamlessly between stage and pit. The production of *Don Giovanni* in 1890 was marked by new emphasis on dramatic effectiveness and changes to long-held performance practices, not only rejecting the derided multi-lingual approach for a performance given solely in Hungarian, but the restoration of some passages routinely cut, and the accompaniment of recitatives by Mahler at a piano placed on the podium (previously, these recitatives had been just spoken). The *Budapesti Hirlap* noted that the result was that 'we heard Mozart's music in its complete stylistic purity, with absolute choral discipline, with fresh tempos and with all its subtlety of nuance. Mahler knows how to clean layers of dust from such a masterpiece and restore it.'[13] Famously, the visiting Brahms was inspired to rise from his seat and congratulate Mahler on stage.

The year 1889 was one of intense personal difficulties for Mahler, with the deaths of both parents (Bernhard in February, Marie in October) and sister Leopoldine, and a period of debilitating ill-health (his haemorrhoids requiring a painful operation). His spirits were, however, revitalized by a very pleasing final rehearsal for the premiere of his First Symphony (billed as a 'Symphonic Poem in Two Parts' with the later-to-be-discarded 'Blumine' included as the second of five movements) on 20 November with the Budapest Philharmonic. But Mahler's symphony, particularly the (then) fourth movement (which begins as a parody funeral march on the nursery rhyme known in German as 'Bruder Martin', but also widely known as 'Frère Jacques') and the finale (with its explosive, dissonant opening, which Mahler called a 'horrifying scream', and tumultuous climaxes), was bound to be provocative and, unlike at two subsequent performances (Hamburg, 1893; Weimar, 1894), the audience was given no programme. (The experience of the Hamburg performance led to significant revisions in orchestration and form, and by the time of a performance in 1896 in Berlin it had become the now familiar four-movement 'Symphony', minus 'Blumine', with no programmatic 'explanation'.) Mahler declared to Bauer-Lechner – with a hint of braggadocio – that the symphony was 'spontaneously' and 'daringly composed', but nonetheless, he admitted, he had 'naively' hoped it would meet with enthusiasm from the Budapest audience as well as the performers, indeed be as easy as 'child's play'. That it did not completely do so clearly skewed Mahler's recollection of the event as a total failure, whose effect, he said, was to turn him into a kind of social pariah. Mahler's deflation is understandable and Bauer-Lechner dutifully called the performance a 'ghastly fiasco'.[14] La Grange follows suit and declares that the symphony completely dumbfounded its audience, but Franklin's position, that the reception was more mixed and reflected the no-holds-barred arena of contest and politicization characteristic of contemporaneous critical discourse, is more judiciously nuanced.[15] The symphony garnered some positive comments, along with responses which reverberated with the sound of political axe-grinding by critics of nationalist and conservative bent who were unlikely to be sympathetic to daringly progressive music by an Austrian Jew who had taken over the podium at the Hungarian opera house.

Politicized interpretations of the First Symphony were surely encouraged by the fact that the rest of the concert (Cherubini, Mozart and a Bach arrangement) was led by the orchestra's regular conductor Sándor Erkel, son of nationalist Hungarian composer Ferenc (who had dominated the opera house prior to Mahler's appointment). In a long review published the day after the premiere in the German-language *Pester Lloyd*, the Moravian-born critic August Beer encapsulated the ambiguity of response to Mahler's symphony. Compositionally, he noted, Mahler 'frankly staggers us by his virtuosity in handling the modern orchestra', but this is deemed as taken to excess, resulting in passages of immoderate 'exaggeration' and incoherence. Beer noted that Mahler began to lose his Budapest audience during the provocative last two movements, but interestingly described the second section of the funereal fourth movement as evoking the 'Hungarian manner'.[16] For Mitchell, the use of violin glissandi in this passage was a 'tactical' gesture towards the home crowd as a recognizable reflection of the performances Mahler would have heard by Gypsy bands in Budapest restaurants.[17] But it was an allusion laced with caustic, darkly comic irony. As a parody of a commercial 'gypsy' style that, after its appropriation in, for example, Liszt's *Hungarian Rhapsodies* (published from 1851) and Ferenc Erkel's opera *Bánk Bán* (1861), was then considered 'Hungarian' national music (a myth later debunked by Bartók), the effect of Mahler's 'child's play' is unsettling and disturbing rather than offering a charm offensive. Theodor Helm repeated Beer's 'Hungarian' ascription (in the same journal) in 1900, but many later responses (famously reflected in Leonard Bernstein's interpretation) identified this same music as 'Jewish'. Gypsy and Jew function as interchangeable musical itinerants, both always vulnerable to conflicting cultural agendas of assimilation and abjection.[18] The reception of the premiere of Mahler's First Symphony therefore established tropes (excess, lack of formal control, striking if not perplexing use of popular idioms) and identity politics (conflations, contradictions, artifices, hybridity) which were to inform critical reaction throughout the rest of his career as a composer.

Bauer-Lechner described Mahler leading a 'very lonely life' in Budapest, and reported that, being so busy at the opera, he was frustrated at having no time to compose or play the piano. Mahler also told her that, after working long hours with Hungarian artists, he longed to hear German sung again.[19] His popularity in Budapest suffered a steep decline in 1890. There was continuing discontent from the orchestra about Mahler's unsparing rehearsal demands, and when Beniczky was replaced in January 1891, Mahler lost an important ally. The incoming, antisemitic Count Géza Zichy wanted to employ the Wagnerian Felix Mottl. Mahler resigned two months later and signed a contract with Bernhard Pollini, director at the Hamburg Stadttheater. (It was Nikisch, not Mottl, who was hired in Budapest, as the game of conducting musical chairs continued.)

Mahler was to stay in Hamburg for six years. At the beginning all was well. He found the north German city congenial and he initially had productive relations with Pollini, who had firmly established Wagner in the theatre's repertory. Mahler had quick success with performances of *Tannhäuser* and *Siegfried* in March 1891: local critic Josef Sittard wrote:

> Herr Mahler is a conductor who has in his command not only the notes in the score, but, what is more, the spirit of the artistic work; and he also possesses the gift of transmitting this spirit to the entire cast and carrying them along with him. There is no entry that is not cued by him, no dynamic shading that remains unobserved; Herr Mahler holds the reins in his hand with an energy which binds the individual firmly to him, draws him, we might say, with magical force into his own world of thought.[20]

Mahler conducted Wagner very frequently, including his first *Tristan und Isolde,* part of a further increase in the proportion of productions devoted to Wagner in Hamburg. In the summer of 1892 he travelled, for what was to be the only time, to London to conduct a series of opera performances, including *Fidelio* and a *Ring* cycle, in a collaboration between Covent Garden and Hamburg (this was the second London *Ring,* after Neumann/Seidl in 1882).[21] After seeing *Siegfried,* George Bernard Shaw described the 'energetic' Herr Mahler as receiving 'several curtain calls . . . he knows the score thoroughly, and sets the tempi with excellent judgement. That being so I hope he will yet succeed in getting a finer quality of execution from his band.'[22] Shaw's tempered enthusiasm (which he attributed more to the orchestra's limitations than Mahler's) contrasted, however, with more thorough acclaim from other critics. Herman Klein, critic of the *Sunday Times,* described Mahler's 'magnetic power', that he reminded him of Richter in his 'strong decisive beat', his 'absence of fussiness or superfluous action' and also through his 'unity of idea and expression'.[23]

A production of *Die Walküre* in 1895 was significant for the Hamburg debut of Anna von Mildenburg in the role of Brünnhilde. Mahler clearly recognized the soprano's talent (and, as we shall see, her physical attributes). He saw potential for greatness and was therefore especially demanding in his training of her as both singer and actor (she was reduced to tears on her first rehearsal with him at the piano).[24] As a devoted Wagnerian committed to the ideal of the total work of art, Mahler was keen to develop theatrical techniques of gesture and movement in his singers. In both Leipzig and Budapest he had already also developed strong aspirations to influence staging. A total work of art required his total control. Walter noted Mahler's 'astonishing agility' on the podium in Hamburg:

> In spite of his absorption in the purely musical work with singers and musicians, on the occasion of stage rehearsals with orchestra the dramatist within him watched with the hundred eyes of Argus, and nothing on the stage, whether connected with the

dramatic performance, with the lighting, or with the costumes, ever escaped him. Everything was under his observation at all times.[25]

Mozart also figured very prominently in Mahler's Hamburg years, especially *The Magic Flute* and *Don Giovanni*, as did Beethoven's *Fidelio*, Weber's *Der Freischütz* and Engelbert Humperdinck's hot-off-the-press *Hänsel und Gretel* (1893). While the Verdi repertory selections are unremarkable there were also more noteworthy performances of non-German opera. In January 1892 Tchaikovsky had planned to conduct the Hamburg premiere of his *Eugene Onegin*, but quickly recognizing Mahler's 'genius' on the podium he handed it over, with great success; and a winning production of Smetana's *The Bartered Bride* in 1894 was followed by the Czech composer's *Two Widows* (later in 1894) and *The Kiss* (1895).[26] In a now familiar pattern, however, Mahler's relationship with his boss, Pollini, deteriorated. Mahler held less control than he had in Budapest, and Pollini had differing priorities to the idealist Mahler. Pollini always had an eye for commercial profit, which drove the appointment of singers and choices of repertory. As ever, there are numerous recollections of tensions in rehearsal. Once again, Mahler's position became increasingly uncomfortable.

The death of von Bülow in Cairo in February 1894 led to Mahler taking over from him as conductor of the Hamburg subscription orchestral concerts for the 1894–5 season. All eight concerts featured Beethoven, and other notable works included Berlioz's *Symphonie fantastique* (which Mahler was to conduct relatively frequently through his concert career) and the second Hamburg performance of Bruckner's Fourth. But Pollini's authoritarian shadow extended from the opera house to the concert hall; the series was not a financial success, and Mahler's contract was terminated at the end of the single season. The series represented, however, a significant opportunity for Mahler to gain conducting experience outside the opera house.

Von Bülow, who in his later years held Mahler in much higher regard as a conductor than he did as a composer, possessed the highest Wagnerian conducting credentials, having been mentored by Wagner as a young man in Zurich and then entrusted with the premieres of *Tristan* (1865) and *Meistersinger* (1868; both in Munich). (Notoriously, his wife Cosima had already by then embarked on an affair with Wagner, whom she married in 1870.) Von Bülow's conducting innovations and his role in developing a post-Wagnerian performing tradition became important models for Mahler's practice. They shared a debt to Wagner's essays 'About Conducting' ('Über das Dirigieren', 1869–70) and 'On Performing Beethoven's Ninth Symphony' (1873), which Wagner wrote after conducting the symphony at Bayreuth in 1872.[27] When combined with the centennial 'Beethoven' (1870) these essays are crucial to Wagner's self-construction as Beethoven's true heir. In his essay on the Ninth Wagner recommends numerous reorchestrations and tempo modifications. Many of these retouchings were designed to ensure a realization of what Wagner called Beethoven's 'melos', the essential lines which were the main carriers of musical expression. Wagner never realized all his proposed Beethoven retouchings in performance. (The Bayreuth concert, the last time he was to conduct the Ninth, was only Wagner's fifth complete performance of the Symphony.) Paul Stefan considered that it was Mahler who realized Wagner's ideal of 'melos', which he judged to be the conductor's main task in bringing a work to 'life'. Both von Bülow and Mahler were reported as singing to the orchestra in rehearsal to convey how they wished lines and phrases to shape and 'breathe'.

Mahler's rethinking of the Romantic performing tradition was to go further than von Bülow, both in the pursuit of timbral and structural clarity and in attempts to realize, through spatial disposition of instruments on and off stage, a symphonic theatre. In a performance of the Ninth with the Hamburg Philharmonic on 11 March 1895 he placed an off-stage band of woodwind to play a march passage in the finale. Walter described the result as sounds moving 'as though from a vast distance into a victorious presence'. For Walter, the alteration was 'audacious', but though Mahler thought (like Wagner before him) that he was realizing Beethoven's unfulfilled intentions he did not try the same trick again. The links to Mahler's own vast symphonic soundscapes are, however, unmissable, and Mahler was to continue his practice of retouching the scores of Beethoven and other composers in preparation for performance, firmly in the belief that they moved the interpretation closer to what the composer intended.[28]

Mahler's work at the Hamburg Opera acquired a growing reputation among Wagner's disciples, with Mottl (conductor at Bayreuth along with Richter and Levi) reporting he had heard that he is 'very gifted, but he is unfortunately a Jew'.[29] So in January 1894 Mahler was asked to prepare Willy Birrenkoven (a tenor at the Hamburg Stadttheater) for the role of Parsifal at that year's Bayreuth Festival. Mahler agreed to do so in large part as a favour to Strauss, who was employed as an assistant to that year's festival. But by the summer Mahler was increasingly enthusiastic about Birrenkoven, and even more overwhelmed by *Parsifal*. Mahler attended the performances at the festival. On a postcard to Justine he wrote: 'Frau Wagner accommodates me really warmly, and these moments are very interesting.'[30]

Cosima Wagner had first encountered Mahler when she attended his performance of *Tannhäuser* in Leipzig on 13 November 1887. In a letter to Levi (19 June 1889) she recalled that 'the performance was worse than I would now have thought possible. But the impression that [Mahler] himself made on me was not wholly insignificant.' Mahler's contribution to the preparations for *Parsifal* in 1894 led her opinion of him to strengthen. She wrote to Levi in May: 'I am in constant touch with Mahler and have nothing but praise for his character and method.' Cosima subsequently invited Mahler to the 1896 festival, at which he heard Richard and Cosima's son Siegfried's conducting debut in a complete *Ring* cycle. Strauss considered the performance to be 'miserable', but Mahler was cunningly warm in his recollections to Cosima. (Eduard Reeser notes an 'almost obsequious' tone in Mahler's letters to Cosima. With the Jewish Levi conducting at Bayreuth did he hold out hopes of some day standing on that 'sacred' podium?) Cosima was suitably chuffed. On 31 October 1896 she wrote to Mahler:

Gustav Mahler, *c.* 1896.

'You have . . . described the performance of my son and the manner in which the creative processes were revealed to you, with an intensity one rarely encounters.'[31] Mahler asked Cosima to take on Anna von Mildenburg for the roles of Brünnhilde and Kundry; Cosima was impressed by the 23-year-old soprano when she went to her in December. Pollini agreed to Anna's temporary release from Hamburg, and after intensive preparation with Mahler, she performed Kundry in the 1897 festival.

When news broke in 1897 of a possible conducting vacancy arising at the Vienna Court Opera due to the failing eyesight of the director, Wilhelm Jahn, Cosima wanted her trusted Bayreuth interpreter Mottl for the post. When Mahler – not Mottl – was appointed she retained cordialities with Mahler and sought to use the relationship to further son Siegfried's composing career. She was happy for Mahler to conduct the Vienna premiere of his first opera *Der Bärenhäuter* (27 March 1899) because of her experiences of his success working with Mildenburg and Birrenkoven, and his sustained enthusiasm for Bayreuth. As a mark of her gratitude, she offered again to help with rehearsing Mildenburg for the role of Isolde. Cosima continued to promote the operas that followed from her son, but they were works of poor quality and Mahler was not to be persuaded to programme them, despite lengthy entreaties from Frau Wagner.

Mahler had begun to plot his departure from Hamburg from the middle of 1896. The Imperial and Royal Court Opera Theatre ('k. und k. Hofoperntheater') in Vienna was always the greatest prize in his eye (it was a strong candidate for the best opera house in the world). He mobilized useful friends and influential professional colleagues to drip-feed recommendations to the Vienna powerbrokers. Head of all Vienna court theatres was Baron Josef von Bezecny, and Lipiner made informal contact in autumn 1896. Friends from Budapest were urged to supply supporting letters. Mahler wrote to Ödön von Mihalovich, director of the Academy of Music in Budapest, on 21 December 1896:

> This is to request you to do me a favour on which the whole pattern of my future depends. The matter of the Conductor or Director post in Vienna is now acute. My name is among those receiving 'serious consideration'. Two circumstances stand against me. First, I am told, is my 'craziness', which my enemies drag up over and over again whenever they see a chance of blocking my way. Second, the fact that I am Jewish by birth. As regards this latter point, I should not fail to inform you . . . that I completed my conversion to the Catholic faith soon after my departure from Pest.[32]

In that last sentence Mahler was being strategically deceptive (not for the only time on this matter). He was not baptized as Catholic until 23 February 1897, at the Kleine Michaeliskirche in Hamburg. Křenek argued that this 'conversion' was part of the

> inner logic of [Mahler's] evolution. His intimate and persistent relation to the subject of death is from the outset determined by the idea of redemption and personal immortality . . . Mahler's work must appear as a most eloquent and consistent manifestation of Christian eschatology.[33]

Fischer, by contrast, considers the baptism to be a 'purely tactical step' to assuage the hindrance Mahler's Jewish origins would be to his ambitions in Vienna.[34] Křenek's view is certainly idealistic. A more nuanced position would be to see the decision as mainly driven by professional necessity, but also partly a stage in Mahler's sustained but ambivalent engagement with Christian theology.

The campaign continued in the new year, with a testimonial from Count Albert Apponyi (a highly influential political and cultural figure in Hungary) attesting to Mahler's success in Budapest. Bauer-Lechner rekindled her connections with the opera: via Natalie and Anna von Mildenburg, Mahler gained the support of the singer Rosa Papier, a close friend of Eduard Wlassack, who was a board member at the Hofoperntheater (though coming on to Mahler's side, he initially considered appointing a Jew to be impossible and urged Mahler to convert). It did Mahler's case no harm that Brahms (who died on 3 April 1897) was known to be an advocate.

But the deal was maybe sealed by a letter from Hanslick, dated 27 March, upon hearing that Jahn's time was up:

> The only two applicants worth considering are said to be Mottl and Mahler. But misfortune could be in store if – in my own humble opinion – Mottl were to become director . . . he loves and performs only Wagner, together with the whole of Wagner's evil imitators of German and French extraction . . . Conversely, it may be assumed on the strength of his achievements in Prague and Hamburg that Mahler will breathe new life into our opera without violating its classical traditions.[35]

It is, of course, a recommendation laced with Hanslick's well-known antipathy for Wagnerism and his advocacy of traditional musical forms, but also with a conviction that Mahler would enliven a dull opera house which had for too long been under Jahn's wilting baton.

On 8 April a brief notice appeared in the *Wiener Abendpost* announcing the appointment of Herr Heinrich Mahler [*sic*] as Kapellmeister.[36] Mahler's preliminary contract was signed on the 15th and on the 24th he conducted a triumphant final Hamburg concert – Beethoven's 'Eroica' and *Fidelio.* At the Vienna Opera he joined a team of conductors which (for the time being) remained under Jahn's directorship. Among them was Richter, with whom Mahler sought to smooth over any initial difficulties with a strategically ingratiating note. But Richter's reply on 19 April was cautiously, even tersely, worded: 'you will find me to be a benevolent and accommodating comrade in the cause of art.'[37] Mahler was irate. They were never to see eye to eye. On 8 May Mahler wrote with disdain on the second and third acts of Richter's *Meistersinger*.

Vienna's German nationalist presses were quick to condemn the choice of Mahler. *Deutsche Zeitung* denounced the appointment as another example of the 'Jewification' of German culture (and likely to lead to neglect of German operatic repertory). That not even Mahler's baptism was sufficient reflects strong anti-clerical

Vienna Opera House, 1890s.

sympathy and a desire to make clear the separation of 'German' Austria from Catholicism.[38] The *Reichspost* screeched its prediction of calamity 'as soon as Herr Mahler starts his Jew-boy antics on the podium'.[39] Mahler was, of course, unlikely to have been surprised by these reactions, but he certainly became anxious, questioning to close confidants whether this really was such a good idea. The wider political context only darkened when, the day after Mahler signed the opera house contract, Karl Lueger, of the nationalist, antisemitic Christian Socialists, was installed as mayor of Vienna.[40]

Mahler was to conduct his debut on 11 May with *Lohengrin*. Bauer-Lechner reports that he was ecstatic at the abilities displayed by the orchestra:

> I got further with them in one rehearsal than after years with all the others. It's true that the acoustics of the Vienna Opera idealize the tone in a quite unbelievable way . . . But the chief credit must go to Austrian musicianship: to the verve, the warmth and the great natural gifts that each player brings to his work.[41]

At the performance Mahler's supporters applauded vigorously from the audience, adoring students swarmed him at the stage door afterwards, and the critics were enthralled. A new age had dawned. Ludwig Speidel wrote enthusiastically (but with a fixation on Mahler's body that quickly became a critical trope, one often imbued with antisemitism):

> Mr Mahler is a small, slender, energetic figure, with intelligent, sharply chiselled features . . . The way he looks is the way he conducts: full of energy and subtle understanding. He belongs to that younger school of conductors, which, in contrast to the statuesque posture of the older Kapellmeisters, has developed more vivid use of expressive gesture. These younger ones speak with their arms and hands, with movements of the whole body.[42]

Theodor Helm in *Österreichische Musik- und Theaterzeitung* was glowing in his description of Mahler's control over all the assembled forces and attention to detail and tempi and favourably compared the interpretation with Wagner's own Vienna *Lohengrin* performance back in March 1876. Even though he also wrote for the nationalist *Deutsche Zeitung*, Helm was less politicized and placed more focus on the musical qualities by comparison with his colleague Hans Puchstein.[43] Mahler was delighted that the antisemitic critics such as Puchstein seemed to be either won over or were (at least for the moment) holding their tongues.

Jahn had programmed Wagner's *Ring* for August – a revival which had begun in April under Richter. Mahler started rehearsals of *Das Rheingold* and *Die Walküre* in early August, devoting particular time and effort to the ensembles (the Rhinemaidens and Valkyries). After the performances Mahler was once again greeted by cheering students, but as they were revivals, not parts of a new production, the performances were not especially noted in the press. However, Puchstein, in *Deutsches Volksblatt*, responded more broadly to Mahler's conducting of the *Ring* and what now seemed to be his likely ascent to the directorship: 'I regard it as obviously improper that a Jew should be appointed to head the first German opera institution' – though (in another barbed observation) he doesn't blame Mahler for taking the well-paid post. *Deutsche Zeitung* offered an unflattering comparison with Richter. This was a relationship which became overtly politicized and racialized, the Jew versus the Teuton.[44]

In a feuilleton published on 1 September in the *Österreichische Volks-Zietung* Balduin Bricht, observing that Jahn was 'exhausted and tired', asked what should be done about the directorship. Richter was an obvious candidate, but Bricht thought he 'suffers from an excess of genius', is 'not a worker' and has eyes more firmly fixed on work in 'Budapest, London, and perhaps even a little towards America' (Richter would gradually withdraw from Vienna, and he left in March 1900). Josef Scheu in *Arbeiter-Zeitung* also developed a comparative assessment of Mahler and Richter, noting that the latter did not have the enthusiasm to direct the required range of repertory and also that ultimately 'it is very questionable whether he would have condescended to take up the thorny office.'[45] The ailing Jahn had retained the title of director through the summer, but it was clear he could no longer fulfil the role. Mahler took over as deputy director in July, as Jahn (now nearly blind) remained on leave and the season was due to begin in just a few weeks. At the end of August Jahn finally agreed to his retirement, negotiations continuing until Mahler was confirmed as director on 8 October (with Wlassack again a key supporter). Mahler had achieved his aim, reaching the summit of his profession.

The Hofoperntheater traditionally celebrated the emperor's name-day on 4 October with a premiere. In 1897 that was to be Smetana's *Dalibor*. Smetana had figured quite prominently in Mahler's Hamburg repertory and both Franklin and La Grange say that the choice of *Dalibor* for this symbolic date was Mahler's.[46] But there is no evidence, and it may have been scheduled by Jahn, who had conducted Smetana in each of his last three years at the Vienna Opera.[47] Whoever had scheduled *Dalibor*, its performance under the freshly and controversially appointed Mahler in the autumn of 1897 raised especially intense political issues. While moderate German nationalists had previously accommodated

Smetana by pointing to his debt to German musical styles, the context had now changed as new language ordinances for Bohemia and Moravia in April 1897 had increased the official use of Czech in those territories and led to dissent and demonstrations in Vienna. Czech nationalists identified with Smetana's work, which was now more likely to be viewed as 'foreign' in Vienna, unwelcome at the 'German' institution. Many felt it was particularly regrettable that it was to be performed on such an auspicious day, even if the performance would (as usual) be sung in German. Czech–German tensions were therefore much greater than in the previous year, when on the emperor's name-day Jahn had also conducted Smetana, but a comedy, *Die verkaufte Braut*, not the tragedy of a legendary hero with a story easily interpreted as nationalistic. Unsurprisingly, at Mahler's *Dalibor* performance Czech parliamentarians were in plentiful presence.[48]

During rehearsals for *Dalibor* Mahler not only insisted on an intensive rehearsal schedule with both soloists and orchestra, he also supervised the scenic and costume designs. More provocatively, he recomposed the finale, the dramatic result being that the eponymous Czech hero, instead of meeting his end in battle, lives to enjoy freedom. As Bauer-Lechner wrote, Mahler then 'added about twenty bars which bring the work to a moving conclusion'. She remarks on the quality of the dramatic staging and casting, the results of Mahler's all-encompassing direction, and a 'brilliant first night'.[49] Hanslick represented the wide consensus that indeed *Dalibor* was an artistic triumph, with no mention of the political context of the rising German nationalist discourse, a case of bad timing for a worthy opera, a point which was noted by others.

Among the more moderate German nationalists, Helm in the *Deutsche Zeitung* still expressed admiration for the opera but jibed at the prominent Czech cheers after the performance. Others in that paper, however, were pointedly antisemitic in their nationalistic defence of ethno-German culture. Mahler's ambiguous relationship to that culture is revealed by his later comments on *Dalibor* to Bauer-Lechner, after a performance he gave on 5 November 1901:

> You can't imagine how annoyed I was again today by the imperfection of this work . . . He was defeated by his lack of technique and his Czech nationality (which hampered him even more effectively, and deprived him of the culture of the rest of Europe) . . . When I'm conducting it I'm practically beside myself; there is a lot more that I should like to cut and re-orchestrate, even re-compose – so unskilfully is it written, in spite of its many beautiful passages.

After which he lauds Mozart, Wagner and Weber as the 'three perfect German opera composers'.[50] What is interesting here (apart from again a manifestation of Mahler's desire to 'retouch' another composer's work) is Mahler's view that as a Czech Smetana can write gorgeous music but lacks the highest level of technical skill, which only training in the German tradition can provide. It's a venerable prejudicial trope: Slavic culture can be wildly beautiful but suffers from being untutored.

Mahler held a comparably conditioned opinion of the grand operas of Meyerbeer. Richter had often conducted Meyerbeer, but though Mahler did so only nine times in Vienna (*Les Huguenots* and *Le Prophète*) his first Kassel production was *Robert le diable* and he had made his debut at Olmütz with *Les Huguenots* in January 1883 (to Bauer-Lechner he recalled: 'it was a splendid performance – and I hugely enjoyed Meyerbeer!'[51]). For a production of *Huguenots* in Hamburg in 1889 he had cut the whole final act; in response to criticism he argued that doing so lent the opera greater dramatic effectiveness, and that pre-Wagnerian works did not suffer from judicious cuts because they didn't have the same degree of unity.[52] (The same aim of dramatic effectiveness lay behind his famously adding Beethoven's third 'Leonore' Overture before the final scene of *Fidelio*, a much more sacrosanct operatic text.) He nonetheless defended *Les Huguenots* against the Wagnerians who denounced it.[53] Mahler aspired to be a 'universal' theatre conductor, and in October 1902 aimed for a definitive Vienna performance of *Les Huguenots*. It was a commercial success, but the critics were less impressed.

In pursuit of a more reverential atmosphere, Mahler quickly sought to eradicate irritating aspects of audience behaviour in the Hofoperntheater. He wanted rid of the claque (paid fan clubs for star singers who would loudly cheer and applaud their every aria) and to ban latecomers from taking their seats until a suitable interval (Richard Hirschfeld noted that at Mahler's largely uncut *Tristan* in October 1897 audience members were still moving into their seats during the prelude[54]). A Wagnerian idealist aesthetic experience comparable with the Bayreuth Festspielhaus was now more realizable through his wider control of rehearsal, performance and production. The orchestra was mostly up to Mahler's aspirations (though there were habits he wanted to eradicate); the singers were sometimes brilliant, but more inconsistent. The admirable von Mildenburg joined the company in June 1898 and sang Brünnhilde to acclaim in a *Ring* cycle that autumn. But Julius Spielmann's debut as Mime was badly received: Mahler told Bauer-Lechner he hated his exaggerated caricature of Wagner's 'personification' of Jewishness – especially as this was Vienna and it played into the hands of the antisemites. He makes a striking comment of self-identification: 'I know only one Mime . . . and that is me! You would all be amazed what there is in the role and how I would want to bring it to light!'[55]

In September 1898 the players of the Philharmonic (which had the same performers as the opera house band) elected Mahler as its new conductor, succeeding Richter (a decision which predictably dismayed the antisemitic *Deutsche Zeitung*). Mahler's first programme for their concert series was Mozart's Fortieth and Beethoven's Third – the latter a bold, perhaps territorial, move as it was a work famously interpreted by Richter. Among many Viennese premieres, Mahler conducted Tchaikovsky's 1812 Overture and 'Manfred' Symphony, Strauss's tone poem *Aus Italien* and excerpts from *Guntram* (of Strauss's operas Mahler only conducted *Feuersnot* in Vienna; he admired *Salome* but it was banned by the Court Opera authorities). French and Slavonic repertory included Franck, Dvořák and Berlioz; in February 1899 he conducted the world premiere of Bruckner's Sixth. He remained in the post for nearly three seasons, each with eight regular concerts from November, which were always a sell-out. He withheld conducting his own work until the Second Symphony at his first so-called 'Nicolai' concert (April 1899), an extra event held at the end of the season to support the pension fund and named after the Philharmonic's first conductor, Otto Nicolai. If Mahler's main reason for not including his music sooner was apprehension concerning critical response then the wildly conflicting reactions that the Second Symphony raised in the audience at the Musikverein (the prestigious home of the Philharmonic) and the negative press reaction would do little to appease his anxiety.

On 18 November 1900 he conducted a performance of the First Symphony to dispiriting critical reception. Hanslick wrote that in the absence of a programme to guide the audience, the effect was 'puzzling incoherence' and (surely in allusion to Wagner's description of the dissonant *Schreckensfanfare* which opens the finale of Beethoven's Ninth) noted the work's 'horrific finale' (*Schreckensfinale*). Mahler the conductor was, however, a different matter for Hanslick. Two years earlier he had written in appreciation of Mahler's interpretation of Berlioz's *Symphonie fantastique*. When he later heard a selection of Mahler's orchestral songs (on 14 January 1900) he remarked how they reminded him of Berlioz. The comparison is musically unconvincing, but it illuminates cultural politics. David Kasunic notes that Hanslick's attraction to Berlioz was not only because he offered models for a modern music that was 'not-Wagner', but because, as part of the 'New German School', while not (of course) actually being German, Berlioz was positioned as an ambiguous figure of 'belonging-while-not-belonging' to German musical culture. Mahler, similarly, was viewed as a 'non-German' offering a symphonic non-Wagnerian newness (his First Symphony may hold debts to the idea of Wagner's music drama but hardly to its style). The First Symphony's perplexing position with regard to the nationalist German tradition of 'absolute' music was such that for Hanslick it was a 'symphony' but not a *Symphony*. Mahler's position as an outsider operating inside was further problematized by him being not only Jewish but a ‘modern’ Jew. Hanslick’s own roots, however, lay in the assimilated Jewish community in Prague. He may, then, have held an empathetic feeling for Mahler as he related to his ‘otherness’ in Vienna, marked both musically (his eschewal of Germanic expectations of the symphonic genre) and physically (the obsession with the bodily and racial). Ultimately, Hanslick’s review of the First has an equivocal tone (Kasunic calls it ‘rhetorical squirming’). He may not now understand it, but it may still be a music of the future.[56]

Mahler sustained his Hamburg practice in deciding some works could be improved by retouching. But his new position in Vienna created more anxiety. During preparations for a performance of Brahms’s Third Symphony in 1899 he was conflicted: Bauer-Lechner reported Mahler felt that the symphony’s

Caricature of Mahler conducting the first performance of his First Symphony in Vienna, 1900.

> one failing . . . is a lack of brilliance in the instrumental setting: but this might easily be taken care of with a few changes in the scoring . . . Also I felt the greatest desire to make a few cuts here and there but was prevented from doing so by my inner reluctance to tamper with the work of one who was so recently alive – not to mention my fear of how the critics and public would attack me.[57]

(Sections of Bauer-Lechner's reminiscences unpublished until 2016 reveal further fascinating comments on Brahms.[58]) He was less restrained with Smetana, Dvořák, Schumann, Bruckner (the Fifth and Sixth, both performed with cuts, to mixed reviews) and, notoriously, Beethoven. Mahler's performances of Beethoven's Ninth on 18 and 22 February 1900 in his retouched version (cuts, dynamic changes and reorchestrations – a fuller string section, alterations to woodwind and brass parts) met with critical outrage. In response, he cited Wagner's recommendations and declared that his alterations more fully revealed the composer's intentions, which were hampered by deafness, the lesser capability of the orchestral instruments in his time and poorer concert halls.

The criticism of Mahler's Beethoven is sometimes cited, rather hastily and unsustainably, as representing new levels of negativity, but for German nationalist sections of the press, Mahler as 'Jew' performing a rewritten Beethoven inevitably raised hackles to new heights. In this regard, reviews tell us more about Viennese culture than Mahler as conductor. While Helm had accepted Richter's 1897 use of Wagner's alterations he compared Mahler's performance unfavourably, finding it 'unrecognizable'. Helm, as often, uses softer language than other critics of nationalist persuasion; by contrast, Josef Scheu called the performance a 'forgery' and Richard Heuberger an 'overpainting' and act of 'barbarism'. At the repeat performance Mahler made the strategic error of publishing an explanation of his changes, which only served to reinforce the opinion of those who held that he could not understand Beethoven's masterpiece (or Beethoven more widely: there were similar comments after his debut concert concerning his introduction of the E♭ clarinet in the

'Eroica', and when he performed his orchestral version of the Op. 95 String Quartet in 1899). At root was the fear that Mahler's corrupted, counterfeit versions would be mistaken for the 'real' thing, a conviction that in place of Beethoven's serene, profound sublimity Mahler offered superficial effect and nervousness, colour instead of formal control, over-interpretation, a conductor trying to be too clever by half, by contrast with the flawless genius of the composer. All of these are classic antisemitic tropes.[59]

Mahler's last Vienna Philharmonic concert was to be at lunchtime on 24 February 1901 (the programme including a cut and retouched Bruckner Fifth) after which, in what now seems like an incredible workload, he swiftly moved from the concert hall to the opera house, conducting *The Magic Flute* on the evening of the same day. That night he suffered severe, potentially life-threatening haemorrhoidal bleeding, which would require an urgent operation. He cancelled the remaining two concerts – they were conducted by staff conductors at the opera, Josef Hellmesberger Jr and Franz Schalk. In April, citing health concerns and the demands of the opera house, Mahler resigned from the Philharmonic (Hellmesberger replaced him). He continued to appear with the orchestra as a guest conductor, mostly to perform his own works.

Mahler's most enduringly renowned Wagner productions during his time in Vienna are collaborations with the artist and designer Alfred Roller, co-founder in 1897 of the Vienna Secession, a group of modernists most famously including Gustav Klimt. Roller organized a Secession exhibition around the unveiling of Max Klinger's Beethoven Monument in 1902. For the opening, Mahler prepared and conducted a wind arrangement of a section from the finale of Beethoven's Ninth (no quibbles on retouching here). In the style of decorative symbolism that typified the Secession's post-Wagnerian aestheticism, Roller produced a nocturnal fresco as backdrop for the sculpture. A mutual high regard quickly developed between Mahler and Roller, leading to collaboration on a groundbreaking new production of *Tristan*, performed in February 1903. Roller held a keen interest in theatre and his artistic aesthetic brought a new level of form and symbolism to the visual dimension within

Emil Orlík, *Gustav Mahler*, 1902, etching.

the *Gesamtkunstwerk* through innovative scenic design, costumes and lighting. For Max Graf, the results approached a kind of synaesthesia, as the lighting for *Tristan* was so subtle it could 'vary the colour of a basic chord, spreading it out and changing it' . . . Roller 'brought something of the subtle Tristan chromaticisms to the world of the decorative arts', as 'musical impressions' were reflected in the 'vibrations of air and colour'.[60] Mahler was effulgent in his praise for Roller's work and appointed him Director of Production. They worked together on twenty productions, including a very expensive *Ring* cycle, of which *Rheingold* was performed in 1905 and *Die Walküre* in 1907 (the third and fourth parts were not performed until after Mahler's departure from Vienna). Graf noted the clear influence of Impressionism in Roller's work on *Rheingold*; in the *Neues Wiener Journal* (January 1905) he described the '*paysage intime* of the moderns, the newer French [painters], the analysts of the effects of light'.[61]

Figaro and *The Magic Flute* were the most frequently performed Mozart operas under Mahler while he was at Vienna. The Mozart anniversary season of 1905–6 offered an opportunity to present a prestigious cycle of innovative productions.[62] Mahler had been very critical of Richter's Vienna performances of *Don Juan* [*sic*] in 1898. In the 1905–6 cycle he conducted a new production, now under its original Italian title, but with a new German translation of the libretto by Max Kalbeck. (Mahler still made cuts to the score, both those of the Romantic tradition and new ones.) Roller's sets demonstrated his technique of framing part of the stage for intimate scenes and the deployment of strong colouristic contrasts which seemed to fit with both music (the variations in tempi) and characters. (Some of the more vivid elements, however, disturbed Walter.) For the new *Figaro* in 1906 (having conducted the old production every year since his appointment) Mahler again asked Kalbeck for a new translation with the aim of creating greater dramatic clarity. Roller designed dynamic, multi-textural sets. Mahler again rewrote sections of the score and enriched Mozart's original recitatives. For the new *Così fan tutte* in the 1905–6 cycle, Mahler reduced the size of the orchestra to provide chamber-like sonorities, inserted the finale of the Divertimento K. 287 before the start of the second act (an addition comparable to his use of the third 'Leonore' Overture before the final scene of *Fidelio*) and composed some new scene-change music based on Mozart's themes.

As with his Beethoven retouches, Mahler's practice with Mozart was very different to today's notion of historically informed authenticity – dramatic and musical effectiveness of the performance was his driving motive. This was also the impulse behind Mahler's frequent revisions of his own symphonies (and his urge that those who follow him should not baulk at doing the same). Antisemitism aside, however, the discourse over Mahler's changes to Beethoven's symphonies in particular reveals the gathering power of the *Werktreue* concept operating in tandem with the emerging notion of an *Urtext* (which held more sway in concert hall repertory than in the more pragmatic opera house). Wagner's recommended modifications remained in practice until quite late in the twentieth century. But Felix Weingartner, who published an essay on interpreting the Ninth in 1906, and Otto Klemperer (who was a close associate of Mahler's, working with him in preparing performances of the Second and Eighth Symphonies) reduced the number of alterations. Heinrich Schenker's book on the Ninth, published in Vienna in 1912, shared much with Wagner's interpretative approach, but he detested Wagner's music and had a very different emphasis to Mahler. For Schenker, structural understanding was a key basis for performance, and he therefore required much greater fidelity to the notes. In this way he prefigured the later move to critical editions, the search for an authoritative text so all conductors are reading from the same page. But this is just to redefine the word 'authentic': Mahler aimed for authenticity through pursuing what he believed were the dramatic and musical objectives of the composer.

By May 1906 Mahler was already considering his future at the Hofoperntheater. He was increasingly frustrated that his production and performance ideals were not being realized, and some of the soloists in the company had seen their best days but trying to replace them had led to conflict. He despaired at recalcitrant critics and felt exhausted by the workload.[63] The house's financial deficits began to increase from 1905 and budgets were tightened. The number of performances he conducted at the house had dwindled, from nearly a hundred in the 1899–1900 season to 36 in 1901–2. Walter had become an increasingly trustworthy assistant but Mahler controversially increased the number of trips away to perform his own works: including the first performance of the Fourth Symphony in Munich on 25 November 1901, the first complete performance of the Third in Krefeld on 9 June 1902, and in 1903 the First Symphony in Lemberg (April), the Second in Basel (June), the Third in Frankfurt (December), and in Amsterdam in late October the First and Third. In 1906 these absences from Vienna became even more frequent, including for the Fifth in Antwerp (5 March), the Fifth and *Das klagende Lied* in Amsterdam (8–10 March), the Sixth in Essen (May), the Sixth again in Munich (November), the First in Brno and the Third in Graz (both December). There were growing grumbles that the director was increasingly out of office promoting his own music.

In early 1907 a sequence of incidents further problematized Mahler's position in Vienna. The year began with negative Viennese reaction to a performance of his Sixth Symphony, which was not done by the Philharmonic but by the far less accomplished Konzertverein. Mahler had previously been disdainful of ballet (a staple at the opera house) but in 1907, influenced by Roller's pan-aestheticism, he sought to reform it. His efforts, inevitably, only led to dismay from the traditionalists who dominated ballet audiences. Critical reaction to the staging of *Die Walküre* in February was very disappointing. In March he took a trip to Rome, returning on 6 April with Alma ill, and more bad press and further ructions about his absence. During April he became increasingly conflicted about his position. Hissing and booing during a performance of *Tristan* hardly improved his mood. May did not bring happier times: his younger daughter Anna contracted scarlet fever (there was to be more tragic family illness that summer: his older daughter, Maria, contracted diphtheria and despite a tracheotomy died on 12 July). He was frustrated at not being able to perform Strauss's *Salome,* which was given its Vienna premiere by the visiting Breslau Opera under the baton of Julius Prüwer at the *Deutsches Volkstheater* on 11 May.

A petition was signed by many of the leading artists and intellectuals urging that he should not leave the opera house, but by 23 May sections of the press were confidently reporting Mahler's resignation. Mahler attempted to clarify his situation. In an interview published on 28 May he declared, 'I have not submitted a written resignation . . . The decision is out of my hands.'[64] Nonetheless, reports on 31 May said that Prince Alfred Montenuovo – the aristocrat to whom Mahler reported – had been appraised of the director's desire to leave.[65] Mahler's enemies in the press gleefully grasped their opportunity. Hans Liebstöckl (*Illustrirtes Wiener Extrablatt,* 11 June) declared: 'Gustav Mahler is going. To the many things at the Hofoper we have to thank him for he has now added something very important – his resignation.'[66] Montenuovo's hopes that Mottl might take over were frustrated and (with misgivings and probably knowing full well that such entreaties were likely to be futile) he tried to persuade Mahler to stay on. Mahler continued to prevaricate and weigh up other opportunities. Hearing rumours, Heinrich Conried, director of the New York Metropolitan Opera, contacted Mahler with an offer. Attempts were made by both parties to keep negotiations discreet, but, after a meeting in Berlin in early June, news broke prematurely in the New York press that Mahler was on his way. Mahler eventually signed a contract with the Met which was sufficiently lucrative to secure the financial future of his family.[67] On 10 August Montenuovo wrote to Mahler confirming that Weingartner would replace him.

Mahler's last performance at the Court Opera was on 15 October with *Fidelio*. His final appearance in Vienna was a performance of his Second Symphony on 24 November in the Musikverein. Mahler wanted to leave with no fuss, and no one at the Opera thought an official farewell ceremony would be appropriate. However, a large assembly of his admirers and friends congregated to say *Lebewohl* at the railway station on 9 December. Among a gathering of around two hundred were Schoenberg, Berg, Zemlinsky, Roller and Klimt.

On 12 December Gustav and Alma sailed from Cherbourg, arriving in New York eight days later. Alma wrote: 'the harbour and all the sights and scenes and human bustle – so took our breath away that we forgot all our troubles. But not for long.'[68] On New Year's Day 1908 Mahler made his Met debut with his calling-card, *Tristan*.[69]

The Met had opened in 1883, funded by the fabulously wealthy Vanderbilts. Soloists were of the highest calibre and the main attraction for most of the audience, which included New York's moneyed and social elite. Conried managed productions, but he was ill and due to leave. Mahler was offered the post of director, but it was not an attractive option given his recent experiences in Vienna and the low production standards he inherited at the Met (stellar singers apart). Already by 20 January he was writing at length to Roller asking him to come to New York. He also spells out to Roller his annoyance at the plan that had been hatched to hire Giulio Gatti-Casazza, director of Milan's La Scala, and the ascendant Arturo Toscanini, with the idea of dividing up the conducting of repertory at the Met along national lines.[70] It was a scheme which would never work, as Toscanini's Wagner performances at La Scala were making waves and he was supremely ambitious. When Toscanini arrived at the Met both he and Mahler wanted to conduct *Tristan* – which Toscanini was promised he could do early the next season, before Mahler was due to arrive in New York, using sets brought over from Milan. Mahler was furious; Toscanini's *Tristan* had to wait. Fischer goes so far as to suggest that from the moment in March when Roller was confirmed as not coming Mahler's 'days at the Met were numbered'.[71]

In January Mahler conducted his first *Don Giovanni* sung in Italian, but with the Met's inadequate staging (to Paul Hammerschlag Mahler wrote: '*in spite of the fact* that the singing was almost unsurpassable, I yearned for my Vienna production, which Mozart too, I think, would have liked better'[72]). Two months later, Mahler's first new production, *Fidelio*, met with some critical success and was all round dramatically stronger (it used reproductions of Roller's stage designs) even if it did not meet all his most demanding aspirations. In mid-March he signed a contract with the Met's new power broker, Otto Kahn, to commit to three months in the following season. Mahler left New York on 23 April after a stint of four months, which Fischer concludes Mahler must have found 'dispiriting rather than inspiring'.[73] Zoltan Roman, however, holds a much more positive view: 'unquestionably, [Mahler's] first season . . . had been a very successful one.'[74] Fischer's judgement is based on Mahler's (perennial) frustration at failure to realize his ideal production values. In the letter to Hammerschlag he pointedly writes that 'the climate, the people and the extremely generous conditions suit me extraordinary well,' but 'I have not changed my views on the nature of the whole institution.' And as the season drew to its close he admitted to 'homesickness that has tormented me all the time'.[75] Roman's yardstick was, one assumes, pragmatically scaled to reflect the sometimes unhappy practicalities Mahler endured.

During the spring of 1908 Walter Damrosch sought to confirm a deal for Mahler to conduct the New York Symphony Orchestra, but because of the terms of Mahler's contract with the Met this couldn't happen until November and December; in the second of three concerts he conducted his Second Symphony, to a rather lukewarm critical reception. New York had many fine orchestral players, but, in a letter to William Ritter, Mahler described the orchestra as 'utterly inadequate'.[76] He had arrived in November for his second season with the Met (after a summer during which offers arrived from Buenos Aires and Berlin). He began, as in his debut season, with *Tristan*. Later highlights were an acclaimed new production of *Figaro* in January, and the New York premiere of Smetana's *The Bartered Bride* in February. By comparison with Vienna, Mahler's workload was light. But his future already seemed clear. After conducting *Figaro* on 26 March he effectively left the Met behind him. For the following 1909–10 season he agreed to conduct only one production, Tchaikovsky's *The Queen of Spades* in March. He was contracted for ten performances but conducted only four. It was to be his last time on the opera podium.

As Mahler's work in the opera house declined, his concert hall activity claimed the focus. With encouragement from Mary Sheldon, the leader of the New York Philharmonic guarantors, there were fleeting hopes of establishing a new 'Mahler Orchestra' to rival the quality of the Boston Symphony. Building a new band from scratch proved to be unrealistic; instead, it was a substantially revamped Philharmonic that Mahler conducted in Carnegie Hall, with a contract announced in February 1909. His first concerts were in March (Beethoven's Seventh, Schumann and Wagner) and April, when his interpretation of Beethoven's Ninth once again caused controversy. The *New York Sun* protested that the timpani 'volleyed and thundered at times so that the melodic instruments could not be heard' (Mahler's direction of his timpanists often aroused critical ire).[77] With the orchestra he would go on to perform his Bach arrangement, much Wagner and Beethoven, and also contemporary works by Elgar (the 'Enigma' Variations in November and December 1910), Debussy, Busoni, Enescu and Richard Strauss.

With the exception of *The Queen of Spades* at the Met in March, his third stint in New York, from November 1909 to April 1910, was devoted to the Philharmonic. Opening with a programme including Beethoven's 'Eroica' and Strauss's *Till Eulenspiegel*, it was a longer, more demanding season with the orchestra. Concert highlights in January 1910 included Rachmaninov's Third Piano Concerto with the composer as soloist (Rachmaninov was 'touched' by the 'devotion' given to the orchestral accompaniment,[78] but Mahler did not think highly of the work) and Busoni (whom he held in very high regard) as soloist in Beethoven's 'Emperor' Concerto. But his own First Symphony was not widely understood when he conducted it on 16 and 17 December: Henry E. Krehbiel of the *New York Daily Tribune* declared that the finale confirmed Mahler to be 'a prophet of the ugly'.[79]

Fischer's assessment is that, while there were elements of success during the season, and Mahler sustained a degree of celebrity status, Mahler's dissatisfaction with the quality of the orchestra and the mixed, negative or befuddled reactions from audiences and critics led to his 'prevailing mood' being a 'mixture of estrangement and mounting homesickness'.[80] In January 1910, however, partly in response to tittle-tattle in Vienna that he was now a slave to institutions beneath him, he wrote to Guido Adler:

> I absolutely have to have some practical outlet for my musical abilities to counterbalance the tremendous upsurgings that go when I compose: and it was my lifelong desire to have my own concert orchestra. I am glad to be able to enjoy this for once in my life (apart from the fact that I keep on finding it *very instructive*, for the technique of the theatre is totally different, and I am convinced that many of my previous inadequacies in instrumentation arose from my being accustomed to hearing music in the totally different acoustic conditions of the theatre). Why did neither Germany nor Austria offer me this?[81]

That rhetorical question is a sign that Mahler is biting back with some bitterness, but there is no doubt that he gained much from conducting the New York Philharmonic regularly, not least in further developing his own understanding of orchestration. He was constantly searching for ideal realizations in the concert hall of the orchestral sounds he heard in his head, in his own pieces as much as with Beethoven. Klemperer recalled, while working with Mahler during rehearsals for the premiere of the Eighth in September 1910, Mahler saying: 'If, after my death, something doesn't sound right, then change it. You have not only the right but the duty to do so.'[82]

The demands during that 1909–10 New York season seemed well within his physical powers, and in a letter to sister Justine written in March he says he is 'happier than I've been in 10 years'.[83] And to Zemlinsky the same month, though admitting he was greatly looking forward to returning to Vienna at the end of the season, he wrote: 'Next winter I shall be back here. We have both come to love this country very much; we are very much attracted by all the freshness, soundness and straightforwardness of the way things are done. There is a *future* in everything.'[84] (When Weingartner resigned from the Vienna Opera later that year Mahler scoffed at rumours he might return to his old post.)

The traumatic personal events of the summer of 1910 will be discussed elsewhere. When he conducted the premiere of his Eighth in Munich in September, despite a raging throat infection, Walter observed that Mahler on the podium 'seemed at the height of his powers'.[85] He was back in New York in late October in a positive mood (perhaps surprisingly given his marital crisis, though he was no doubt buoyed by the performances of the Eighth). He conducted 46 concerts with the Philharmonic that season and in December took the orchestra on a successful tour of northeast cities. The Cleveland critic Miriam Russell (after a concert of Mahler's Bach Suite arrangement, Beethoven's 'Pastoral' and three chunks of Wagner – the 'Prelude and Liebestod' from *Tristan*, the *Siegfried Idyll* and the Prelude to *Die Meistersinger*) wrote:

> Little Mahler with the big brain! Little Mahler endowed with the strength of a giant! Little Mahler with a great musical imagination! Little Mahler with the mighty force that makes other conductors look like pygmies . . . And this from little Gustav Mahler, that mere wisp of a man, with the slight form, the long slender hands, the loose shock of black hair standing away in all directions from the delicate, ascetic face. Little Mahler, the giant![86]

Russell's image of a potent mini-Mahler combines the comic with the sublime. It is almost Hoffmannesque and also curiously evokes that combination of monumentalism with miniature materials that is so characteristic of his music.

In the New Year of 1911, however, matters soon became fraught. Critics were more bewildered than bewitched by two performances of a revised version of the Fourth Symphony. Mahler started programming more repeats, audiences were declining and the press were less than enthralled. Toscanini increasingly attracted the New York limelight. Members of the Philharmonic committee were spurred to consider replacing Mahler (Weingartner and Henry Wood were both considered as successors). Provocatively, they also looked to form a committee to supervise programming. In February there was a confrontational meeting with Mary Sheldon (whom Alma had come to loathe as meddling and disrespectful). And then there was the onset of the final, fatal illness. On 20 February Mahler fell sick with a high fever and infection. Contrary to the advice of his friend and physician Dr Joseph Fränkel, Mahler went ahead with the next day's concert, conducting a programme including (with darkly prophetic symbolism) Busoni's *Berceuse élégiaque*. It was to be his last time on the concert podium. A few days later, the *New York Times* reported Mahler being indisposed: 'he is said to have had a light attack of grippe' (an old term for the flu).[87] But the debilitating effects of acute bacterial endocarditis (an inflammation of the heart valves today treatable with antibiotics) meant that when the Mahlers left their hotel on 8 April to begin the arduous journey back to Europe, Gustav looked so weak he was offered a stretcher from the hotel. He refused.

Assessments of Mahler's achievements in New York vary. Joseph Horowitz's judgement is comparable with Fischer's in its ambiguity: Mahler's impact at the Met was, Horowitz decides, 'great but ephemeral' – it left little legacy; at the Philharmonic he was 'admired but controversial', New Yorkers found him both 'inspirational and irritating'. For Horowitz, La Grange's pervasively positive spin on these years lapses into hagiography, the product of writing from a European's view, of an insufficient comprehension of New York society, a failing that La Grange shared with Mahler. Horowitz also argues that La Grange (like Mahler) seriously underestimated the quality of musical culture in New York prior to Mahler's arrival, a prime example of which being Seidl's symphonic concerts in the 1890s.[88] Brought over at enormous cost, Mahler 'remained a chronic outsider'.[89] He misunderstood his audience as a kind of *tabula rasa* (to Carl Moll, Alma's stepfather, he wrote: 'I now regard [America] as an awkward youth'[90]), he never mastered English and showed no enthusiasm for getting to know American music. He could be prickly, elitist and self-obsessed. Mahler's intention was in strong part to 'educate' his new audience (particularly through a series of 'historical' concerts), but this stoked resentment from American critics towards an expensive European import viewing them as nouveau-riche gatecrashers to high culture.

Roman, however, emphasizes the 'freshness and flexibility' which broadly characterizes contemporaneous American music critics; even Krehbiel, widely identified as Mahler's critical nemesis, 'must be acknowledged for his initial, commendably open-minded attempts to understand and interpret Mahler's music and music-making'.[91] But unease in their relationship quickly developed, intensified by the fact that Krehbiel was also the programme writer for the Philharmonic concerts. Before the December 1909 performances of the First Symphony he requested a 'programme', but programmes had long since become at best problematic for Mahler so one was not forthcoming. After the concert Krehbiel bellowed: 'the symphony has no justification without a programme.' As so often in Europe, Mahler's interpretation of Beethoven's Ninth was again a lightning rod for critical opprobrium: a performance in the last concert of the 1909–10 season provoked Krehbiel to pen a damning critique. Krehbiel, whom Feder describes as an 'American chauvinist who was quick to take umbrage at any perceived superior or patronizing old-world attitude', sustained his attack on Mahler to the end (and beyond). Fischer calls his 'infamous' obituary of Mahler 'a classic example of a posthumous character assassination'.[92] Feder describes it as a piece of 'perverse criticism' – 'one is left with the impression that if Krehbiel could have resurrected the dead Mahler in order to destroy him, he would have done so.'[93] Horowitz offers a more sympathetic analysis, pointing out that New York critics such as Krehbiel were familiar with the interpretations of Seidl and Nikisch (when Mahler's old Leipzig rival visited New York with the Boston Symphony). Mahler's performances posed a problematic alternative to their preferred Wagnerian Romantic style.[94]

Other critics pointed to exaggerated contrasts in Mahler's interpretations. James Huneker described the sound Mahler obtained from the Met orchestra in a performance of *Tristan* as (somewhat paradoxically) a demonstration of 'logic', one lacking 'sensuousness' but which 'laid bare the nerves of the music'; he did admit that, in its way, Mahler's interpretation offered a viable new way forward.[95] Horowitz makes an interesting comparison with the aesthetics of the Vienna Secession:

> [Mahler's] eschewal of Romantic *Innigkeit*, in his predilection for kaleidoscopes of sound pursued by adding or modifying

> wind and brass parts, and in his preference for a mosaic of instrumental voices cancelling the Romantic cathedral sonority of dominant strings and recessed winds

is, he suggests, a parallel to Gustav Klimt's 'flat, polyphonic canvasses'.[96] As with many attempts to parallel music with visual arts, Horowitz's metaphors are seductive but problematic.

The famous final photograph of Mahler on deck during the voyage home from New York remains deeply affecting. His body is broken and weary. Fischer says 'it is impossible to look at it for long,' but only does so after quite a long and detailed description of Mahler's physical condition.[97] Mahler's body ('Little' Mahler's body) always attracted scrutiny, sometimes to obsessive degrees. (To counter the myth of Mahler as 'unattractive, puny, ugly, a fidgeting bundle of nerves' Roller wrote an extraordinary, fetishized, eroticized recollection of gazing at Mahler sunbathing naked: his body was 'the perfect male torso', 'beautifully made' with 'well-defined musculature'.[98])

Conducting is in large part a choreographic art. The movements, gestures and shapes of the conductor's body are a focus for both the performers and the audience (if they can see it in the dimmed lights of the opera house). Mahler's performances become less a body of work and more a work of the body. William Ritter recalled Mahler rehearsing his Seventh Symphony in Prague in 1908:

> [Mahler] threw himself about like a madman, seated, standing, dancing, leaping like a jack-in-a-box, in all directions at once, conducting to the right, to the left, in front, behind, completely oblivious of me and giving me several hefty kicks in the kidneys.[99]

Gutmann's description of Mahler stepping up to conduct the premiere of the Eighth is even more striking:

> In this moment, here were no singers and no listeners, no instruments and no sounding boards, only one single body,

Mahler on the crossing back to Europe from New York, April 1911.

with many, many veins and nerves, that was waiting to have the blood and breath of art course through it . . . The name and purpose of this body was the concept of the communality of art! And Mahler began to beat with his baton – animating blood throbbed rhythmically through his body.[100]

The image of Mahler's conducting body as a bundle of nervous energy and frantic gestures is frequently found in the contemporaneous critical discourse, where it often denotes notions of modernity (the character and topics of Modernist art and the agitating experience of the modern urban world), but also an antisemitism which could be overt. When Max Graf, in his 1900 *Wagner-Probleme und andere Studien*, contrasted Mahler with Richter's 'strong and manly' presence on the podium (which offered 'more roast beef and less nerves in his body'), the image is explicitly gendered as well as culinary. At this time Graf considered Richter and Mahler to be positively complementary (but Mahler responded coolly to Graf's request to dedicate the book to him). Later, in a 1945 recollection, however, Graf's 'Mahler' is couched in antisemitic terms: Mahler was 'a demonic man' from whom 'streams of nervous energy emanated', a 'small man with sharply chiselled features, pale and ascetic-looking', a 'wicked dwarf'. That final characterization inevitably recalls Wagner's antisemitic characterization of Mime.[101]

Mahler's conducting style may have become rather calmer in his American seasons, possibly in part due to the diagnosis of his heart condition in 1907, but also as a mark of greater artistic maturity. Even if it did so, however, hair-raising associations with Mahler's physiognomy remained: the *New York Daily Tribune*'s 1910 'character sketch' described 'his slight, almost emaciated figure, his fine, dome-shaped head, his crown of black hair tinged with grey, every strand of which, erect, self-supporting, appeared charged with the full force of the energy which animates the man himself'.[102] Mahler's physical character remains a critical trope to this day: Fischer, though insistent, stretches the boundaries of persuasiveness when he writes that Mahler in his American years

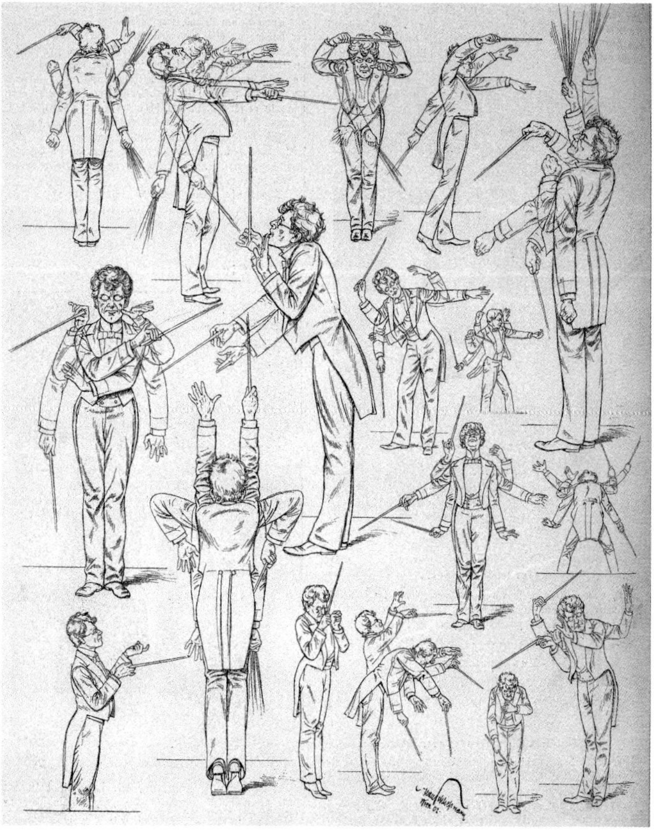

Caricature of Mahler titled 'A hypermoderne conductor: Kapellmeister Kappelmann conducts his Symphony diabolica', by Hans Schliessmann, 1901.

abandoned the eccentric gestures of his youth and adopted a stricter and more economical style of conducting. Moreover, he preferred a Wagnerian sound that was lean-textured and yet muscular, embodying the phenotype closest to his own physical appearance – such links do indeed exist and are by no means far-fetched.[103]

Some in the European press, in part echoing Alma, sought to blame the strains and stresses of Mahler's time in New York for his premature death. Krehbiel's excoriating obituary was among many American responses to vehemently refute that claim. The Philharmonic concerts on 23 and 24 November 1911, under the new director Josef Stransky, were dedicated to Mahler's memory. The programmes included the funereal first movement of his Fifth Symphony, the 'Good Friday' music from *Parsifal*, and one of Mahler's own conducting calling-cards, Beethoven's 'Eroica' (the second movement funeral march of which was one of his most famous interpretations).

Mahler the conductor cut a contentious and physically fascinating figure in the performative, political theatre of a series of urban spaces (Leipzig, Prague, Budapest, Hamburg, Vienna, New York), a musical maestro in the maelstrom of the modern metropolis. But it was an activity whose demands he frequently felt were a distraction from a higher calling to composition. To pursue that creative aspiration he sought rural retreat, a relief from, but also a complement to, his experience of performing in the city.

4

Mahler Composing in the Country

I have realised today that articulate art is greater than inarticulate nature.

Mahler, on conducting Beethoven's 'Pastoral' Symphony after a visit to Niagara Falls, 1910[1]

O earth, my beloved earth, when, ah, when will you give refuge to him who is forsaken, receiving him back into your womb? Behold! Mankind has cast him out, and he flees from its cold and heartless bosom, he flees to you, to you alone! O, take him in, eternal, all-embracing mother, give a resting place to him who is without friend and without rest!

Mahler, letter to Joseph Steiner, 17 June 1879[2]

Mahler's effusive and depressive letter to Steiner, written when he had not yet turned nineteen, is a cliché-ridden example of late adolescent angst. It is a flagrant conflation of borrowed images – the earth as Mother, a yearning for death as a return to an original state of rest, an idyllic refuge from feelings of alienation and loneliness. And yet the letter has often been cited because, for all the rather immature gush, its images and emotions remained central to Mahler's poeticized, symbolic relationship with nature. The challenge, given it has been so widely recognized and long discussed, lies in bringing a fresh approach to this part of Mahler's world view and creative stimulus. It is a challenge to which several Mahler scholars have risen in recent years.

The *Lieder eines fahrenden Gesellen*, composed just a few years after that letter (1883–5; but not orchestrated until 1893 or perhaps as late as 1896) are often identified as Mahler's first mature music. In strong part this judgement is based upon the cycle's effective portrayal of an ambivalent relationship with, and characterization of, the natural world. The five songs are settings of Mahler's own poems, which are closely comparable with the stylized folk tone of Brentano and von Arnim's *Des Knaben Wunderhorn* (1805–8). Contrasts are played out between the lover's sorrow and nature's loveliness; the figure of a weeping and woeful suitor is set against the landscape's beauty. Nature has an ambiguous presence: cherished by the lovelorn subject, but effectively indifferent to his predicament. No consolation is found. In the opening of the second song, 'Ging heut" Morgen über's Feld', the joy of walking over dewy morning fields contrasts with the gloomy prognosis for an amorous relationship, encapsulated in the song ending on an unresolved dominant. Mahler's debts to Schubert (especially *Winterreise*) may be overt, but freshness lies in the already idiosyncratic switches between lightness and darkness. The songs are often linked with his youthful yearning for Johanna Richter, but while a self-identity may be partly at play, the familiar figure of the wanderer also stands (or moves) more broadly for the lonely outsider. Though the vigorous Mahler hardly cut a figure who walked in a forlorn Romantic fashion, there is no doubt that country walks could provide a therapeutic as well as inspirational quality, facilitating conversations (especially with Bauer-Lechner) in which Mahler would overtly indulge in 'self-fashioning' in tandem with ruminations on the significance of the landscape around them.[3]

Mahler reused the opening theme of 'Ging heut"' in the opening movement of the First Symphony. The bulk of the compositional work on the Symphony was achieved (possibly in only six weeks) in early 1888, while he held the conducting post in Leipzig. One of the most startling aspects of Mahler's symphonic debut is the manner through which 'nature' is effectively given qualifying inverted commas; the 'natural' is always staged as a construction. While hardly without precedent (Schiller confirmed that in the modern world the idyllic could no longer be directly, naively evoked in art), Mahler's musical presentation and manipulation is especially provocative. It is immediately apparent through the Symphony's overt theatricality. As musicologist Thomas Peattie has noted, this theatricality marks the Symphony as a product of modern 'metropolitan culture', a piece of constructed sonic scenery.[4] Many critics have described Mahler's symphonic style as theatrical or operatic because traditional form is ruptured through dramatic events, the breakthroughs (for example in the finale of the First), culminations and catastrophes. Sceptics considered these as markers of symphonic failure, but for Adorno they were marks of Mahler's authentic modernity. Adorno described Mahler's symphonies as *opera assoluta* (absolute opera, a typical Adornian paradox) to reflect narratives, passions and tensions more akin to opera and the novel than conventionally found in 'absolute' symphonic music.[5] As many commentators have observed, Mahler's experience of opera conducting (especially *Fidelio* and Wagner) was key to his expansion of the formal characteristics and range of musical materials of the symphony. It led to a generic ambiguity reflected in the shifting title of the First. At its Budapest premiere (1889) it was billed as a 'Symphonic Poem', with five movements grouped in two parts. In the 1893 Hamburg performance it carried the title 'Titan', after Jean Paul's novel. Only in 1896, when performed in Berlin (now as a more conventional four-movement work, omitting the original second, 'Blumine'), did it become 'Symphonie in D-dur für grosses Orchester'.[6] The twists between novelistic and generic titles encapsulate both the ambiguity of the work's character and the composer's uneasy relationship with programmatic explanations.

The First Symphony expands upon the 'latent theatricality' of Beethoven's Ninth.[7] But Mahler's opening slow music is very different to the gradual thematic emergence with which Beethoven begins. Mahler assembles sounds in space to create a sonic tableau. During the final stages of revision Mahler added a telling indication to the passage: 'wie ein Naturlaut' ('like a sound of nature'). The key word is 'like': it is a simulacrum, a representation, a fabrication. Nature sounds in Mahler are never compositional attempts to parallel the observational detachment of the 'real' typical of contemporaneous literary naturalism. They are contributions to the conflicts in late Romantic subjectivity, and particularly the tensions between idyll and elegy, communion and alienation. 'Distance' in the opening of the First Symphony is not only spatial: it also conveys the divisions between culture and nature, and that widening gap invests the music with an expressive, psychological edge. Mahler uses romantic pastoral conventions (a long pedal note, imitations of birdsong, soft horn calls) but the sustained string harmonics are eerie, cloaking the sounds in a 'denaturing' effect. Something sounds awry. The lightly tripping tune from 'Ging heut'' may begin leisurely (*gemächlich* in the score) but it arrives on a scene of gently ambiguous artifice.

Another side of Mahler's musical 'nature' presents a more overtly disturbing denial of beautifully benign pastoralism. For the 1893 Hamburg performance of the five-movement version of the First, the parodic slow fourth movement was titled 'funeral march in the manner of Callot'. Mahler was probably not directly familiar with Jacques Callot (a seventeenth-century engraver) but most likely knew of him through the characterization in E.T.A. Hoffmann's *Fantasiestucke in Callots Manier*, an 1814 collection of novellas for which Jean Paul wrote a preface. Hoffmann's own prefatory paragraphs encapsulate the unsettling effect of Mahler's music:

> Irony, in that it sets man and animal in conflict, derides man with his paltry works and endeavours; it resides only in a profound soul, and Callot's grotesque forms, created out of animal and man, reveal to the serious, deeper-seeing observer all the hidden meanings that lie beneath the cloak of absurdity.[8]

Man and animal are in darkly farcical relationship. In the Hamburg programme Mahler also pointed to a 'parodistic illustration familiar to children from fairy-tale books'. This is the 'Hunter's Funeral Procession', of which a woodcut by Moritz von Schwind from 1850 is an oft-reproduced version. Though it may not be the version Mahler was referring to in his programme, the unsettling image of animals carrying (in dark and mocking retribution) the body of the hunter is apposite in its grim humour.

The Hunter's Funeral Procession, woodcut after drawing by Moritz von Schwind, 1850.

Settings of texts from the *Wunderhorn* collection were a recurring compositional preoccupation for Mahler from 1887 and right through the 1890s. Writing from Hamburg to Marschalk in December 1896 (in a letter in which he also complained about being 'chained' to the opera house, only being able to compose on his 'day off', a phrase around which Mahler places inverted commas; he clearly felt he never had any respite) he called his *Wunderhorn* songs 'humoresques'.[9] Mahler would soon drop this title, but many of the songs are characterized by passages of rustic humour. They also carry sophisticated and troubling undercurrents, an ironic humour in the manner of Jean Paul, an inverted sublime in which sensuous, perhaps perky or impertinent particulars stand in place of profound perturbations. It is a self-conscious humour in which the bucolic coexists with the potential for suffering and dark destruction: the world of the *Wunderhorn* encompasses both a child's view of heaven ('Das himmlische Leben' (1892)) and children dying of hunger ('Das irdische Leben'). Foreshadowings of the ambiguous tone of Mahler's *Wunderhorn* songs can be seen in von Schwind's painting *Im Walde des Knaben Wunderhorn* (In the Forest (The Youth's Magic Horn), *c*. 1848). The conjunction of spontaneous musical inspiration and nature is pictured as apparently blissful. But the way in which the curvilinear shape of the boy and horn contrasts with the jagged angularity of the looming tree suggests latent conflict and threat, and beyond the tree lie troubling, dark shadows.

It was during his time at Hamburg (1891–7), when 'days off' from duties at the opera house were few and far between, that

Moritz von Schwind, *In the Forest* (*The Youth's Magic Horn*), *c.* 1848, oil on canvas.

Mahler established a routine of primarily composing from June to August. These years saw the prolonged gestation of his Second and Third Symphonies. The summer of 1893 was his first at the stunning setting of Steinbach am Attersee (a location that sister Justine and Bauer-Lechner had identified the previous spring as suitable for Mahler's compositional retreat). Here Mahler quickly settled into a disciplined routine (La Grange describes him leading an ‘ascetic life’[10]), completing several *Wunderhorn* songs and two movements of the Second Symphony. The compositional tasks were intimately related, as the *Wunderhorn* song ‘Des Antonius von Padua Fischpredigt’ became the basis of the symphony’s third movement scherzo. With the church empty, the holy man preaches to the fishes, but after seeming to listen attentively they are as unmoved by the saint’s message as humankind. Whether addressed by hunter or saint, nature has the last laugh. During this summer Mahler orchestrated another *Wunderhorn* song, ‘Urlicht’ (composed the previous year), as the Second Symphony’s fourth movement: images of nature’s exquisite forms (the symbolic red rose at the opening) coexist with existential woe as hopes for heavenly redemption are questioned. A revised version of the ‘Todtenfeier’ movement that Mahler had composed in the summer of 1888 would form the first movement of the Second Symphony, but the redemptive finale was not completed until the summer of 1894 (the story of inspiration drawn from von Bülow’s memorial was told in the Prologue).

Mahler followed the Romantic tradition (established in large part by Goethe) of using organic aspects of nature to characterize his process of artistic creation. In recollections of the summer of 1893 in Steinbach, Bauer-Lechner reports Mahler describing how ‘Fischpredigt’ grew into the Scherzo of the Second as ‘potentialities lay hidden within it like the plant within the seed.’[11] Mahler would repeat this organic metaphor for his composition process when speaking to Webern after the premiere of his *Kindertotenlieder*:

> Our model on this matter is nature. Just as the whole universe has developed from the original cell – through plants, animals, men, to God, the highest being – in music too a whole piece should be developed from a single motif, a single theme, which contains the germ of all that is to follow.[12]

The conjunction of artistic beauty and pain led to him drawing on another natural process: ‘the creation of a work of art resembles that of a pearl, which, born of the oyster’s terrible sufferings, bestows its treasure on the world.’[13]

Organic metaphors proliferated. When Mahler drafted the introduction to the first movement of the Third Symphony during the Steinbach summer of 1896, Bauer-Lechner reports him describing an overtly evolutionary process:

> It has almost ceased to be music; it is hardly anything but sounds of nature. It's eerie, the way life gradually breaks through, out of soulless, petrified matter. (I might equally well have called the movement 'What the mountains tell me'.) And, as this life rises from stage to stage, it takes on ever more highly developed forms: flowers, beasts, man, up to the sphere of the spirits, the 'angels'.[14]

The ascent to the heavenly describes the trajectory of the whole symphony and so Mahler betrays the fact that work on the first movement in 1896 was actually the final stage of composition – the evolutionary process was to some extent reverse-engineered. But initial (embryonic, one might say) ideas for the opening of the symphony may go back to 1892, the year of many *Wunderhorn* songs, with some further preliminary planning undertaken in 1893. Indeed, a sketch Mahler gave to Bauer-Lechner in the summer of 1896, which survives with a date of '1893 Steinbach' (though not in Mahler's hand) contains material clearly related to the first movement. Bauer-Lechner reports that she found the sketch with a note from Gustav: 'On 28 July 1896, a curious thing happened: I was able to present my dear friend Natalie with the seed of a tree, that, nevertheless, is now grown to full size.'[15]

Characteristically, however, the Third contains substantial ambiguity in the relationship of materials symbolizing rural and urban environments. Ryan R. Kangas notes that Vienna, as a staging post on Mahler's journey between Hamburg and Steinbach, mediates the binaries of winter (Hamburg, conducting in the city) and summer (Steinbach, composing in the country). This is reflected in the way in which nature and culture become more 'enmeshed' in the Symphony. Mahler uses marches in the first movement to signal the approach and arrival of summer, evoking a collective human activity of motion as symbol for seasonal change – nature is thereby 'anthropomorphized'. Moreover, through the associative meanings attached to marches, nature is politicized: the arrival of summer is a signal of change, of progress, but one which battles through conflicting forces of resistance. On the fair copy of the score of the first movement, Mahler annotated one of these marches as the 'mob' (this is not in the published score).[16] During the summer of 1895 Bauer-Lechner noted Mahler commenting: 'I need a regimental band to give the rough and crude effect of my martial comrade's arrival . . . Such a mob is milling around, you never saw anything like it!'[17] Thus, Kangas concludes, 'nature and natural metaphors provide routes towards understanding urban life and politics, rather than avenues for escaping from them.'[18] The tense relationship between the two worlds is sustained: the posthorn calls in the scherzo of the Third, for example, sound as symbol of civilization's expanding intrusion on nature. They also turn the nature–culture/simple–complex binary on its head: the posthorn is a 'voice from Vienna' that is ironically naive, its simplicity contrasting with the complexity of the pastoral world.

Mahler was consistently concerned that his audiences understood nature's symbolic complexities. When Nikisch conducted the second movement of the Third Symphony on its own, under the title 'What the flowers in the meadow tell me', with the Berlin Philharmonic in November 1896, Mahler was apprehensive that it would mislead the audience into pigeonholing him as a benign, picture-postcard pastoralist. (The complete symphony would not be performed until June 1902.) In a well-known letter to Richard Batka in the month of that Berlin performance he feared he could be cast as a '"meditative", finespun "singer of nature"'. 'Of course', Mahler continued,

> no one gets an inkling that for me Nature includes all that is terrifying, great and also lovely (it is precisely this that I wanted to express in the whole work, in a kind of evolutionary development). I always feel it strange that when most people speak of 'Nature' what they mean is flowers, little birds, the scent

of the pinewoods, etc. No one knows the god Dionysus, or great Pan.[19]

For Mahler, 'the sound of Nature' includes difficult lessons from gods of uncontrolled drives, disturbances and panic.

The issue boils down to the degree of separation Mahler sought from the bourgeois pastoral idyll, a distance achieved through reducing superficial imitation (tone painting) and giving space to invoking an inward turn, expressed in a self-reflective, often ironic, 'discourse on nature'.[20] In the summer of 1897 Mahler explained to Bauer-Lechner the multiple, shifting relationship of the artist with nature:

> We probably derive all our basic rhythms and themes from Nature, which offers them to us, pregnant with meaning, in every animal noise. Indeed, Man, and the artist in particular, takes all his materials and all his forms from the world around him – transforming and expanding them, of course. He may find himself in a harmonious and happy relationship with Nature, or alternatively in painful and hostile opposition to her. He may even seek to have done with her, looking down upon her with humour and irony from a superior vantage-point – and this attitude provides the basis, in the most precise sense, for the sublime, the sentimental, the tragic and the humorously ironic styles in art.[21]

Mahler's understanding of art and nature is therefore notably complex. But over-simplified and idealized images of Mahler's creative process stubbornly persist. Here is La Grange, his most monumental biographer:

> when he was composing, Mahler seemed to live in a state of perpetual enchantment, inhabiting a world apart and entirely absorbed by the mystery of his own creative powers. The music he composed each day was written not with ink but with his own blood. It contained everything he had experienced and suffered.[22]

The ink/blood metaphor is a tired romantic cliché; the last sentence hopelessly overblown. What is certainly tenable is Mahler's desire for peace and isolation while composing. In spring 1894 a hut was built by the lake at Steinbach, to provide more seclusion. The small construction contained a table and chairs, stove and a baby grand piano. During the summer of 1894, when he completed the enormous finale of the Second, his hut routine began with rising early and working all morning (on some days until later). Noisy intrusions remained a constant concern. Bauer-Lechner wrote:

> Mahler, who suffers so much from noise and disturbance even in the country, tells me that when he was a child he used to wish that the good Lord had equipped human beings in such a way that, the minute they got too noisy, something like an internal 'jack-in-the-box' [*Knüppel aus dem Sack*] would pop out, and, belabouring them vigorously, reduce them to silence.[23]

He became unhappy with Steinbach's imperfect seclusion, irritated by the weather and disappointed with the food. After a productive summer on the Third in 1896 he left Steinbach with mixed feelings.

Mahler's composing hut at Steinbach.

He would not return. But Mahler had three fruitful composing summers there, and he wept on seeing his hut for the final time.

During the next two summers Mahler was compositionally frustrated: in 1897 by the all-encompassing demands of his new role at the Vienna Court Opera, the following year by convalescence after an operation. He resumed his summer composing routine in Altaussee in June 1899, where he sketched one of the most powerful of his *Wunderhorn* songs, 'Revelge', the idea apparently coming to him while sitting on the toilet after taking a laxative.[24] In mid-July he began work on the Fourth Symphony (whose *Wunderhorn* preoccupations are revealed by its rejected title 'Humoreske') but it was only a few weeks until he had to return to duties in Vienna. His creative work felt curtailed, and he also yearned for the solitude of a composing hut. But now lucratively ensconced in his Vienna post he was financially well-placed to buy a suitably quiet, and spectacularly scenic, lakeside plot at Maiernigg on the Wörthersee on which a house would be built for his future summers. Crucially, there was nearby space just a stroll up the hill for a new hut. Though construction on this hut was completed in time for Mahler's arrival in June 1900, the new house was still being built, necessitating a sojourn at the Villa Antonia, a twenty-minute walk away. The location and atmosphere of the hut delighted him, 'a piece of truly enchanted virgin forest', whose 'Dionysian marvels and enchantments . . . far surpass even those of the little cottage on the meadow at Steinbach which he so loved'.[25]

The main task in that first summer at Maiernigg was the composition of the Adagio of the Fourth. But Mahler struggled to pick up the threads of his symphony. Noises off once more seemed intrusive: 'even in his little house . . . the birds torment him with their singing, in spite of scarecrows and the firing of blank cartridges . . . sometimes the sound of a barrel-organ, or a military band on the opposite side of the lake, wafts over.'[26] Given the presence of many of these sounds in his music the intensity of Mahler's reaction (especially the attacks on birdlife!) may seem surprising. It becomes understandable when it is recalled that during composition these types of sound are radically transformed in their character, that Mahler never sought simply to imitate. An inward turn was crucial to both his working environment and his musical discourse. The latter is encapsulated in his famous description of the character of the Fourth:

> Think of the undifferentiated blue of the sky . . . this is the basic tone of the whole work. Only once does it become overcast and uncannily awesome [*spukhaft schauerlich*] – but it is not the sky itself which grows dark, for it shines eternally blue. It is only that it seems suddenly sinister to us – just as on the most beautiful day, in a forest flooded with sunshine, one is often overcome by a shudder of Panic dread.[27]

The final clause recalls Mahler's comments on the presence in nature of symbolic, unsettling and ancient gods in his letter to Batka on the Third.

The Maiernigg house, designed by the amateur but skilled architect Friedrich Theuer, was ready for the following summer, 1901. Sister Justine had set about making it a home. Mahler was elated; he considered the view over the lake to be 'too beautiful'. The work achieved during the productive summer which followed is often considered to mark a turning point in Mahler's compositional style. There was a final, funereal *Wunderhorn* song of a doomed, incarcerated drummer ('Der Tambourg'sell'), three of the *Kindertotenlieder* (whose poems Friedrich Rückert had written after the death of two of his children) and four further Rückert songs, including one of his most beautiful and famous expressions of withdrawal from the world into contemplative stasis, 'Ich bin der Welt abhanden gekommen', which Mahler said came to him while alone with nature (again, one might recall the daydreaming boy Gustav). As well as these vocal works he composed substantial parts of the Fifth Symphony. Alma reports two completed movements; Bauer-Lechner says the third movement scherzo was composed first; La Grange decides that the first two movements, the funeral march and torrid Allegro, must both be from 1901 as they are so closely related.[28]

Mahler's summer house at Maiernigg.

This impressive body of work represents, among other things but especially prominently, a powerful musical expression of sorrow and suffering. Biographers and critics have often pointed to Mahler's serious health scare (the severe, potentially fatal, haemorrhoidal bleeding) of the preceding February as a direct, or at least likely cause. While it is important to be sceptical of simplistic life–art relationships, it is persuasive in this instance that, now recovered and in his lovely country home, Mahler pursued new compositional explorations of death.[29] (La Grange calls the scherzo of the Fifth a 'song of thanks of one restored to health'.[30]) As is also widely noted, his creative rethinking was accompanied by significant changes in musical style, pointing towards the 'late style' of *Das Lied von der Erde* and the Ninth Symphony. Aspects of the Rückert songs especially adumbrate *Das Lied*, but though the topics of death and withdrawal might be ascribed to autobiographical stimulus the stylistic changes of 1901 (including greater use of counterpoint, clarity of texture, and tonal dissonance) cannot simply be assigned to this motivation. Recall the comments of Mahler, Lipiner and Boulez discussed in the Prologue: though the gap between life and art may sometimes appear close, it is never closed.

Composition of the Fifth (completed in 1902) certainly marked a turning point in Mahler's symphonic output, the first of three symphonies composed between 1901 and 1905 in which he eschews texts and voices for purely instrumental movements, often in structures which are closer to tradition than those deployed in his previous symphonic works. The Sixth was written during the summers of 1903 and 1904 and was completed shortly after writing the two remaining songs of the *Kindertotenlieder*. During August 1904 he also composed two 'Nachtmusik' movements for the Seventh Symphony. Both the Sixth and Seventh sustain and intensify the complex relationship of art and nature. In the first movement of the Sixth, the urgent, thrusting development section is interrupted by 'nature' music (*Naturlaut*) that sounds as a static, subversive intrusion into an otherwise pulsating symphonic process. The effect is to create a sense of separation, of distance and withdrawal, but the symphonic context also marks the moment as liminal, as a threshold between the earthly and the heavenly, and between culture and nature. When the driving, progressive march rhythms return, the beautiful moment's fragility is confirmed, as is the impossibility of fulfilment, of ascending to the sunlit summit.

The most notorious element of Maher's *Naturlaut* in the Sixth and Seventh is the use of cowbells. Julian Johnson notes, however, that while they can sound like 'the most appalling piece of tourist kitsch', affirming the bourgeois ideology of a benign 'nature' of leisure and escape, the contexts in which they are heard and the transformations they undergo generate ambiguities. They may bring a landscape of Alpine tourism into the concert hall but by their very placement in symphonic forms and the sound-world of the orchestra they are invasive, imprecise, unruly and disruptive, and therefore paradoxically unsettling.[31]

In a footnote to the revised (1906) score of the Sixth Mahler wrote:

> The cowbells must be treated with great discretion so as to produce a realistic impression of the bells of a grazing herd of cattle whose sounds drift from the distance, sometimes alone, sometimes in groups, sound in high and low pitch. It must be made explicit that this technical remark does not allow for a programmatic interpretation.[32]

Mahler's comment again reveals a concern to avoid his audiences mistaking the music as *Tonmalerei* (tone painting). But the cowbells coexist in a shifting relationship with human subjective presence and this raises deeper prospects for interpretation. In the first movement of the Sixth the score indicates the bells must be 'in Entfernnung aufgestellt' (placed at a distance). Tinkling and clanging across conventional orchestral artifices of 'nature' music (celeste, high strings, long bass pedal notes), they precede the introduction of a woodwind theme symphonically coded as 'feminine' (it is a 'grazioso', lyrical transformation of the second subject) but one which is fragile and ephemeral, petering out before the brutally sudden return of developmental dynamism. In the two occurrences of cowbells in the Andante moderato movement, by contrast, they are in the orchestra, embraced within a more sustained thematic eloquence. But detachment and alienation return in their role and placement in the tragic finale. The symphony confirms the human figure's ambivalent place in an ambiguous sonic environment.

The spatial mobility of cowbells in the first 'Nachtmusik' of the Seventh (composed during the summer when the Sixth was finished) is comparable with their trajectory across the Sixth. They are first heard from a distance (indeed, they were a compositional afterthought), then blended.[33] Mahler's comments, reported by Edgar Istel, at a rehearsal for the Seventh in Munich again evoke the position of the solitary human in a symbolic landscape:

> he imagines that he was standing on the highest peak, facing eternity. And as the one who roams above the peaks perceives the last greeting of living beings only through the fading sound

of herds grazing afar, so Mahler perceives this sound as the only one symbolizing the loneliness afar from the world.[34]

Johnson decides that 'never are the creatures of Mahler's symphonies domesticated'[35] but as Anna Stoll Knecht points out, 'the cowbells, here, refer to nature *domesticated*, to the human appropriation of nature.' There is a stage of removal from, and human intervention in, nature (we do not hear the sound of bovine 'mooing' which might bring us closer to nature). In the cowbell sections both animal and human presence is implied. The human presence is fourfold: first as herder (tamer of nature), second as feminized ideal (embodiment of nature's beauty), third as wanderer (as lost and lonely outsider) and fourth as listener (the receptive creator of desired meaning).

The first, third and fifth movements of the Seventh Symphony were composed in 1905, with a full draft of the whole work completed by mid-August. The Seventh has always suffered from, at best, a mixed reception. From a dark beginning, where funereal rhythms underpin the striking sonority of a solo tenor horn playing a theme in which Mahler once told Specht 'here nature roars,' the Symphony projects an affirmative sometimes comedic alternative to the bleak tragedy of the Sixth. Deryck Cooke called it the 'Cinderella among Mahler's symphonies', 'enigmatic, inscrutable' and with a finale which is 'largely a failure'.[36] The scholar who has come closest to being the Seventh's fairy godmother is Anna Stoll Knecht. For Knecht, the Seventh seeks to uncover truth through music which often sounds like an (ambiguously) abstract theatre and elsewhere evokes the spectacle of a circus as a metaphor for life – the conjuring of illusions, the clown who weeps and grimaces, the unpredictable licence of the carnivalesque, the precarious, ever-present threat of danger in performance.[37] Peattie hears the Seventh as reflecting 'new modes of perception' experienced in modern modes of travel and leisure, specifically through projecting a 'kaleidoscopic unfolding' parallel to the perspective of a shifting panorama seen when (as Mahler often did, not always pleasurably) travelling in a railway carriage.[38] Perhaps, then, this 'Cinderella' symphony's carriage awaits: 'she' shall, after all, go to the ball.

The Seventh has also suffered from a reputation for apparent lack of unity. In part such judgements reflect the sustained influence of the Romantic requirement of 'organic' unity in an artwork. But Knecht comments that they are in part also tied to the history of the Symphony's creation itself being fragmented, in contrast to the Romantic ideal of the teleological, 'organic' creation of music from beginning to conclusion. As with the Third, however, Mahler indulged in mythmaking through invoking an experience during the summer of 1905 as the work's initial stimulus. Ignoring (surely not simply forgetting) the fact that the first movement was not the first to be composed, in October 1908 he told William Ritter:

> So you see, this Seventh Symphony . . . there was not a note composed . . . I went to the Dolomites for three days, and when I came back, crossing the lake, as soon as I stepped into the rowing boat, at this moment my mind began to work; everything I thought, saw, and felt was doing 'ta-tatata-tatata' (and he indicated the funeral march-like rhythm of the first movement).[39]

The moment of inspiration is once again identified with the interaction of man and nature (the oars breaking the surface of the water). But Mahler's trip on the lake occurred after two movements had already been drafted the previous summer. In a letter to Alma of 8 June 1910 he is more chronologically precise when he says that after the inspirational boating trip 'within four weeks the first, third and fifth movements were completely finished,' but here he is keen to emphasize that 'in art, as in life, I rely entirely on spontaneity.'[40] (Knecht points to the letter's important context: Gustav seems to have wanted to explain his spontaneous, even capricious spirit to allay Alma's distress by his recent behaviour.) In both these descriptions Mahler follows the common tactic of an artist 'attempt(ing) to tie up their works with their lives to form a whole, just as biographers are tempted to make order in their subject's lives to build a coherent narrative'.[41]

Mahler's self-characterization as an artist driven by impulsive moments of inspiration also surfaces when, in the same letter to Alma, he recalls the summer of 1906:

> on the first morning of our summer at Maiernigg, I went up to my hut . . . as I entered that all-too-familiar room, the creator spiritus took possession of me, held me in its clutches and chastised me for eight weeks, until the work was all but finished.[42]

Mahler is, of course, talking of the monumental Eighth Symphony, whose first movement sets the hymn 'Veni Creator Spiritus'. The speed of Mahler's composing, to Stephen Johnson, 'defies credibility'.[43] It is certainly impressive, even if a sketchpad page in the Paris La Grange archive suggests some preliminary ideas for the Eighth may date from the previous summer. There was also some finishing off to do during the following summer.

In 1907, after months of mounting professional difficulty and personal strain in Vienna, the Mahlers finally arrived at Maiernigg at the end of June. Anna had just recovered from scarlet fever, but Maria, 'Putzi', their older daughter who was still not five, contracted the illness and diphtheria. She died, after enduring the terrible ordeal of a tracheotomy, on 12 July. After Alma and grandmother Anna Moll had both fainted at the sight of the beloved girl's coffin, a doctor was summoned for consultation. During his visit he also found trouble with Gustav's heart. A specialist in Vienna confirmed a valve defect and demanded stringent limits to Mahler's exercise regime. The beautiful Maiernigg house was now a site of deepest tragedy and emotional trauma. The family could not bear to stay. They spent the rest of that summer at a hotel beside Lake Toblach. Mahler's last three summers were spent at a farmhouse in Alt-Schluderbach, just outside Toblach (Dobbiaco), whose grounds on the edge of the forest included his final composing hut. Here, in 1908 and 1909, he composed *Das Lied von der Erde* and the Ninth Symphony. During the final summer of 1910 he worked on the incomplete Tenth.

Acknowledging the obvious differences between an artistic canvas and holiday snap, it is instructive to compare a famous photograph of Mahler walking in the Dolomites near Toblach in 1909 with Caspar David Friedrich's now well-known *Wanderer above the Sea of Fog* (*c.* 1817; Friedrich's work had fallen into prolonged obscurity until an exhibition in Berlin in 1906). The human presence in Friedrich's painting is a *Rückenfigur*, a subject who is seen, from behind, doing the seeing. (It seems especially close to what Mahler described to Istel concerning the Seventh: the solitary human in a symbolic landscape 'imagines that he was standing on the highest peak, facing eternity'.) The landscape is staged as if it were a projection of the wanderer's imagination. Ordered (to the extent that it is 'ordered') around or by him, the landscape is posed as not only a view but a vision: it seems to emanate 'from his gaze, or more precisely, from his heart', as an 'extension of his subjectivity'. The resulting relationship of human figure and nature confirms the thinking of Mahler's beloved Kant (in the *Critique of Judgement* (1790)): sublimity lies not in the natural landscape itself but rather in the subjective effect on a human mind. The wanderer also 'stands as a kind of trope for origins', for the creative act, and thereby also confirms Friedrich Schelling's concept, in 'On the Relation of the Fine Arts to Nature' (1807), that the artist is both 'faithful to, and separate from, nature in the production of his art', which is therefore not merely the imitator of natural forms.[44] (Fredric Jameson made a similar point when arguing that the cowbells of the Sixth are intended to convey not a pastoral landscape but 'another world beyond our own'.[45])

The face of Friedrich's 'Wanderer' is unseen, so the figure is a universalized, anonymized Everyman, and his distant gaze offers no obvious line of sight or way through the landscape. Mahler, by contrast, looks almost straight to camera; he stands on a well-trodden valley path, the erosive mark of humanity's presence. His garb and stance are favoured ones – gentlemanly tweeds, resting on his walking stick. Mahler is a tourist at leisure. But his facial expression and wistful smile suggest a relationship with the landscape of both pleasure and pain. Freud's short essay 'On

Mahler walking in the Dolomites, near Toblach, 1909.

Transience', written in 1915 for a commemorative volume *Das Land Goethes*, contains thoughts on recalling a walk in the Dolomites in the summer of 1913. His unnamed poet companion (if only it could have been Mahler!) was 'disturbed by the thought that all this beauty was fated to extinction'. The inevitable decay of summer's beauty raises the value of the moment's enjoyment while at the same time bringing sorrow at its ephemerality. A multiple

Caspar David Friedrich, *Wanderer above the Sea of Fog*, *c*. 1817, oil on canvas.

response is required, including the recognition that by contrast with the natural cycle of regeneration the fate of the human subject is terminal. Freud's poet (our ersatz Mahler) demands a 'revolt against mourning' and pursues the aspiration of immortality through creative work.[46]

Hill walking was a vital complementary activity to Mahler's withdrawals into his composing huts. These buildings were partially primitive, partially domesticated spaces (with rudimentary cooking equipment). They were in marginal locations, a place where the Muse might visit, on a threshold between culture and nature where the composer could indulge in the 'part surrender of voluntary control implicated in the practices of the Romantic imagination'. The huts – liminal, impermanent places of occupation, a choice of what might be seen as a sign of impoverishment but one based on an act of privilege – had a double function as partial shelters from both nature and the home.[47] They are, in a quotidian modern-day sense, precursors of the garden shed, the 'man cave' or, most recently, the trend for shepherd huts famously embraced by British politician David Cameron. These are all spaces facilitating male fantasies of (just enough) freedom and self-expression. The 'Mahler hut' also becomes a symbolic site of creative origins. In the opening of Russell's *Mahler* film (with the English Lake District framed as an ersatz Alpine landscape) the hut explodes into flames, a blazing 'metaphor for the way inspiration would often engulf Mahler'.[48]

In recently discovered letters to Theuer, architect of the Maiernigg house, Mahler deploys a newly fashionable term by describing his hut as 'mein Study'.[49] Technological, economic and social developments in the early twentieth century altered perceptions of living spaces. In a cultural politics of domesticity, spaces are disciplined, invested with power, through the work of capital and gender. There was expectation of a non-negotiable manly space of privacy, regulated solitude, undisturbed male (in)activity, separated from homely spaces for family, servants and receiving guests. The study, a means of control over and escape from clock time, feminine diversions and the strictures of domestic routine, was often in a high or distant corner of the home. It was a singular, cerebral, privileged space of culture and separateness, by contrast with multiple rooms of nurture and socializing in the rest of the house. Mahler's huts amplify this division of space and labour and extend the functions of the male study into, and beyond, the garden. The Mahler pilgrim might be deflated to find that the site of the Steinbach hut is now a camping ground. It seems particularly ironic, however, that before being restored it was for a while appropriated for a domestic chore, temporarily serving as a laundry.

The creative and psychological significance of the composing hut for Mahler stands in marked contrast with that which accrued to the main house at Maiernigg. Theodor Reik (young associate of Freud in Vienna, and a devotee of Mahler's music) considered that the house became a 'symbolic representation of woman', a space identified for Mahler with functions of nurturing and procreation, and from 1902 specifically with Alma as wife and mother. (But Alma hated the furnishings and called the house a fortress.) Reik is rather speculative in arguing that during the summer of 1900 Mahler was unconsciously composing the Fourth in a race with the progress on building the house, a manifestation of his 'hypochondriacal fear of impotence'.[50] A more persuasive psychological identification of house with maternal function emerges from an intriguing aspect of the 1904 manuscript of the final song of the *Kindertotenlieder*, where children seek shelter from a storm. Mahler substituted (in a Freudian slip?) Rückert's 'in der Mutter Haus' with 'in der Mutter Schoss' (womb) (unlike many other poets he set, Mahler seldom altered Rückert). When he sent the final version for publication to the copyist in 1905 Mahler changed the word *Schoss* back to *Haus*, but the telling performance instruction 'like a lullaby' was retained.[51]

Alma, along with Mahler's other significant women, has waited long enough in the lobby of this account of his 'lives'. It is time to move from Mahler the ascetic, antisocial, hut-bound composer to Mahler the lover, husband and father.

5

Gustav and Alma

Almschilitzilitzitzili!

Mahler, letter to Alma, 5 September 1910[1]

Mahler's relationship with Alma (née Schindler, 1879–1964) has generated abundant accounts and analyses. Among them, recently, a novel (Joseph Horowitz's *The Marriage* (2023)) and a misfiring film scene (the error-strewn interview at the opening of Todd Field's excruciatingly pretentious Cate Blanchett vehicle *Tár* (2022)).[2] No single chapter can hope to offer a comprehensive response. However, as Feder has pointed out, key aspects of the emotional character of Gustav's relationship with Alma are foreshadowed in earlier romantic liaisons.[3] Mahler's youthful infatuation with local Iglau girl Josephine Poisl, which blossomed in autumn 1879, appears largely to have been unreciprocated. The relationship that developed with soprano Johanna Richter in 1883–4, while he was working at the Hoftheater in Kassel, seems to have been more mutual. But in both, Mahler's anxiety and lack of confidence, manifest in a propensity to be highly disturbed by the smallest suspicion that his beloved might harbour doubts or hold flimsier passions, was a constant. In response to these early romances Mahler made efforts to repair his 'psychic wounds', to use Feder's term, through writing poetry and music, creative reconstructions of life as art formed as attempts to master feelings of yearning and loss. The unrequited passion for Poisl led to outpourings reminiscent of the manner of Hoffmann's Kreisler. He wrote poems during the early spring of 1880 on amorous unfulfilment and set three of these as songs, inevitably dedicating them to Josephine. They foreshadow the love poems he wrote for Johanna Richter, which are an important aspect of the genesis of the *Lieder eines fahrenden Gesellen* (1884).

Three years later, his dashed hopes of eloping with the married Marion von Weber, for whom he had fallen during the completion of *Die drei Pintos* in Leipzig in 1887–8, can be tied with the 'Blumine' movement which was originally part of the First Symphony. Marion may have possessed a copy of an early version of the 'Blumine' score, with the movement carrying the dedication 'To M., on the occasion of M.'s birthday' (this is according to Willem Mengelberg;[4] the copy is now lost). The movement may therefore partly be a declaration of love, which Mahler decided to remove from the symphony's final version. It is possible, furthermore, that Mahler's suppression of programmatic explanations of the First Symphony was in part driven by this being a very personal, indeed therapeutic, work (Bauer-Lechner suggests that Marion's inspirational encouragement was vital in Mahler's return to writing his own music). Bruno Walter called the First Mahler's *Werther*, as in Goethe's famous novel, in which 'a heart-breaking event is acted out by means of art.' The creative attempt to deal with failure to find romantic happiness ties it with the symphony's best-known literary parallel, Jean Paul's *Titan*, which is itself, in part, a satire on Goethe's *Werther*.[5]

In the relationship that developed in Hamburg from 1895 with the Wagnerian soprano Anna von Mildenburg, Feder characterizes Mahler as a Pygmalion who attempted to fashion her into the sound and form of his ideal woman, training her unsparingly in both singing and in the way she moved her body. The relationship certainly became intense and passionate, and developed into what may have been Mahler's first full sexual relationship. But it once more reinforced Mahler's vulnerability as he again slipped quickly into anxiety when Anna seemed silent or withdrawn. On his move to take up the conducting post in Vienna in 1897 he ended their liaison, but their professional association was to continue, when, to Mahler's surprise, she was engaged at the Vienna Court Opera.

Anna von Mildenburg, 1900.

He made it clear to her that the boundaries around their behaviour must now be very different. (Alma reported that in response Anna became hysterical, but her comments on her husband's ex-lover must be taken with some scepticism.) By comparison with the way he struggled with his earliest romances, Mahler is now wielding more power, finding greater control in handling a romance through regulating its relationship with his professional work.

Another singer, Selma Kurz, was Mahler's *affaire de cœur* between Anna and Alma. She made her Vienna debut in September 1899 and possessed a breathtaking coloratura voice. Her relationship with Mahler became intimate in early 1900 and developed rapidly in impassioned intensity. But it was short-lived. She was fifteen years younger than Mahler and probably sexually inexperienced; she struggled under the imbalanced power dynamic that played out in their affair. Fischer considers that 'it is all too easy to understand that Mahler should time and again have fallen for his female singers' and yet 'Mahler's notorious passion for his female singers was highly problematic.'[6] Kurz was unable to handle the situation, and it was she who ended the liaison.[7]

Through all this, with estimable if ultimately self-delusional powers of patience, stood the loyal Natalie Bauer-Lechner. She had first met Mahler while playing violin in the student orchestra at the conservatoire (she had previously graduated, aged fourteen). She was a highly accomplished musician, one-time lover of Lipiner and held progressive views on politics and sex. She was married at seventeen (to a much older man), but divorced without bearing a child ten years later, in 1885. After travelling to meet Mahler in Budapest in 1890, she became a regular companion, accompanying him during nearly every summer from 1893 to 1901. As a professional viola player she could appreciate Mahler's musical musings. Their relationship became one in which, through long conversations, Mahler could construct an idealized self-image, and also get some things off his chest. At times there was a cathartic element to these discussions for Mahler, and Bauer-Lechner was an assiduous and sympathetic amanuensis. The preparation for publication (after Mahler's death and in the face of opposition from Justine and Alma) of those parts of her diaries pertaining to her relationship with Mahler was a complex, incomplete process leading to a substantial proportion not being included in the published versions (first, in 1923, then expanded in 1980 and again in 1984).

A maternal aspect informed Bauer-Lechner's tireless attentiveness (sometimes, much to Mahler's irritation). But she longed for more. She was wildly jealous of von Mildenburg. On at least two occasions, her relationship with Mahler appears to have become erotic. They are events she judiciously omitted from her published reminiscences. In a recently discovered letter of 1917, however, she characteristically described the first (which happened in 1892) by idealizing the encounter through quoting Goethe and then alluding to Wagner's *Tristan*:

Natalie Bauer-Lechner, 1900.

> would it not have been a wonder, even a sin, if such a transfiguration and consummation of life had not been followed by the highest expression of love? And so it came to be: 'In the coolness of the night of love/ Where the silent candle glows/ There higher feeling seized us' . . . our psyche and physis melted into each other.[8]

But it led nowhere. When, in the same letter, Bauer-Lechner wrote of Mahler's 'chaste lifestyle' and stated that there was no sexual dimension to his relationship with von Mildenburg (which was highly unlikely), this is probably an attempt to cope with Mahler's lack of erotic interest in her beyond what were essentially a couple of fleeting encounters. The end of the relationship, which preceded Mahler's fateful meeting with Alma in November 1901, was likely precipitated by her despair that there was no amorous commitment from Gustav after their sexual liaison a few weeks before. She continued to record her reminiscences into the beginning of 1902, but then she disappears from Mahler's life. She called hers a 'sacrificial love'. Alma is rather cruel: 'she was old and ugly' and 'was in love with Mahler and hoped for the return of her passion'.[9] Bauer-Lechner died, in impoverished circumstances, in 1921.[10] Her voice needs rehearing in fuller, more complete form. The promised forthcoming publication of the remaining manuscripts and copies of her Mahler reminiscences (which were purchased by La Grange) is long anticipated;[11] meanwhile, Beate Thalberg's docu-drama *My Time Will Come* (2010) offers a sympathetic cinematic rendition.

In her diaries Alma recorded seeing Mahler's performance of Wagner's *Siegfried* on 11 February 1898. At the end of that year (4 December) she writes, after hearing him conduct a Philharmonic concert, 'As for Mahler – I'm virtually in love with him.' On New Year's Eve 1898 family friend Dr Pollack gave her an autographed picture of 'Mahler, my beloved Mahler'. Her comments may be little more than distant, youthful hero-worship (she was nineteen years old), but they are based on her appreciation of Mahler as a conductor. The admiration drove her own aspirations. On hearing him conduct the Preludes to Acts 1 and 2 of Strauss's *Guntram* (on 19 February 1899) she enthused: 'Mahler is a genius through and through. Music has never pervaded me as it did today. Suddenly I burst into tears. It's my wish – just once – to write a symphonic work.'[12] The character of her connection with Mahler at this time is shown in her reaction when the family happened to encounter him while he was out on his bicycle the following summer (he had recently sent her a signed postcard having been told it was for an admirer of his work):

> Judging by the way he looked at me, he appears to have perceived the connection between myself and the postcard – which I found most embarrassing. Anyway I feel absolutely no urge to meet him. I love and honour him as an artist, but as a man he doesn't interest me at all. I wouldn't want to lose my illusions either.

But by the following February 1900, she wrote 'I longed to meet him.'[13]

That meeting would not be until 7 November 1901, at an evening gathering in the home of Berta and Emil Zuckerkandl, who were well known for hosting Vienna's elite artistic circle. In the recollections she published some decades later, Alma describes being hesitant at accepting the invitation because of Mahler's promised presence. She knew him 'well by sight' ('small, fidgety . . . with a fine head') and as a conductor (source of 'his mysterious and powerful fascination'), less favourably as a composer (his First Symphony, 'I had thoroughly disliked and even angrily rejected') and for his rumoured reputation as a womanizer. She went 'feeling rather intimidated'. The gathering included two prominent artists who had erotic designs on her: Gustav Klimt, with whom she had a brief, non-consummated liaison, and Max Burckhardt (once director of the Burgtheater), whom she admired for his artistic achievements but loathed for his physical advances (he was 25 years older than her). Alma recalled Mahler's growing impatience as he watched her talking enthusiastically with Klimt and Burckhardt, and him chipping in to a discussion on beauty:

> 'Beauty!' Mahler said, 'the head of Socrates is beautiful.' I agreed and added that in my eyes Alexander von Zemlinsky . . . was a beauty. He was the ugliest man I had ever seen – and yet the force of his intellect was felt in every glance of his eyes and in every one of his abrupt movements . . . Mahler shrugged his shoulders. That was going a bit too far he thought.[14]

Zemlinsky, who was unable to attend that evening, was then Alma's composition teacher. They were also becoming deeply involved emotionally, and increasingly erotically. She argued with Mahler on the merits of Zemlinsky's music. Afterwards, when she reflected on the evening's events in her diary, she began to wonder what to say to Zemlinsky: 'I must say, I liked [Mahler] *immensely* – although he was dreadfully restless . . . The fellow is made *entirely* of oxygen. When you go near him, you get burnt. Tomorrow I shall tell Alex *some* of this . . .'[15]

Mahler was impressed by Alma's intellectual curiosity and artistic enthusiasm. He invited her to visit him at the Opera House the next morning. On Alma's arrival he confessed to having had a sleepless night. His poetic muse was again rekindled, writing her flowery lines in admiration. Mahler began to usurp Zemlinsky's place in Alma's affections, but not without considerable soul searching. Her diary tells the story. On 20 November: '*Mahler's* picture is graven in my heart'; 28 November: 'I believe I love him [Mahler!]' (her emphasis and underlining); 30 November: 'a battle is raging within me. Alex against Mahler.'[16]

But Alma remained unimpressed by Mahler's music. (A year previously, on 18 November 1900, she had attended the Vienna premiere of the First Symphony and declared it not 'beautiful': 'Certainly, it's done with talent, but with the greatest naivety and refinement, and not in the best sense of the word. An unbelievable jumble of styles – and an ear-splitting, nerve-shattering din.'[17]) When Mahler sent her his songs as their relationship intensified in late November she wrote that they 'disappointed me because they struck me as insincere. I shall tell him so as well.' Two days later, as she sang them through, she was only slightly more appreciative: 'I'm beginning to like some of them. It's pretty dour stuff.' When Mahler visited on 2 December their physical passion was growing rapidly, but she still did not care much for his music and retained strong feelings for Zemlinsky (here identified as the 'other'): '[Gustav] told me that he loved me – we kissed each other. He played me his pieces – my lips are sealed . . . His caresses are tender & agreeable. If only I knew! He or – the other.' At heart, she was concerned that they would not be able to understand and support each other musically (something she was much more confident about with Zemlinsky): 'Can I really love Mahler as he deserves and as I am really able? Shall I ever understand his art, & he mine!? With Alex the sympathy is mutual. He loves every *note* of me.' 'One question plagues me: whether Mahler will inspire me to compose – whether he will support my artistic striving – whether he will love me like Alex.'[18]

Other doubts emerged, on both sides. Alma was concerned about Gustav's health, which scurrilous speculations suggested was poor. On 18 December she wrote: 'he's a sick man . . . no longer young.'[19] Mahler, now away from Vienna for several days on conducting assignments, began to express his own worries about the age gap (she was 22, he 41), though such differences were not uncommon in bourgeois marriages at that time. He had, however, rapidly moved to talk of marriage. The relationship with Justine therefore required careful handling. Alma was annoyed when Gustav became critical of how she engaged with his sister: 'I take the greatest pains to make friends with Justine, and she observes me with an eagle eye – every word, movement and sensation – and promptly passes on her <u>fears</u> to Gustav.' Justine, writing to brother Gustav on 12 December of her meeting with Alma, described that after initial awkwardness on both parties 'I liked her *quite* a bit.' Faint praise indeed. Later the same day Gustav replied: 'I beg of you, really look at Alma with your cooler, feminine eyes; I am basing quite a lot on your judgement.' Three days later Justine wrote again to him, describing Alma as a girl who was very interested in Gustav's library but 'seems *very* young to me'. Justine confessed that in her eyes no woman would be a good enough wife for him.[20] Alma later described Gustav's relationship with his sister in strong terms, and falsely claims that it was the reason why Mahler, until then, had eschewed the pleasures of the flesh: 'Mahler was extremely puritanical. Up to now he had been in a sense married to Justine. He regarded himself as bound to her by vows of fidelity and deliberately eluded all temptations.'[21]

On 19 December, while in Dresden, Mahler sent Alma his most notorious letter. After writing of his disagreement with Nietzsche's views on the relationship of men and women, and his concerns about what will happen 'when the first passion is spent (which happens very quickly) and our relationship has become one of friendship', he asks (with insistent underlinings): 'From now on, would you be able to regard my music as if it were your own?' In other words, she must relinquish her own compositional aspirations. There was room for only one composer in this relationship. He knew that this was a big ask: 'This letter will come as a dreadful shock to you – I know it, Alma, and even if this is only cold comfort, you can well imagine that I am suffering just as much.'[22] Alma took time to allow the demands to sink in. In her diary entry two days later, upon rereading Mahler's letter (no doubt for the umpteenth time), and sharing it with her mother, she writes: 'What if I were to *renounce* [my music] *out of love* for him?'. . . 'Yes, he's right. I must live *entirely* for him, to make him happy . . . I long for him *boundlessly*.'[23] Her later public recollections are more ambivalent: 'I buried my dream and perhaps it was for the best. It has been my privilege to give my creative gifts another life in minds greater than my own. And yet the iron had entered my soul and the wound has never healed.'[24]

Gustav's matrimonial mandates and Alma's response have elicited numerous analyses. In an often-problematic biography of Alma, Oliver Hilmes argues that Mahler 'presented his intended with this difficult choice, so he could be absolutely certain that Alma really suited him. Alma mythologized: Mahler did not forbid her to compose; he didn't force her into a decision. She had a choice.'[25] Antony Beaumont, co-editor of the English translation of Alma's diaries, also deemed that Alma had free will to choose. But Beaumont also has a very low opinion of Alma's musical abilities and suggests that Gustav was perhaps concerned at being professionally embarrassed if she had continued to compose as his wife. Beaumont's co-editor, Susanne Rode-Breymann, considers this verdict to be harsh on Alma, who had wide artistic tastes, and also points to the unresolved question of when she wrote the songs that were published years later (perhaps she worked on them during the marriage, as compensation for her unhappiness and what we have now is therefore more accomplished than her work before 1902).[26] What is clear is that right from the start, problematic, ultimately damaging, power dynamics informed their relationship. More on this later.

Gustav and Alma were privately engaged on 23 December, in the company of Alma's mother Anna, her stepfather Carl Moll and Justine. Mahler wanted the engagement kept out of the papers, but the news leaked four days later. Meanwhile, their relationship quickly moved towards consummation. In her diaries Alma, until then a virgin, was candid: on 30 December, 'Today we all but joined in wedlock. He let me feel his masculinity – his vigour – & it was a pure, holy sensation, such as I would *never* have expected.' On New Year's Eve: 'His beloved hand explored my body, and mine his.' The following day a failed attempt at intercourse was deeply distressing for both, but Alma's exultations on 3 and 4 January require no interpretation: 'Wonne und Glück'; 'Wonne über Wonne' (Bliss and Joy; Bliss upon Bliss).[27]

Social life as an engaged couple did not begin well. The guests at a dinner party that Gustav hosted on 5 January included his old friend Lipiner and old flame Anna von Mildenburg, sister Justine and Arnold Rosé (leader of the Philharmonic Orchestra, whom Justine announced was now her fiancé). Lipiner held deep misgivings about Alma's suitability as a wife for his friend. On her side, Alma despised Lipiner, later describing him as a 'bogus Goethe' and 'haggling Jew'. Indeed, she observed that all the guests at the dinner were 'conspicuously Jewish. I could find no bond.'[28] Time spent privately together offered much happier moments, notably the day after the awkward dinner party, when they played through Gustav's new Fourth Symphony at the piano. By contrast with her previous responses to her fiancée's music, Alma noted in her diary that it 'pleased me very, very much'.[29] (Later, however, her opinion of the Fourth is harsher: 'I resented an archaizing that had no relation to our time.'[30]) They were married on 9 March 1902 in a small family ceremony at the Vienna Karlskirche. (Justine and Arnold's wedding was the following day; Gustav and Alma did not attend.) A honeymoon was tagged on to Mahler's professional obligations in St Petersburg later that month. By then, Alma was two months pregnant with their first daughter.

Their first summer together was hardly one of easy marital pleasures. Alma experienced extreme mood swings. Between moments of feeling deep love for her husband there were frequent bouts of weeping. In her published memoirs she ironically uses the title 'splendid isolation',[31] one of Mahler's favourite turns of phrase. She often felt neglected and missed her Vienna social life. Mahler's indefatigable work ethic meant he was uninterested in social gatherings. Her sense of loneliness would sometimes become acute as for long hours Gustav retreated into silent seclusion to compose in his hut. A behavioural pattern was established which would continue through all their summers together. Alma's memoirs often strike a tone of despair: 'I cancelled my will and my being . . . He noticed nothing of all it cost me . . . I separated myself inwardly from him . . . He saw in me only the comrade, the mother and housewife,' and he had no time for the frivolities of fashion, travel, jewellery.[32] She discerned a conflict in Mahler's personality: he 'loved cheerfulness and gaiety . . . but some dark principle or other held him back. He would laugh uncontrollably, but if anybody else laughed it got on his nerves.'[33] Hilmes is characteristically dismissive of Alma's description of the marriage:

> she styled herself as the victim of a workaholic, ascetic genius . . . the constant laments about being lonely, not having any more friends, not being allowed to work with Zemlinsky, being suppressed by Mahler – none of this took place in reality.[34]

Even if Alma can lean towards exaggeration and obfuscation in some passages of her memoirs, it seems an unfair judgement.

Alma's musical abilities were allowed a subservient outlet – copying parts from the manuscript as Gustav completed the Fifth Symphony. The famous Adagietto fourth movement, according to Mengelberg's reminiscences and score annotations, was composed as an expression of love for Alma.[35] As Mahler became aware of his wife's unhappiness he took time out from work on the symphony to compose a song setting of Rückert's 'Liebst du um Schönheit' as a gift: the poem opens 'If you love for beauty, O love me not' (conceptions of beauty and ugliness were a favourite topic of conversation, often explicitly identified with themselves – the beautiful Alma, the ugly Gustav) and closes with 'If you love for love/ Ah yes love me!/ Love me forever/ I shall love you evermore.' Alma was delighted. She recalled Mahler secreting the manuscript in a score of *Die Walküre* in the hope she would surprisingly find it (Alma spent much time playing Wagner at the piano) but losing patience and picking up the score himself to let it fall out in her presence.[36]

Mahler characteristically continued to combine asceticism and athleticism. On the one hand, 'his one aim', Alma recalled with no little hint of lingering frustration, 'was to be unconscious of the body'.[37] He held a fastidious concern with diet (apples were always his favourite snack; he was very fussy with breads) and assiduously monitored and reported on the condition of his unreliable digestive system: among many such comments he wrote to Alma with relish on 1 September 1903: 'bowels tip-top'.[38] On the other hand Alma would accompany Mahler on his characteristically vigorous walks across open, sometimes hilly countryside. These excursions were taken during her pregnancy: the complications of the birth on 3 November of their first child, Maria Anna (she was named after the two grandmothers, but always to be affectionately called 'Putzi'), may be partly a result of overexertion. Mahler was also ever the aesthete: when Alma's labour pains signalled the imminent birth of their second daughter (Anna Justina – 'Gucki' – was born on 15 June 1904) Gustav 'did all he could think of to mitigate my pain. But the best he could think of was reading Kant aloud. I sat at his writing-table and writhed in agony. The monotonous drone of his voice drove me crazy.'[39]

Mahler with his daughter Maria, 1905.

Many accounts describe Mahler's devotion to his daughters. Their arrival seemed to motivate broader changes in his domestic habits: 'the children had a great effect on our lives,' Alma recalled, and

> Mahler had more time for us; he could hardly tear himself away from the two little girls, with each of whom he had an intimate, oddly individual relationship. More friends were allowed to come, and he himself became more human, more communicative.[40]

It was incomprehensible to her, therefore, that during the summer of 1904 (which she described as 'beautiful, serene and happy', with Gucki a babe in arms and Putzi a delightful toddler) he would turn to composition of the *Kindertotenlieder* and completion of the tragic Sixth Symphony. She held superstitious fears of tempting fate and would later declare that the brutal hammer blows in the Symphony's finale were prophetic of the three blows of fate in 1907 – resignation from the Court opera house, the tragic death of Putzi and the diagnosis of Mahler's heart problem. This is nonsense, of course. Others have sought for more persuasive analysis of the extreme dissonance between Mahler's life and art at this time: for example that, 'true to his character, Mahler gave this happy phase of his life inverse artistic expression.'[41] Feder's psychoanalytical approach identifies deeper unconscious connections with death, that after suffering the near-fatal haemorrhage in February 1901 Mahler's impulse for marrying Alma was a desire to gain immortality through having children, and that 'when Mahler's creative thinking . . . turned to children, these thoughts were imbued with mourning' because of the losses of multiple siblings in his own childhood.[42]

Alma's antisemitism was often plainly expressed. She was hardly unusual in this regard in the social circles of turn-of-the-century Vienna. Different biographers of Alma have laid varying emphasis on it. Hilmes was the first to use Alma's unpublished diaries from 1902–44 with the aim of revealing the unvarnished truth. He portrays her as seeking the power to redeem gifted, ugly, Jewish

Alma Mahler with daughters Anna and Maria, 1906.

male artists. If things had turned out only slightly differently at the Zuckerkandl dinner she could possibly have gone on to marry the Jewish, 'ugly' Zemlinsky. They had met in spring 1900. He cut a famously unhandsome figure, but by that summer she wrote of her teacher: 'I don't find him strange – nor is he ugly, for his eyes glow with intelligence – and a person like that is never ugly.' (This alludes to the kind of inner beauty that Mahler was pointing to in setting Rückert's 'Liebst du um Schönheit' as a love offering to her.) But when Alma contemplated standing at the altar with the outwardly unattractive and vertically challenged Zemlinsky ('I, so lovely – so tall') and considered the prospect of 'bring[ing] short, degenerate Jew-children into the world'[43] the thought of marriage to Zemlinsky turned sour. Clearly, Alma's emotional relationship with Zemlinsky was deeply ambivalent. His most attractive characteristic was an ardent enthusiasm and understanding of the music of her beloved Wagner (author, of course, of the notorious 'Judaism in Music'). In her later memoirs she wrote that Zemlinsky

> was a hideous gnome. Short, chinless, toothless, always with the coffee-house smell on him, unwashed – and yet the keenness and strength of his mind made him tremendously attractive . . . He played *Tristan* for me, I leaned on the piano, my knees buckled, we sank into each other's arms.[44]

Alma had two years before declared *Tristan* to be 'my favourite opera'; its effect, she wrote, was one of 'sheer rapture';[45] Zemlinsky's Wagnerism played a strong role in overriding Alma's aversion to his Jewishness.

But Mahler's credentials as a conductor of Wagner, and increasingly of *Tristan*, were by 1901 unimpeachable and it was his Wagner interpretations that had first attracted him to Alma's attention. (That the style of Mahler's compositions is in many ways far from Wagnerian was undoubtedly a major reason why she was so often disappointed or perplexed by them.) While Gustav was away in Berlin during their relationship's very early days she saw *Tristan*: 'in every note, in every bar, my thoughts were with him.'[46] Later, on hearing her new husband conduct the 'Liebestod' in St Petersburg, she recalls, 'That uplifted face, those open lips! There was a divine beauty in his expression when he conducted. I trembled.'[47] The fashion of the day was for 'Tristanizing' every passionate affair – every glance must be intoxicating, the desired climax must achieve *Verklärung* or fail. (This context makes more persuasive the allusion to *Tristan* in the expression of love that many hear in the Adagietto of the Fifth.) Bauer-Lechner also often played this game. In her analysis of Mahler's affair with Marion von Weber she wrote:

> what lost them both . . . or rather what captured them in most blissful ill-fated love, was *Tristan,* which they used to play four-hands. As if through the power of a magic potion, they were suddenly overcome by the knowledge of their most intimate oneness.

And as we saw, she also turned to 'Wagnerizing' to describe her own ill-fated lovemaking with Mahler.

A key aspect of the question of Jewishness in Mahler and Alma's relationship lies in the then commonly held distinction between the assimilated, acculturated Viennese Jew and the 'Ostjuden', the Jews from lands to the east, who were deemed to be beyond hope of transfiguration (though a counter-discourse emerged placing value on their supposed closeness to nature, with a resulting tension between aspirations of assimilation and authenticity).[48] The Ostjuden were often seen to embody abject Jewish suffering. Alma recalled that during a brief stop in Warsaw on returning from their St Petersburg honeymoon they gave loose change to 'an old Jewish match peddler. This poor old Jew, in one instant, made me see the whole of Israel's burden and suffering.'[49] Poland recurs as a site of Jewish abjection. Gustav wrote to Alma from Lemberg (Lviv) on 2 April 1903 describing 'a filthy place . . . And one couldn't imagine anything dirtier than the Polish Jews here.'[50] In a letter to Alma from St Petersburg (22 October 1907) he describes two 'enchanting hours' at Warsaw station:

> I was quite horrified to be served tea by a crotchety old waiter with a greasy tailcoat and grimy shirt. I couldn't bring myself to order anything else from the buffet, as it was swarming with bluebottles (even at this time of the year the Poles manage to attract hordes of them) . . . Then I wandered around in search

> of our old Jew. I couldn't find him, but I did find a number of younger ones (I thought it better not to bring one back as a souvenir for you). All the same, I had a most amusing time. It's a strange experience to observe such exotic people at close hand.[51]

There seems little that is attractive in such letters, in which the jarring paradox of Jewish antisemitism is unmissable. But it is interesting to recall that when Mahler told Bauer-Lechner how he disliked Spielmann's exaggerated caricature of the dwarf Mime, Wagner's personification of abject Jewishness, he wrote: 'I know only one Mime . . . and that is me! You would all be amazed what there is in the role and how I would want to bring it to light!'[52] Mahler often told Alma that the most profound beauty is one marked with suffering, and a simulated self-identification and self-abjection with ugliness and affliction, embodied most overtly in the Eastern Jew, plays a part in this construction. Interestingly, in his 1985 'television essay' *The Little Drummer Boy*, which focuses on hearing Jewishness in Mahler's music, Leonard Bernstein adds, spuriously, Polishness to his construction of Mahler's hybrid identity, by implication turning Mahler into part Eastern Jew. Hostile critics of antisemitic inclination had long since shifted Mahler's 'Jewishness' eastwards, to make it more unpalatable. Rudolf Louis wrote in his *Die Deutsche Musik der Gegenwart* (Munich, 1909):

> If Mahler's music would speak Yiddish, it would be perhaps unintelligible to me. But it is repulsive to me because it *acts* Jewish. This is to say that it speaks musical German, but with an accent, with an inflection, and above all, with the gestures of an eastern, all too eastern Jew. So, even to those whom it does not offend directly, it cannot possibly communicate anything.[53]

In 1907 many of these Ostjuden symbolic identifications re-emerged when, while in Toblach, Alma met the Russian pianist and conductor Ossip Gabrilowitsch (who had impressed Mahler in 1906 and would remain an associate). Alma's brief relationship with Gabrilowitsch to some extent recapitulates aspects of the Zemlinsky affair. She describes him as 'an ugly young man whose whole face seemed out of joint' and quotes Emil Zuckerkandl saying that he 'looks like a Russian Jew *after* a pogrom'. Alma then adds in parentheses: '(Of course, this may also have been what attracted Mahler, the perpetual grief-seeker, who kept telling me that there were not enough lines of suffering in my face.)' Also telling is Alma's declaration that 'It was natural for us to fall in love'; Gabrilowitsch was a man sufficiently attractive in Alma's favoured Jewish figuration to override his Eastern Jewishness. Furthermore, Gabrilowitsch's confession of love in Paris in autumn 1907 convinced her that she remained sexually desirable, and not 'old and ugly'.[54]

The flirtation with Gabrilowitsch was nipped in the bud, probably in large part because it came quickly on the heels of the traumas suffered during the previous summer. The pain of the tragic death of daughter Maria can hardly be over-emphasized. Mahler's heart diagnosis, though in itself not a death sentence, had been profoundly troubling. The loss of Maria was acutely felt as Alma and Gustav spent a lonely first Christmas in New York, with their precious younger daughter Anna staying in Vienna. Even during the following summer of 1908 in Toblach, 'grief and anxiety' were still raw, according to Alma, during which time Gustav worked on the composition of *Das Lied von der Erde*. The New York spring of 1909 saw a robust Gustav being more energetic in pursuance of his conducting duties, but Alma, despite the diversions of the American metropolis, was in poor physical and mental condition. On her return to Europe she took a health cure in Levico. She may have been recovering from a miscarriage or abortion (perhaps not for the first time). That summer was a low point in their relationship, and Alma's reliance on alcohol was increasing.[55]

The following summer Alma took another health cure, this time at a sanatorium in Tobelbad. The stay was fateful. In her published accounts Alma resorts to either awkward attempts at anonymity or more 'Wagnerizing', describing that she met 'an architect, X',[56] an 'extraordinarily handsome German who would have been well cast as Walther von Stolzing in *Die Meistersinger*'.[57] The affair with Walter Gropius began in June. Mahler, away on tour, became unsettled by Alma's lack of response to his frequent letters. In July his anxiety at her silence rises further. Unlike all but one of her letters to Mahler (the only one she didn't destroy is a letter of 29 November 1901) Alma's letters to Gropius survive. They express an intense physical attraction. Alma rejoined Mahler at Alt-Schluderbach in mid-July. She was in good health but withheld herself from Gustav sexually. La Grange's assessment is that Mahler 'loved her deeply, and trusted her utterly, and was thus unprepared for the catastrophe which occurred on the morning of 29 July'.[58]

The mail that morning included a letter addressed to 'Herr Direktor Mahler'. It was a passionate missive from Gropius meant for Alma (this letter is now lost). Many years later Gropius told La Grange that the incorrect addressee was simply a terrible, inexplicable mistake.[59] Alma was horrified at Gustav's anguish when he opened and read the letter, but equally must have been dismayed by her lover's reckless error. La Grange's analysis is that Alma quickly turned the blame onto Gustav: 'she made Mahler responsible for her betrayal' through 'accusations of neglect'. La Grange is unsparing on Alma, whom he describes as becoming a 'tigress' now aggressively exercising, with little compassion, a new-found power. Gustav became overwhelmed with a sense of guilt. 'From now on', La Grange writes,

> Gustav's one effort, invested with all the more intensity and passion because he believed the cause was a lost one, was to woo Alma as if she were an angry goddess, an all-powerful and dangerous mother whose favours could only be won with offerings.[60]

By contrast, Carr is more judicious in weighing up the crisis:

> [it has been] easy to see [Alma] alone as the guilty party and Mahler as an innocent victim. It is a role which rarely fits him and it does not do so here. Alma was frequently flighty, jealous

> and deceitful but Mahler was moody and authoritarian at least as often.[61]

Alma, despite the intensity of her feelings for Gropius and the unhappiness of her marriage, felt compelled to stay with Gustav. She recalled in her memoirs:

> After we had laid bare the causes of our division with the completest honesty, I felt as strongly as I ever had that I could never leave him. When I told him so, his face was transfigured. His love became an ecstasy. He could not be parted from me for a second.

She can't leave him not only because she knows his love is 'limitless', but because of his fragility: 'I knew that my marriage was no marriage and that my own life was utterly unfulfilled. I concealed all this from him, and although he knew it as well as I did we played out the comedy to the end, to spare his feelings.'[62] La Grange adds another, and for him primary if unspoken, reason: Alma wished to avoid the damage to her social standing that a scandal would cause.[63]

Gropius impetuously decided to meet the Mahlers at Toblach to compel a resolution. Gustav told Alma she must choose. She decided to secretly hold on to both (with encouragement from her mother Anna – of whom Gustav was very fond, but who was a role model in the practice of infidelity, having cheated on Alma's father with Carl Moll). Hilmes paints a rather pathetic picture of Mahler: 'by and large, clueless and full of hope about his marriage', he showered Alma with love offerings.[64] To her he dedicated the Eighth Symphony, now in the advanced stages of preparation for its premiere (none of his previous symphonies have dedications). He suddenly felt remorse at his ban on her composing: on playing through her songs Alma says he declared 'What have I done?'[65] And his literary muse was once more inspired, as he wrote a succession of poems to her through the month of August. More disturbingly, he watched her from the door as she slept at night (they had always had separate bedrooms). Beaumont sees Mahler's behaviour as manifesting a 'state of submission and emotional regression'.[66]

Remarkably, Mahler still found the mental powers to compose. But as he worked on the Tenth Symphony he plastered the manuscript with impassioned, desperate annotations expressing his emotional trauma. Franklin notes that these are 'often painful to read', and 'have consistently inspired more embarrassment than post-revelatory awe'.[67] The 'Purgatorio' third movement was likely composed after the exposure of the Gropius affair. Feder interprets the Tenth as in large part 'tragic autobiography encoded'. Some of the heart-wrenching exclamations on the manuscript are derived from Wagner (*Parsifal*, *Die Walküre*), others are overtly biblical ('O God! O God! Why hast thou forsaken me?' – Gustav had read the Bible during Gropius's confrontational visit) and, in the finale, direct addresses to Alma: 'To live for thee! To die for thee! Almschi!' Feder analyses these collectively as expressions of 'symbolic suicide' (though, unlike brother Otto, this does not mean Gustav intended or contemplated the act).[68] The five-movement work was left incomplete at his departure from Toblach, but with hopes for a return to his compositional desk in the summer of 1911, and future work at a new house he planned to build at Semmering. But the Tenth was to remain unfinished.

Alma became very concerned for Mahler's mental health. Feder argues that encouragement to approach Freud probably came from Alma, because of her family connection and greater initial sympathy for psychoanalysis (Bruno Walter had previously consulted Freud in 1906, but Mahler had been sceptical).[69] An appointment was sought between the end of Mahler's composing stint in Toblach and the Munich rehearsals for the Eighth in September. After several postponements (cancellations which La Grange sees as indicating a combination of Mahler's neurosis, doubts, illness and dedication to work on the Tenth Symphony[70]), on 25 August he set off to meet Freud in Leiden. The next day, during a four-hour stroll, Mahler had his 'peripatetic psychoanalytic consultation'.[71] While hardly constituting a comprehensive or conventional analytical session (the 'patient' Mahler was ambulatory, not recumbent) it is a famous meeting of two great Viennese minds. Freud shared many of Mahler's literary and philosophical interests (especially Schopenhauer, Nietzsche, Dostoyevsky) but held little interest in music. He would not have known Mahler's compositions but was fully aware of his stellar musical reputation and may have heard him conduct at one of his infrequent visits to the opera house.

The tantalizingly incomplete record of what was discussed has encouraged multiple attempts to reconstruct and extend its findings. The meeting has also formed the basis of a film, *Mahler auf dem Couch* (dir. Percy and Felix Adlon, 2010), to which many critics responded favourably, though the reviewer in *Variety* (28 June 2010) baulked at the dissonant moments of 'cheap comedy' and characterization of Mahler as a kind of 'Teutonic Woody Allen'. (In what is presumably an unintentional conflation of Alma's beloved 'ugly' Jews, the actor playing Mahler, Johannes Silberschneider, was previously cast as Zemlinsky in the Alma biopic *Bride of the Wind* (dir. Bruce Beresford, 2001), in which Jonathan Pryce plays Mahler.)

In the absence of any case notes two secondary sources have provided partial reports of the Freud–Mahler dialogue. In a conversation recorded in an unpublished diary (1925) by Freud's disciple, Marie Bonaparte (1882–1962, a distant relation to Napoleon), we read that Freud was encouraged by Mahler's immediately sympathetic grasp of the aims of psychoanalysis. Freud pointed out that Gustav had married a 'Marie' (his mother's name; Alma's middle name was Maria), while Alma had married a (homophone) 'Maler', German for painter, the occupation of her father, Emil.[72] In a letter to Reik ten years later (1935) Freud writes (in his seventy-ninth year, and with a partially failing memory – he incorrectly says the year was 1912) that Mahler 'withdrew his libido' from Alma, something which Mahler appears to have predicted in the infamous letter he wrote her during their courtship ('when the first passion is spent (which happens very quickly) and our relationship has become one of friendship'). Freud famously concluded that Mahler's 'personal conditions for love' were dominated by his 'Holy Mary complex (*Marienkomplex-Mutterbindung*)', a psychologically debilitating idealization of the 'Mother', even if the informal consultation was only partially insightful: 'No light fell at the time on the symptomatic façade of his obsessional neurosis. It was as if you would dig a single shaft through a mysterious building.'[73] In the Freudian reading all of Mahler's adult emotional relationships with women were profoundly modulated by his attachment to mother Marie.[74] Alma claimed that though 'Freud's analysis reassured Mahler . . . he did not want to hear of his mother fixation. He shunned such concepts.' She then turns to her unhappy marital experience, imagining Freud's words: '"Your mother was careworn and ailing – and that, unconsciously, is how you want your wife." How right he [Freud] was!'[75]

In the account given in her autobiography, which (like others) moves towards imaginary extrapolation, Alma tilts the focus more fully onto herself, claiming Freud had close knowledge of her personality: '"I know your wife. She loved her father and she can seek and love only his type. Your age, which you are afraid of, is just what attracts your wife."'[76] While Alma's claims of Freud's personal acquaintance may be challenged, there is widespread agreement of the 'diagnosis'. Many comments from Alma corroborate the deep admiration for, and psychological attachment to, her father, the trauma she experienced on his relatively early death at the age of fifty (when she was thirteen), and the effect on her later relationships with men. In *And the Bridge Is Love* she wrote: 'My father was profoundly musical'; when she saw him lying in his coffin, 'He was beautiful. He looked like a fine wax image, noble as a Greek statue.' After his death, she continues, 'with my father in mind, I looked for help in maturing to older, knowledgeable men of our artists' circle.'[77] And when she began looking for more amorous attachments, she confessed she 'always looked for a small, slight man, who had wisdom and spiritual superiority, since this is what I had known and loved in my father'.[78]

Reflecting the psychoanalytical gaze back at Alma, Feder sees her elaborations, attempts to make her a larger topic in Gustav's 'consultation', as a manifestation of narcissism. Though, to be fair, he also comments on Mahler's own narcissism, recurrent bouts of depression and psychosomatic illnesses.[79] Others appear not to be so psychoanalytically even-handed. (Feder was alone in the major Mahler biographers in being a trained psychoanalyst.) La Grange wrote of Alma's 'boundless narcissism'. In his estimation her diaries reveal a 'spoilt and hugely egocentric teenager' with an 'insatiable desire to wield power over others' and a sadistic tendency to confirm her power through hurting people. La Grange's opinion is that, for some time, Alma's 'more or less permanent state' was one of 'psychological crisis'. He describes her as an alcoholic 'too self-centred to devote close and lasting attention to a creative artist', a woman who had a 'near-pathological craving' for 'admiration and devotion'.[80]

In his review of La Grange's account of Mahler's final years, Horowitz lambasts the overt 'hostility towards Alma'.[81] But La Grange is not alone. Hilmes, to whom La Grange is greatly indebted, lays emphasis on diagnosing Alma's 'hysteria' (a psychoanalytical concept defined by Freud and Josef Bauer in 1895); 'there are', he observes, 'many traits of the hysterical woman even in the young Alma.' For Hilmes, Alma had an 'hysterical personality disorder' which 'is probably traceable to her extremely close attachment to her father'. Hilmes sees this neurosis manifest in Alma's 'constant vacillation between emotional frigidity and erotic extravagance', her 'flawed sense of identity . . . acute inferiority complex' and rather deluded opinion of her own beauty. 'Her much-cited erotic attractiveness', furthermore, 'had nothing to do with genuine sensuality. For her, sexuality was no more than a kind of kick; a pathetic bit of playacting. That is the home turf of a hysterical woman.'[82]

Hilmes offers a devastating verdict. But there are alternative, more sympathetic ways of 'reading' Alma. First, one can reconsider the question of whether her histrionic expressions, particularly in the diaries, are consciously constructed stylistic markers, simply her adopting mannerisms of the time (for example, all that 'Tristanizing'). In the most recent full-length biography, Cate Haste declares that: 'I like Alma,' especially what she reads in the diaries of 1888–92, and describes a woman of paradox and 'extraordinary complexity'.[83] And second, as in Rode-Breymann's more scholarly German study, one might shift away from the power of the male gaze to allow a fairer portrait of Alma to come into view.[84] Most recently, Gustav and Alma have entered the #MeToo debate. Nancy Newman seeks to change the discourse by taking more account of the sexual politics between an older, professionally powerful man and a much younger and inexperienced woman, between 'the accomplished and the aspiring'.[85] Newman reassesses the role of consent and Gustav's 'gaslighting' (a strategy to undermine the other's self-confidence and perception of reality), for which Alma was primed by the recent experiences of being 'groomed' (a testing of her sexual availability) by a succession of older men: Klimt (who was 17 years older than her) and Max Burckhardt (who was 25 years older). Eleonore Büning emphasizes the double standards then attaching to marriage and sexual licence and the contrast between Mahler's 'callous' approach to numerous pre-marital affairs (including Bauer-Lechner) and Alma's torments over both her virginity and her one infidelity, as she struggled with the 'humiliating' restrictions women endured at that time.[86]

Newman asks us to listen to Alma with a will to believe. In this respect she considers the perspective offered in *Mahler auf der Couch* to be 'brilliant' as it does not discredit Alma's words, by contrast, for example, with the approach of Beaumont in his introduction to the diaries, who casts Alma as quite delusional. Newman urges due recognition for Alma's attempts to articulate a self-identity while living under the principle of 'coverture', in which a married woman's rights are subsumed by their husband, and the obstructions created by the ideological division of labour and gendered functions of public and private spaces. Newman's #MeToo discourse requires a rethinking of Mahler's notorious demands in his letter of 19 December and Alma's response. Alma had long declared that she had destroyed it, only for the letter to be found by La Grange in Alma's papers after her death. Newman focuses on La Grange's difficulties with how the letter depicts Gustav and how this acts as a preface to his launching an 'assault' on Alma's character and her distortion of Mahler's marital demands in her memoirs.

La Grange's speculations generate a grim analysis of Alma's motives. First, she yielded to Mahler's demands, he argues, because it allowed her to ascend in social status, to attain power through propinquity, gaining prestige which acted as a substitute for love, of which she seemed incapable. Second, he argues, Alma knew that as a woman she couldn't achieve her ambition to become a creative artist (and when she had the freedom to attempt to do so in later life she didn't take up composition again).[87] Against the proposition that Gustav's demands were posed as if Alma genuinely had freedom to choose, Newman and Büning both point to the massive asymmetry of power: absolving Gustav through an appeal that he was only behaving in line with the sexual politics of the times relies on an exaggerated level of sympathy and a neglect of the fact that in pursuing this relationship his strategic decision was to keep all the strong cards tight to his chest.

Mahler's effusive exclamations on playing through Alma's songs in the days after the Gropius affair broke reveal, for Feder, the likelihood that trauma had compromised his judgement of their musical quality. Too much, too late, Gustav. Recent decades have seen several reassessments of Alma as a composer (seventeen songs now survive, but this is surely a small proportion of her output). Notable impetus came from Susan Filler's work in the 1980s, whose positive, but overcompensating, assessment of Alma's music identified 'astonishing compression' and an 'adventuresome' quality beyond what Mahler was composing at that time.[88] Alma certainly held strong convictions about what women composers should strive to achieve. She was castigating when expressing her disappointment with the salon-style music of Cécile Chaminade, declaring 'she's a disgrace to her sex.'[89]

Diane Follet's attempt at 'redeeming' Alma begins by taking aim at an easy target, Tom Lehrer's comic song 'Alma', written after he had read Alma's obituary in December 1964 (the 'juiciest' he had ever read):

> Their marriage, however, was murder.
> He'd scream to the heavens above,

> 'I'm writing *Das Lied von der Erde*,
> And she only wants to make love!'[90]

Her verdict is that 'Alma's music is evocative, occasionally excessive, and her compositional choices reflect her volatility – she vacillates between conventional harmonic progressions and startling chromaticisms, not quite settling into one or the other.'[91] Follet admits that what she describes is only a picture of the youthful Alma, but her approach is little better than that pursued by Hilmes, who decides that:

> Alma's composing was a kind of self-expression, something intimate, similar to writing in her diary. Her songs are reminiscent of emotionally laden improvisations and are more like dreamy soliloquies than thought-out compositions based on the rules of music theory.[92]

Alma's songs display more qualities of serious-minded composition than Hilmes's assessment allows, though there are passages which, either through clumsy textures or unconvincing harmonic progressions, reveal an ambition then beyond her technical capabilities. It should always be recalled that the music that survives is (mostly, as far as it is possible to be sure) the product of a student composer. Unsurprisingly, Alma's work is much closer in style to some of her teacher Zemlinsky's *Gesänge* of the late 1890s (his Opp. 5 and 7) than to anything by Mahler. Its appreciation should neither fall into gendered clichés, nor lead to over-valuation as art because of its fascinating documentary status for history or biography. Those precautions, of course, should apply to judgements of all music. In some criticism, however, Alma's songs have been especially susceptible to such treatment, because of who she was and how she has been characterized (so often, to this day, only as either 'muse' or 'monster').

Mahler's music can tell uncomfortable things about discourses of gender, in particular the power-play in relationships between subjects heard as 'masculine' and 'feminine'. Processes towards thematic unity, tonal closure and formal control are pursued in ways which can suggest the exercise of 'male' power moving disturbingly close to violence. Where these powers are queried or set awry Mahler's well-known musical irony (which can be tragic or comic) can rise to the surface. In lighter comedic tones, a scene in the 1990s–early 2000s U.S. sitcom *Frasier* made a comparable point by reversing the role of Mahler's music as gendered symbol of male power. The submissive, effete Niles, with his marriage to the domineering Maris apparently broken, reminisces about how he would lovingly play Mahler to her at their piano. Brother Frasier interjects, in effect telling Niles he's been the subject of gaslighting: 'You hate Mahler . . . besides Maris, who doesn't?' Why is Mahler in this joke? Mahlerian Maris is the one who wields all the power (invisibly; she is never seen on screen). Niles is the deluded, subservient spouse, feminized ('Almarized') by his role of playing piano reductions of Mahler's music at his wife's behest. (It is also a joke about *passé* taste, a snobbish Mahler put-down; enough already of the Mahler fad, his music is kitsch.)[93]

Some of the most powerful interpretations of gendered musical discourse in Mahler's music have been tied to his relationship with Alma. In the finale of the Fifth Symphony the amorous theme of the Adagietto is transformed into a bright and breezy, even coquettish 'grazioso'. This is a subject lacking the *Individualität*, of which Alma had learned from conversations with Burckhardt. In his notorious letter to Alma of 19 December 1901 Mahler defined *Individualität* in a manner implicitly masculine, as something which 'can be attained only through a long process of struggle, anguish and experience, and then only by those capable of profound and vigorous development'. All these things, he says, Alma lacks (instead, she is 'boundlessly delightful'), and, actually, so do Burckhardt and Zemlinsky, because Mahler considers them to be too narrow-minded.[94] *Individualität* required safeguarding against diversionary, potentially weakening forces. In the finale of the Fifth, the controlling function of counterpoint (a learned musical topic) and climactic chorale (symbol of profundity) combine in a masculine redemptive process which sacrifices, or brings under control, the flighty feminine other. Interestingly, Alma had initial misgivings about the character of the finale's chorale passages, and expressed a sense that the Adagietto 'lacked something'.[95]

The Sixth, by contrast, is tragically ironic. Alma's recollection that in 1904 Gustav had 'tried to express me' in a 'great soaring theme', the second subject of the first movement of the Sixth,[96] is widely cited and has been crucial in generating the work's wider reputation as overtly autobiographical. Seth Monahan has shown how rethinking the coexistence of the tragic and domestic in the Sixth is possible through hearing the role of the 'Alma' theme in the structure and meaning of the whole work, rather than isolating it as a vignette.[97] Nineteenth-century musical discourse traditionally identified the two contrasting themes of a sonata form movement with masculine (primary) and feminine (secondary) subject positions. In the opening movement Monahan hears a 'strained' relationship between the two main themes and asks how it might 'reflect the tense and complex psychomechanics of the Mahlers' relationship'. In a close reading, Monahan notes how critics have often couched the 'Alma' theme in problematic terms: gushing, overwrought, sickly sweet, kitschy, offering no ironic saving grace, a momentary lapse in taste. Especially suggestive, however, is the way it is closed (brought under control) by recollections of the 'masculine' marching first subject. Monahan finds this moment disturbing. It not only changes the way 'Alma' is heard but changes the character of these 'masculine' materials, as they are shifted into a space more intimate, private and domestic than the public strut of the first subject march. The result problematizes the gendered characters of the themes and their relationship.

It has become a critical commonplace to note an apparent dissonance between the image of the Mahlers' domestic life in the summer of 1904 and the tragic Sixth (which has helped promote the myth that the work is somehow prophetic of later traumas). But Monahan persuasively challenges the view that the summer was domestically happy, as Alma and others have sought to portray. In Monahan's hearing the 'brash' and 'manic' quality of the 'Alma' theme (atypical for romantic 'feminine' second subjects, which are usually gently lyrical and rather static), and the diversity of its subsequent mutations, 'calls to mind Alma's own notoriously protean personality'. But Monahan resists a single interpretative answer: is this a manifestation of misogyny ('that Mahler was a misogynist can hardly be disputed,' he writes, even if of a more benign bent than many contemporaneous views), or Mahler composing outside his 'comfort zone' in a failed attempt to express feminine empowerment or the possibility of female emancipation? The strain is especially apparent in the affirmations of 'Alma' in the movement's final paragraph, which can sound 'coercive', as the theme is drummed into shape by masculine musical forces (Gustav?). The symphony's bleak finale revokes any affirmative quality attaching to the first movement.

Monahan's 'psychobiographical' approach to the Sixth is comparable with Feder's hearing of 'tragic autobiography encoded' in the Tenth: for example in the way the Tenth's finale moves from the echoes of the drum stroke from the fireman's funeral procession that he and Alma had heard in the street below their New York apartment, through the most screamingly dissonant climax Mahler ever composed, to the return of redemptive synthesis out of purgatorial abyss, with – Feder suggests – Alma as guiding muse. In the Tenth Symphony's closing phrases it is also possible to hear an allusion to 'Ging heut" Morgen über's Feld', the second of the *Lieder eines fahrenden Gesellen*,[98] and therefore a touching reminiscence of Gustav's first real heartbreak, the romance with Johanna Richter. But as Monahan tells us, these types of reading, rather than a revelation of 'truth' driven by a 'naively deterministic view of art/life relations', are among many possible metaphorical or speculative interpretations.

After the tumultuous summer of 1910 Mahler arrived in Munich in early September as final preparations for the premiere of the Eighth gathered pace. Freud's partial analysis apparently provided him succour and new hope. A letter of 5 September opens with his most extravagant amorous appellation – 'Almschilitzilitzitzili!' He goes on to ponder:

> Freud is quite right: this utter dependence on you has always been latent in me . . . But just as love always engenders love, fidelity always wins through to fidelity, and as long as Eros remains the master of men and gods, I too shall succeed in winning back what was once mine, in regaining the heart that once beat for me.

And once again he turns to their typical 'Wagnerizing': 'How right Tristan is when he says "I am immortal – for how could Tristan's love ever die?"'[99] But Alma and Gropius continued to arrange secret assignations. Mahler never seemed to suspect. Feder therefore proposes that Gustav may have been 'too reassured' by Freud.[100] Mahler's behaviour, however, may also suggest a sustained over-compensation, for example when he smothered Alma's hotel room with roses to celebrate her arrival in Munich.

On 12 September, Mahler conducted the triumphant first performance of what was now 'Alma's' Symphony, the beginning of his last, incomplete season on the podium.

6

The Late Gustav Mahler

There is a land of the living
and a land of the dead,
and the bridge is love,
the only survival, the only meaning.
Thornton Wilder, 'The Bridge of San Luis Rey', 1927[1]

Thracymachos: 'To be brief, what am I after my death? Now, be clear and precise!'
Philalethes: 'Everything and nothing.'
Schopenhauer, 1851[2]

The premiere of the Eighth Symphony in Munich on 12 September 1910 was Mahler's greatest moment of public triumph as conductor of his own music. The success of the Symphony of a so-called 'thousand' (a symbolically large round number conjured up, to Mahler's chagrin, by the concert's promotor, the impresario Emil Gutmann) appears to confirm Boulez's opinion that the epic is Mahler's natural artistic range.[3] In his own voluminous *Oxford History of Western Music* Richard Taruskin reinforced the reputation of Mahler as the composer who did most to 'maximalize' the symphony, producing works representing the culmination of the post-Beethovenian project of symphonic expansion.[4] Mahler is hailed as a musician who assailed his audience with massive sound, the masterful manipulator of the monumental style.

Sitting among the many cultural heavyweights in the vast space of the Munich Exhibition Hall for that first performance of the

Mahler rehearsing for the premiere of the Eighth Symphony, Munich, September 1910.

Eighth, Thomas Mann listened in awe. When he met Mahler in the hotel afterwards he was tongue-tied. He wrote to the composer a few days afterwards: 'I was incapable of saying, that evening in the hotel, how deeply indebted to you I was for the impressions of 12th September . . . [the symphony] expresses the art of our time in its profoundest and most sacred form.'[5] After experiencing gargantuan profundity, Mann struggled with how adequately to respond. One option, to turn to the small, is not as absurd or incongruous as it may seem. Later in life, on pondering the 'sorrows and grandeur' of Mahler's beloved Wagner, Mann observed that a 'love of the very small' is the obverse of the monumental grand style of the late nineteenth century.[6] The miniaturism to which Mann alludes may be a radical reduction of the large, in which complexity is compressed within small shapes, with a consequent intensification of detail. The overwhelmingly vast is condensed and encapsulated.

Anton Webern, zealous pursuer of the modern musical miniature, was also in Munich for the Eighth. His ear was drawn to a moment of 'stillness and tenderness' in the symphony's second part, the colossal setting of the final scene of Goethe's *Faust*. He noted the delicate, hushed effect in Mahler's instrumentation and choral writing: '5 harps, celeste, mandolines, pianoforte, harmoniums with soft woodwinds and muted brasses and *pp* singing by three women's voices canon diminuendo right down to *pppp* – entry of the Chorus Mysticus! It is indescribable.'[7] Webern's tiny Orchestral Pieces, Op. 10 (1911–13), the shortest of which is only six bars long, are mini mirrorings of effects he heard in the Eighth, suggesting in a few seconds what is proposed at magical moments within Mahler's immense symphonic movement. Webern recognized that Mahler was a skilful miniaturist. It is reflected in Mahler's pursuit of the intense moment, the expressive qualities he produced through reduced orchestration, formal compression and the calling forth of intimate lyricism (Webern was particularly taken with this aspect of *Das Lied von der Erde*). After the tumult speaks a still small voice.

Mahler had arrived in Munich with very little voice. He was suffering from a severe throat infection that left him seriously debilitated. Many friends noted with deep concern Mahler's unhealthy appearance at the rehearsals and were astonished at how, despite his ailments, he was able to command and control the massive musical forces he had marshalled on the platform. As Bruno Walter commented: 'he seemed to be at the height of his power – the uplifting of his soul once more had given back to the tired heart its one-time vigour.'[8] Julius Korngold, however, described the impression of Mahler as a 'frail and diminutive figure' who conducted 'with the gestures of a Hoffmannesque ghost'.[9] Eight months after this all-conquering performance Mahler was dead.

Mahler's final New York season began in late October. It was a busy one which he initially pursued in good spirits. But after his collapse on 20 February it was cut short, and the Mahlers left New York on 8 April. The sailing was arduous for both the declining Gustav and the deeply distressed Alma. They disembarked at Cherbourg on 16 April. The Austrian writer Stefan Zweig, who had been on the same Atlantic crossing, recalled in 1915:

> He lay there, deathly pale, motionless, his eyelids shut . . . skeletal hands lay folded wearily on the blanket. For the first time I saw him, the pillar of fire, in his frailty. The silhouette –

unforgettable, unforgettable! – was set against the grey infinity of sky and sea. There was boundless sorrow in this sight, but also something transfigured by greatness, something resounding into the sublime, like music.[10]

The next day dawned with Mahler seemingly revived. Alma was ecstatic, but it was cruelly deceptive. La Grange paints the moment in biblical tones, as a 'station on the Way of the Cross upon which Mahler was travelling towards his painful end'.[11] Two days later Gustav seemed resigned to death, confiding to Anna Moll of his wishes to be buried next to 'Putzi' in Grinzing cemetery (he had bought the plot in 1909 and his daughter's body was moved there).

On arrival in Paris treatments were administered by the bacteriologist André Chantemesse. Justine travelled in haste to her brother, rekindling the tetchy relationship with Alma. Walter also rushed to Paris and encouragingly talked with Mahler of performing the Eighth in Vienna. But the medications were failing to halt Mahler's decline. Daily updates on his health were sent to a voracious Viennese press. Another leading medic, the Viennese Franz Chvostek, arrived on 11 May and in mock breezy tones advised Mahler to travel to Vienna (he feared the worst and knew that even if Mahler were to survive he would be severely incapacitated). Journalists jostled at every stop along the gruelling journey on the night train of 11–12 May. The press went into full, sensationalizing grief mode (a contest of 'crocodile tears' as Fischer calls it[12]), including the usual hagiographical and hypocritical rewritings of their views on Mahler's status and achievements.

In Vienna Mahler was taken straight to the Loew Sanatorium. Daughter Anna, 'Gucki', who was not yet seven years old, made a heart-rending visit to her father's bedside. He contracted pneumonia, and on 17 May fell into a coma. As the end approached, Alma, the Molls and Walter were at Gustav's bedside. In her reminiscences Alma turned to Christian imagery in attempting to describe the events. During Gustav's final decline, she wrote: 'he was washed and his bed made. Two attendants lifted his naked emaciated body. It was taken down from the cross.'[13] Alma recalled that the death rattle, after lasting several hours, ended during a thunderstorm on the night of 18 May.[14] On Chvostek's medical advice, however, she was not in the room when, soon after 11 p.m., Mahler died. Alma described Chvostek's instructions as 'humiliating' (and there may well be paternalistic over-protection of supposed feminine fragility at play). Of the family, only father-in-law Carl Moll witnessed Mahler's demise. After composing so many deaths of 'Mahler', those artistic substitutes for the inadequate endings of 'real' lives, the way Mahler came to terms, or not, with his own end remains an enigma. Mahler's thinking on such matters was constantly developing, right up to his last days, when he was reading Eduard von Hartmann's *The Problem of Life* (1906), a speculative combination of philosophy and evolutionary science. Contemplating the death mask Carl Moll made on the evening of the 19th, Adorno noted a curious smile 'in Mahler's face, which seems both imperious and full of a tender suffering, there is a hint of cunning triumph, as if he wished to say: I have fooled you after all.' Mahler's 'cunning', Adorno suggests, is that for all the 'unfathomable sorrow' of his last works their open-endedness allows for the possibility of 'hope'.[15]

The following day, Mahler's body was taken to Grinzing cemetery chapel. It lay there until the 22nd, when it was carried to the parish church for a short and simple blessing (he had wanted neither pomp nor ceremony). In worsening rain at around 5 p.m. the coffin was taken in procession to the hearse. A large group of mourners (perhaps some five hundred, including many of Vienna's cultural elite) followed the cortège through grimly wet weather to the graveside. In poeticized meteorological imagery, Paul Stefan recalled that when the coffin was lowered 'the rain had ceased, a wonderful rainbow became visible, and a nightingale's voice was heard through the silence.'[16] Carl Moll and Arnold Rosé tossed the first handfuls of earth into the grave, and Mahler was laid to rest.

At this point few biographers resist citing Alma recounting, in her introduction to the 1924 first edition of Mahler's selected letters, that the boy Mahler's response to the ubiquitous 'what do you want to be when you grow up?' was (note the exclamation mark)

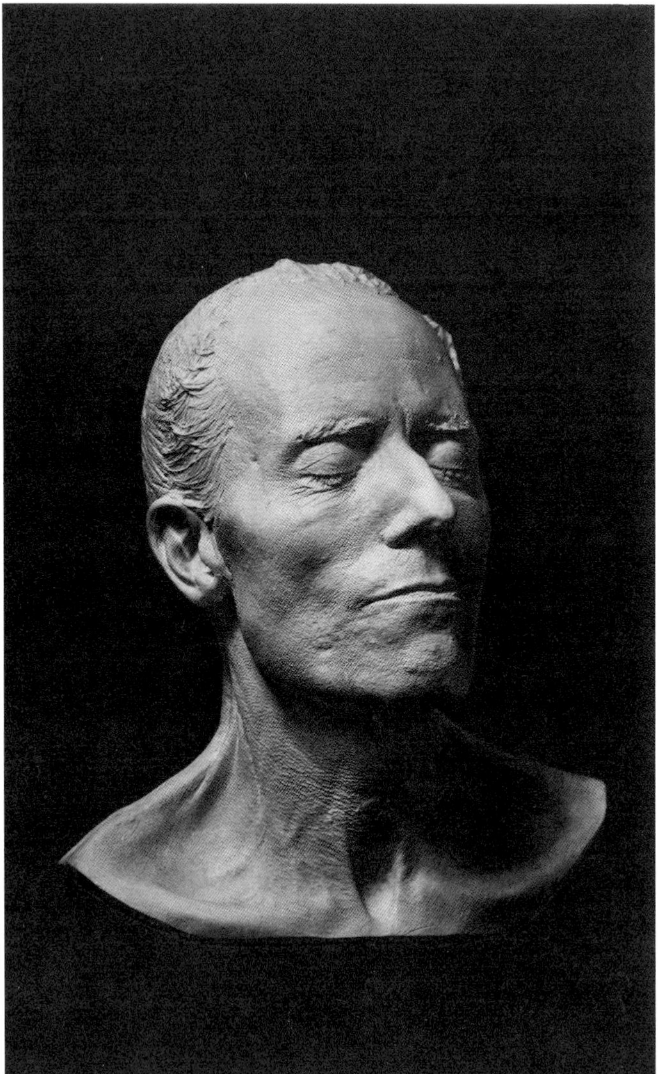

Gustav Mahler death mask by Carl Moll, 1911, plaster.

'a martyr!'[17] Schoenberg considered Mahler to be a 'saint' who was 'martyred' by his critics. He was incandescent with those who now 'pollute the air with their obituaries, hoping to enjoy at least one more moment of self-importance; for those are the moments when dirt is in its element.'[18] Many obituaries recapitulated old Mahler tropes. Julius Korngold described Mahler as

> the most typical representative of the modern musician in whom nervous energy is the driving artistic force. Here nervous sensitivity engenders strength, not weakness . . . from his beat spring many of the strange sounds and remarkable gestures in his music.

Korngold deploys the customary (and often antisemitic) focus on Mahler's supposed nervous intensity and peculiar gestural modernity. He continues by characterizing Mahler in terms suggesting a kind of religious masochism:

> What really singles him out among contemporary composers is the fact that he reveals a profoundly agitated soul concerned with matters of life and death, a soul engaged in a search for the truth that springs from a profound and impassioned emotion bordering upon self-mortification.[19]

The description may seem exaggerated, but it compares with Mahler's self-identification with Jacob wrestling with an angel to overcome suffering and pursue the truth, a struggle in which he was injured and thereafter always carried a limp (Genesis 32). Bauer-Lechner recorded Mahler saying:

> A magnificent symbol of the creator is Jacob, wrestling with God until he blesses him. If the Jews had been responsible for nothing but this image, they would still inevitably have grown to be a formidable people – God similarly withholds his blessing from me. I can only extort it from him in my terrible struggles to bring my works into being.[20]

Similar terms inflected Robert Hirschfeld's obituary, in which Mahler is discussed from the 'perspective of energism'. Mahler possessed 'energy often discharged like a hostile force'. The identification with struggle is once again prominent: 'He did not seek faith through love. Rather, with all the energy of a fighter he sought to gain it through struggle.' Of his conducting Hirschfeld recalled 'the energy of his fascinating movements on the podium' which he managed to suppress when conducting Mozart, but not Beethoven. His negative verdict on Mahler as composer deploys familiar antisemitic tropes: 'his invention was derivative', the result of a 'flickering restlessness'.[21] Paul Bekker, later to become a prominent advocate, called Mahler a 'dictator' on the podium, whose 'nervous energy literally sparked from his fingertips; it was also expressed in his loud manner of speech. Mahler always sounded irritated and fierce.' At this point Bekker's judgement is that Mahler 'belongs to that class of composers who lack a language of their own and therefore speak in many'. He may exhibit 'technical mastery' but 'the necessary inner coherence of form and content – is mostly missing in Mahler.'[22]

None of these critics had heard any of the music Mahler composed after the Eighth Symphony. During the summers of 1908 and 1909, and even part of 1910, Mahler had been back at his most compositionally prolific, returning to levels of inspirational fluency comparable with when he wrote the Eighth in the summer of 1906. After the traumatic and unproductive summer of 1907, *Das Lied von der Erde* was rapidly composed in summer 1908. Composition of the Ninth Symphony, by contrast with the protracted genesis of so many of his earlier symphonies, occupied a single summer in 1909. When Stephen Hefling argues that during these years Mahler was 'more aware than ever that the next work might be his last',[23] perhaps the urgency of his creative process is explicable as a kind of fevered fecundity. Correspondingly, Mahler's last works have frequently been 'medicalized': scrutinized for sounding symptoms of psychological trauma or physical collapse. Alban Berg described the first movement of the Ninth (which he considered to be Mahler's towering masterpiece) as a 'presentiment of death';

Bekker suggested that the subtitle of the whole symphony could be 'What Death Tells Me'.[24] Since then there has been a plethora of psychoanalytical studies identifying Mahler's 'death wish' and its manifestations in his music. Feder's work is the most distinguished in this field, and La Grange cites him extensively. But Fischer is dismissive.[25]

While La Grange considers it misleading to hear Mahler's last works as 'anticipatory of his *own* death',[26] Mitchell retains the contentious characterization of Mahler as preoccupied with his own looming demise in 1908, but ultimately adopts a nuanced position: 'Der Abschied', the final movement of *Das Lied*, composed 'in the shadow . . . of his own threatened life', was

> both a dramatization of how Mahler saw his fate and at the same time the means by which he transcended it, by his turning life (and death) into the enduring work of art that generates its own life and laws and achieves independence of the experience that gave it birth.[27]

To return to the opening of this book, what might be heard in this music are deaths of 'Mahlers'. He composed these figurations while in fine creative fettle. Reflecting on the crisis of 1907 he wrote to Walter in early 1909: 'I see everything in such a new light – am in such a state of flux, sometimes I should hardly be surprised suddenly to find myself in a new body. (Like Faust in the last scene.) I am thirstier for life than ever before.'[28] The following summer, while composing the Ninth in Toblach, he seemed in good spirits and unusually sociable, fussing about domestic arrangements in perky if characteristically prickly manner. Mahler need not be considered morose or fatally diseased to persuasively hear the works from 1908 onwards as, in part, evocative of farewells or reckonings.

Das Lied and the Ninth and Tenth Symphonies have become archetypes of 'late style' and the 'late work' (now almost, perhaps, to the point of cliché). Karen Painter wrote of Mahler's 'perfect self-fashioning of lateness'; Stanley Cavell went further, saying Mahler's work 'was always late'.[29] Late style ubiquitously accrues high critical value, particularly in nineteenth-century Romanticism. Before Mahler, Beethoven's 'late' quartets and Wagner's *Parsifal* are musical paradigms; the second part of Goethe's *Faust* is a literary comparator. Artistic lateness is a critical and historical construct, not a symptom of the geriatric. Schubert's 'late' works may be heard to mark the poignancy of an unfinished life. This biographical trope is recapitulated in the reception of Mahler. But it is intensified by the sense of cultural lateness, the late stages of Romanticism and the myth of *fin-de-siècle* Vienna. Late works need not be defined by their relation to individual biography. Foreshadows of the 'late style' features of *Das Lied von der Erde* – the preoccupation with ending; inward withdrawal; the approach towards stasis; an irony more prominently tinged with nostalgia – have often been heard in the Rückert songs, for example 'Ich bin der Welt abhanden gekommen' of 1901 ('I am lost to the world . . . It may believe me to be dead') and, as Adorno notes, in 'Liebst du um Schönheit' (1902), when the voice finishes on the unresolved sixth 'it does not finish its utterance; expression becomes a sobbing.'[30]

The six movements of *Das Lied* are settings of Hans Bethge's relatively free paraphrases (he called them 'Nachdichtungen') of Chinese poetry collected in his *Die chinesische Flöte* (1907), to which (indulging in his characteristic interventionism) Mahler made his own alterations and conflations. In passages of pentatonicism (especially in the third movement, 'Von der Jugend'), Mahler employs an exotic musical device which by 1908 was already rather old hat. But Mahler had always been interested in recycling fabricated materials. Adorno pointed out that in their eloquent inauthenticity the 'Chinese' elements in *Das Lied* were similar in function to the fake folk songs of Mahler's 'Wunderhorn' period. In their expression of otherness, outsideness and (recalling the ambivalent identification with the suffering of the Ostjuden) their supposed 'eastern' provenance, Adorno also heard the chinoiserie as a 'cover' for Mahler's Jewish element. Opening with a drinking song ('Dunkel ist das Leben, ist der Tod' ('Life is dark, and so is death')) the work is generically ambiguous, or perhaps better a hybrid. Initially it closely resembles an orchestral song cycle, but

'Der Abschied' is a long finale that is more overtly 'symphonic'. At the close, multiple repeats of 'Ewig', the incomplete melodic descent (the 'farewell' 3-2-1 motif minus its ending, the final tonic), added sixth chord on C and magical orchestration, combine to form one of Mahler's (indeed European music's) most famous endings.

One of the most provocative of recent commentaries on 'Der Abschied' has come from Andrew Deruchie, who argues that here Mahler proposes a new way of thinking about death. By contrast with the nineteenth-century paradigm of an individual's story moving through life's suffering to transfiguration in an ecstatic death (famously expressed in Wagner's *Tristan*), Deruchie hears Mahler becoming more concerned with the 'epistemology of death' than with the death of a subject, with the search for an alternative to prevailing attitudes to dying through shifting emphasis onto the regenerative totality of nature. Deruchie rather underestimates the complexities of death's figuration in Mahler's earlier work (in which narratives of life and death and wider epistemological questions are almost always both at play), but offers a particularly interesting analysis of an anonymous drawing of Mahler's deathbed which appeared in *Wiener Bilder* the day before Mahler died. For Deruchie, this illustration reveals attitudes to death that had become prominent by the beginning of the century. The Romantic age of the beautiful death, and its associated deathbed rituals (recall Dickens's Little Nell), was over. Dying became medicalized and technologized. In the drawing Mahler looks gaunt, but no one is looking at him. Alma stares out of the picture (though she is holding Gustav's hand); everyone else is looking to the doctor, who in turn is looking at his medical instrument, not his patient. The diagnosis of fatal disease is the focal centre, not the subject who is dying. Deruchie notes that Mahler's version of the poem of 'Der Abschied', and the expressive manner of his musical setting, offers a very different shift of attention from the dying individual. The poem changes from 'I' to the third person, from subjective expression to detached meditation on the eternal cycles of nature's renewal in which the voice of a dying subject is absent.[31] At this endless end there is no longer even a 'Mahler'.

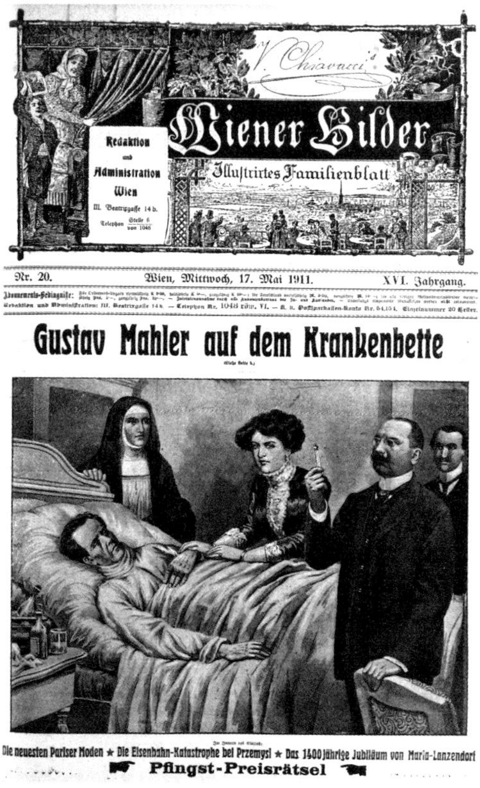

Mahler's deathbed, *Wiener Bilder*, XVI/20 (17 May 1911).

But 'Mahler' returns, as if from the brink of death, in the persistent compulsion to consider the Ninth Symphony as autobiographical, encapsulated by those who hear his weakening heartbeat in the halting, syncopated rhythms of its opening bars. Fischer diagnoses this cardiac unrest as 'extrasystolic arrhythmia';[32] Bernstein famously said the same in his 1973 Harvard Lectures.[33] But La Grange is clear: there is no evidence Mahler had such a symptom.[34] In fact, Bernstein heard premonitions of three deaths in this opening: Mahler's own, the death of tonality and the death of a culture. The music expresses a triple crisis of personal existence, of musical language and of humanity. The Adagio finale, widely heard as grief-laden, is burdened with expressing an extended *morendo* approach towards these multiple losses.

Walter explicitly linked *Das Lied* and the Ninth (whose first performance he conducted on 26 June 1912) by calling the latter 'The Farewell'.[35] It is clear that propositions of a 'farewell' Ninth such as Walter's were in large part projections onto the music of personal grief at Mahler's death. Interpretations of this kind have gained sustained currency through the appeal of popularized and mythologized aspects of Mahler's biography, the aura that has accrued around Mahler's annotations on the Ninth's draft score, and a selective focus on marked qualities of the musical materials, for example the hymn-like opening of the finale and the fleeting allusion to *Kindertotenlieder* as the end is approached.[36] The tenacious influence of this reading of the Ninth has prompted resistance. La Grange points out that Mahler's annotations in the orchestral draft of the first and last movements express farewells to youth, beauty and love, not to life, and cautions against the dominance of the first and last movements in characterizations of the symphony, to not neglect the second movement's double dance of waltz and Ländler and the virtuosic ironies of the 'Rondo-Burleske'.[37]

Adorno heard the opening of the Ninth as a superb example of Mahler's miniaturism: 'the making essential of the inessential through miniaturization' through which, in a predominantly D major field, 'almost vanishingly insignificant features' – a single note (B♭) and a single sonority (horns and cellos) – stand as synecdoche for the symphony's dark side, the 'minor pole' (those notes and keys belonging to D minor).[38] Specht, clearly invoking Mahler's burial (he was writing in 1913), heard the rhythm at the opening as 'Distant bells; like the soil that falls on a fresh grave'.[39] Both these hearings – miniaturism and mourning – combine in Schoenberg's Little Piano Piece, Op. 19, No. 6 (composed in the summer of 1911), which can be considered a musical companion to his painting titled the *Burial of Gustav Mahler* (1911).

In just nine bars Schoenberg presents tolling bells, a restricted vocabulary of chords partially (and possibly deliberately) reminiscent of Mahler's most advanced harmonies (from the

Seventh Symphony particularly), and evocative solo melodic lines (which in one moment faintly recall the woodwind melody at the opening of Part II of the Eighth). Heartfelt tribute is expressed beyond that which words can say. In the end, of course, as a creative response the piece tells us more about Schoenberg (and the putative relation of *his* work and life) than Mahler. But in its condensed borrowings and allusions to conventions, evocations of real but symbolic sounds (bells) and musical lyricism, it movingly reinvents, in Schoenberg's own new musical language of the expressionistic aphorism, key aspects of the 'Mahlerian'. While it is called 'Piano Piece', rather than 'Mahler ist tot', and therefore might be considered determinably abstract and resistant to any singular or conclusive meaning, it strives for expressive eloquence. It speaks of a personally poignant death and reflects on the life lived and lost. Schoenberg's piece commemorates a life in just a minute, without hesitation, deviation and only a little repetition.

As a minuscule 'In Memoriam Gustav Mahler', Schoenberg's piece suggests how to encapsulate response to a life of enormous achievement in a miniature manner. The creation of a man riven by grief, the music echoes with the sense of 'broken beauty'.[40] Argument, development and fulsomely articulated form are not merely inappropriate, they are impossible. The final gesture is marked, like the end of Webern's six-bar Op. 10, No. 4, '*wie ein Hauch*' ('like a breath'). It is neither resolution nor cathartic closure, but a low gasp, an exhalation. It can sound as a remembrance of Mahler himself at his most poignant, as he used the same striking metaphorical expressive marking in the slow movement of his tragic Sixth Symphony.

These little musical sighs echo Josef Bohuslav Foerster's description of when Mahler was interred:

> It was at this moment – not a word was spoken throughout it all – that the world seemed to stand still for an instant, and a great sigh was uttered by all who were present. Then, as before, there followed a silence as sublime as it was hallowed. All that was transient in Gustav Mahler was lost from sight for ever . . .

Arnold Schoenberg, *Burial of Gustav Mahler*, 1911, oil on canvas.

> A bird sang a disjointed springtime melody and I was inevitably reminded of the final movement of Mahler's Second Symphony. There, above a world shaken to its very foundations by the horrors of the Last Judgement, a solitary bird soars aloft.[41]

Foerster's purple prose references both the Second and Eighth Symphonies: the former explicitly as Mahler himself described a flute passage as the 'bird of death above the last grave';[42] the latter allusively by echoing the Chorus Mysticus at the end of Goethe's *Faust*. Foerster's original text was in Czech, but the published German version reads: 'Was an Gustav Mahler vergänglich war, verschwand für immer dem Auge.'[43] Goethe's famous, and almost untranslatable, couplet reads:

Alles Vergängliche
Ist nur ein Gleichnis

All things transitory
Are but an allegory.

As Webern's reaction at the premiere of the Eighth highlighted, when Mahler turned to the small in the midst of his grandest projects the effect is particularly arresting. The fourth movement of the immense Second Symphony, 'Urlicht' (a poem from Mahler's much-loved *Des Knaben Wunderhorn*), is a five-minute miniature immediately followed by the overwhelming outburst of noise that launches the monumental finale (whose substantial sublimity is only outdone by the Eighth). In a response to 'Urlicht' the poet Jonathan Williams wrote: 'the world of the little hears little Mahler.'[44] The line should not be misread as a belittling. 'Urlicht' exemplifies how Mahler's music tells us how we might find life's significance in a series of moments, how a life may be revealed in small pieces rather than the falsifications demanded by a grand, all-encompassing master narrative. The urge to miniaturize may be driven by the sense that something is just too big to comprehend at 'life-size'. It may also be driven by an attempt to capture the transitory through an imaginative attempt at direct and effective means of expression. If art may too often be obscured by the panoptic accumulation of information concerning an artist's sometimes mundane, sometimes extraordinary, sometimes chaotic, life, then maybe a life can on occasion be illuminated by the microscopic acuteness of artistic moments. In this sense, Mahler's music provides a model, in the way its sonic singularities so often seem to stand as synecdoche for the universal. A critical life shaped in artful miniatures may be offered as a complement to Lipiner's aphorism that 'Art is a symbolic abbreviation of life.'[45]

Perhaps, therefore, there is no better way to end these short stories from the multi-stranded life of Mahler than with the words of 'Urlicht'. In just ten lines, they capture many of the preoccupations of his life and work: beauty, struggle, hope, resistance to exclusion, the yearning to be recognized, and the endless search for a path towards redemption. Read them and reflect on the life of the man who set them. Then listen (again) to Mahler's music.

> O red rose,
> Man lies in direst need,
> Man lies in direst torment,
> I would rather be in heaven.
> Then when I came to a wide path,
> An angel came and wanted to turn me back,
> Ah no! I refused to be turned away.
> I am from God and want to return to God,
> Dear God will give me a light,
> It will shine on my way to eternally blessed life.[46]

References

Prologue: Mahler's Deaths/Mahler's Lives

1 Philip Roth, *The Human Stain* [2000] (London, 2005), pp. 312–13.
2 Letter of 28 March 1896; Knud Martner, ed., *Selected Letters of Gustav Mahler* (London, 1979), p. 180; Mahler's own emphasis.
3 Stuart Feder, *Gustav Mahler: A Life in Crisis* (New Haven, CT, 2004), p. 62.
4 Henry-Louis de La Grange, *Gustav Mahler*, vol. I: *The Arduous Road to Vienna (1860–1897)*, revd edn (Turnhout, 2020), p. 37.
5 Sigmund Freud, 'Thoughts for the Times on War and Death' [1915], in *The Penguin Freud Library*, vol. XII: *Civilization, Society and Religion: Group Psychology, Civilization And Its Discontents and other Works* (Harmondsworth, 1985), pp. 77–89.
6 See his letter to Marschalk; Martner, ed., *Selected Letters*, p. 180.
7 Natalie Bauer-Lechner, *Recollections of Gustav Mahler*, trans. Dika Newlin, ed. and annotated Peter Franklin (London, 1980), p. 53.
8 Handwritten text reproduced and translated in Donald Mitchell, *Gustav Mahler: The Wunderhorn Years. Chronicles and Commentaries*, 2nd edn (Woodbridge, 2005), pp. 179, 183.
9 Charles Youmans, *Mahler and Strauss in Dialogue* (Bloomington, IN, 2016), pp. 107–20.
10 Stephen Hefling, 'Mahler's "Todtenfeier" and the Problem of Program Music', *19th-Century Music*, XII/1 (1988), pp. 27–53 (p. 30).
11 Martner, ed., *Selected Letters*, p. 179.
12 See Stephen Hefling, 'Siegfried Lipiner's "On the Elements of a Renewal of Religious Ideas in the Present"', in *Mahler im Kontext/Contextualizing Mahler*, ed. Erich Wolfgang Partsch and Morten Solvik (Vienna, 2011), pp. 91–114.

13 Trans. of Pierre Boulez, 'La Biographie, pourquoi?', preface to Henry-Louis de La Grange, *Mahler* (Paris, 1979), pp. 2–3.
14 Claire Dederer, *Monsters: A Fan's Dilemma* (London, 2023), p. 49.
15 See Adam Phillips, *Darwin's Worms* (London, 1999), pp. 93, 107–8.
16 Peter Franklin's 'uneasy' biography opens with just this suggestion; *The Life of Mahler* (Cambridge, 1997), p. 1.
17 Martner, ed., *Selected Letters*, p. 201; Mahler's emphasis.
18 Andreas Dorschel, 'Life's Work: Wagner's *Tristan* and the Critique of Biographism', in *Life as an Aesthetic Idea of Music*, ed. Manos Perrakis (Vienna, 2019), pp. 63–78.
19 Henry-Louis de La Grange, *Gustav Mahler*, vol. II: *Vienna: The Years of Challenge (1897–1904)* (Oxford, 1995), p. 718.
20 Letter of August 1908 to Adele Marcus; Martner, ed., *Selected Letters*, p. 326.
21 Alma Mahler, *Gustav Mahler: Memories and Letters*, trans. Basil Creighton, ed. Donald Mitchell and Knud Martner, 4th edn with additional notes and commentaries (London, 1990), p. 103.
22 Bauer-Lechner, *Recollections*, p. 30.
23 Eugene L. Stelzig, *The Romantic Subject in Autobiography: Rousseau and Goethe* (Charlottesville, VA, 2000), pp. 1–23; Stelzig's emphasis.
24 Peter Conrad, *Shandyism* (Oxford, 1978), pp. 180–82.
25 Bruno Walter, *Gustav Mahler*, trans. James Galston (New York, 1941), p. 138.
26 E.T.A. Hoffmann, *The Life and Opinions of the Tomcat Murr*, trans. and annotated Anthea Bell (Harmondsworth, 1999).
27 Guido Adler, 'Gustav Mahler' [1914], trans. in Edward R. Reilly, *Gustav Mahler and Guido Adler: Records of a Friendship* (Cambridge, 1982), pp. 13–74 (p. 37).
28 Norman Lebrecht, ed., *Mahler Remembered* (New York, 1998), p. 41.
29 Paul Stefan, *Gustav Mahler: A Study of His Personality and Work*, trans. T. E. Clark (New York, 1913), p. 6.
30 Ernst Křenek, 'Biographical Sketch', in Walter, *Gustav Mahler*, p. 166.
31 Walter is writing in 1912; trans. in Lebrecht, ed., *Mahler Remembered*, p. 81.
32 Walter, *Gustav Mahler*, p. 4.
33 Ibid., p. 138.
34 Lebrecht, ed., *Mahler Remembered*, p. 64.
35 Ibid., pp. 82–3.
36 Vera Micznik, 'Is Mahler's Music Autobiographical? A Reappraisal', *Revue Mahler Review*, 1 (1987), pp. 47–75.

37 Michael Kennedy, *Mahler*, revd 2nd edn (Oxford, 2000), p. 103.
38 See Julian Johnson, *Mahler's Voices* (Oxford, 2009).
39 Mark Evan Bonds, *The Beethoven Syndrome: Hearing Music as Autobiography* (New York, 2020).
40 Karen Painter, *Symphonic Aspirations: German Music and Politics, 1900–1945* (Cambridge, MA, 2007), pp. 26, 28.
41 David Charlton, ed., *E.T.A. Hoffmann's Musical Writings: Kreisleriana, The Poet and the Composer, Music Criticism* (Cambridge, 1989), p. 238.
42 Keith Chapin, 'Lost in Quotation: Nuances behind E.T.A. Hoffmann's Programmatic Statements', *19th-Century Music*, XXX/1 (2006), pp. 44–64 (p. 46).
43 Letter of 5 December 1901; Alma Mahler, *Mahler: Memories and Letters*, p. 206.
44 Chapin, 'Lost in Quotation', pp. 50–51.
45 Letter to Max Marschalk, 17 December 1895; Martner, ed., *Selected Letters*, p. 172.
46 Ben Winters, *Music, Performance and the Realities of Film* (Abingdon, 2014), p. 121.
47 Joseph A. Gomez, 'Mahler and the Methods of Ken Russell's Films on Composers', *The Velvet Light Trap* (Winter 1975), pp. 45–50; see also John C. Tibbetts, *Composers in the Movies: Studies in Musical Biography* (New Haven, CT, 2005), pp. 189–94.

1 Mahler's Childhood

1 Henry-Louis de La Grange, *Gustav Mahler*, vol. I: *The Arduous Road to Vienna (1860–1897)*, revd edn (Turnhout, 2020), p. 32.
2 *Der goldene Topf*, in Henry-Louis de La Grange, *Mahler* (Paris, 1979), p. 102.
3 Ibid., p. 834; poem dating from the mid-1880s.
4 Guido Adler, 'Gustav Mahler' [1914], trans. in Edward R. Reilly, *Gustav Mahler and Guido Adler: Records of a Friendship* (Cambridge, 1982), p. 36.
5 The following paragraphs are indebted to Carolyn Steedman, *Strange Dislocations: Childhood and the Idea of Human Interiority, 1780–1930* (Cambridge, MA, 1995).
6 Natalie Bauer-Lechner, 'Mahleriana', unpublished manuscript; trans. in La Grange, *Mahler: The Arduous Road to Vienna*, p. 1.
7 Natalie Bauer-Lechner, *Recollections of Gustav Mahler*, trans. Dika Newlin, ed. and annotated Peter Franklin (London, 1980), p. 131.

8 Many fascinating documents about the Mahler family are reproduced in Petr Dvořák, ed., *Počátek Cesty: Gustav Mahler a Jihlava v archivních pramenech* [Journey's Beginning: Gustav Mahler and Jihlava in Written Sources] (Jihlava, 2012).
9 Alma Mahler, *Gustav Mahler: Memories and Letters*, trans. Basil Creighton, ed. Donald Mitchell and Knud Martner, 4th edn with additional notes and commentaries (London, 1990), p. 9.
10 Peter Franklin, *The Life of Mahler* (Cambridge, 1997), p. 4.
11 Bauer-Lechner, *Recollections*, p. 69.
12 Alma Mahler, *Mahler: Memories and Letters*, p. 63.
13 La Grange, *Mahler: The Arduous Road to Vienna*, p. 13.
14 Donald Mitchell, *Gustav Mahler: The Early Years*, revd and ed. Paul Banks and David Matthews (Woodbridge, 2003), p. 1.
15 Norman Lebrecht, ed., *Mahler Remembered* (New York, 1998), pp. 16–17.
16 Natalie Bauer-Lechner, 'Mahleriana', unpublished manuscript; trans. in Lebrecht, ed., *Mahler Remembered*, p. 12.
17 Mitchell, *Mahler: The Early Years*, pp. 4, 12.
18 La Grange, *Mahler: The Arduous Road to Vienna*, p. 14.
19 Bauer-Lechner, 'Mahleriana'; Lebrecht, ed., *Mahler Remembered*, pp. 7–8.
20 This summarizes the interpretation in Stanley Steinberg, 'Tragic Absurdity in the Music of Gustav Mahler', *Psychoanalytic Review*, LXXXVI/6 (1999), pp. 853–75. There are many other similar psychoanalytical studies of Mahler's childhood.
21 Ernest Jones, *Sigmund Freud, Life and Work*, vol. II: *Years of Maturity, 1901–19* (London, 1955), pp. 88–9.
22 Stuart Feder, *Gustav Mahler: A Life in Crisis* (New Haven, CT, 2004), pp. 229–30.
23 Ibid., p. 237.
24 Jonathan Carr, *The Real Mahler* (London, 1997), pp. 11–12.
25 Dika Newlin, 'Mahler's Brother Syndrome: Necropsychiatry and the Artist', *Musical Quarterly*, LXVI/2 (1980), pp. 296–304.
26 Mitchell, *Mahler: The Early Years*, p. 21.
27 Alma Mahler, *Mahler: Memories and Letters*, p. 135.
28 Bauer-Lechner, 'Mahleriana'; Lebrecht, ed., *Mahler Remembered*, pp. 9–10.
29 Mahler's school reports are reproduced in *Počátek Cesty*, ed. Dvořák, pp. 125–74.
30 Bauer-Lechner, 'Mahleriana'; Lebrecht, ed., *Mahler Remembered*, p. 8.
31 Bauer-Lechner, *Recollections*, pp. 19, 33.

32 Bauer-Lechner, 'Mahleriana'; Lebrecht, ed., *Mahler Remembered*, pp. 9–10.
33 Bauer-Lechner, *Recollections*, p. 155.
34 Alma Mahler, *Mahler: Memories and Letters*, p. 7.
35 Bauer-Lechner, 'Mahleriana'; La Grange, *Mahler: The Arduous Road to Vienna*, pp. 36–7.
36 La Grange, *Mahler*, p. 16.
37 Mitchell, *Mahler: The Early Years*, p. 13.
38 Trans. in La Grange, *Mahler: The Arduous Road to Vienna*, p. 37.
39 Carr is particularly cautionary, *The Real Mahler*, p. 15.
40 Sigmund Freud, 'Creative Writers and Day-Dreaming' [1907, published 1908], in *The Pelican Freud Library*, vol. XIV: *Art and Literature: Jensen's 'Gradiva', Leonardo Da Vinci and other Works* (Harmondsworth, 1985), pp. 129–43.
41 Feder, *Mahler: A Life in Crisis*, pp. 229–30.
42 Franklin, *The Life*, p. 23.
43 Knud Martner, ed., *Selected Letters of Gustav Mahler* (London, 1979), pp. 54–5.
44 Lebrecht, ed., *Mahler Remembered*, p. 15.
45 Adler, 'Gustav Mahler', p. 19.
46 Stuart Feder, 'Gustav Mahler: A Composer's Childhood. The Auditory Environment', in *Neue Mahleriana: Essays in Honour of Henry-Louis de La Grange*, ed. Günther Weiss (Berne, 1997), pp. 27–38.
47 Ryan R. Kangas, 'Classical Style, Childhood and Nostalgia in Mahler's Fourth Symphony', *Nineteenth-Century Music Review*, VIII/2 (2011), pp. 219–36.
48 Bauer-Lechner, *Recollections*, pp. 152–3.
49 Ibid., p. 32.
50 Ibid., pp. 11–12. For confirmation of the song's identity see Jiři Rychetsky, 'Mahler's Favourite Song', *Musical Times*, CXXX/1762 (1989), p. 729.
51 Alma Mahler, *Mahler: Memories and Letters*, p. 109.
52 Jeremy Barham, 'Mahler and Socio-Cultural Nomadism: The Case of the Fifth Symphony', in *Beiträge z. symposium 'Ferne Heimatklänge – Gustav Mahler und die Moderne' Köln May 2010*, ed. Arnold Jacobshagen (Stuttgart, 2011), pp. 57–68.
53 Gustav Mahler, *Letters to His Wife*, trans. Antony Beaumont, ed. Henry-Louis de La Grange and Günther Weiss in collaboration with Knud Martner (London, 2004), p. 356.
54 Cited in Barham, 'Mahler and Socio-Cultural Nomadism', p. 60.

2 Mahler the Reader

1 Letter to Friedrich Löhr, spring 1894; Knud Martner, ed., *Selected Letters of Gustav Mahler* (London, 1979), p. 153.
2 Natalie Bauer-Lechner, *Recollections of Gustav Mahler*, trans. Dika Newlin, ed. and annotated Peter Franklin (London, 1980), p. 146.
3 For example, Stephen McClatchie, 'Hans Rott, Gustav Mahler and the "New Symphony": New Evidence for a Pressing Question', *Music and Letters*, LXXXI/3 (2000), pp. 392–401.
4 Uwe Harten, 'Hans Rott and Gustav Mahler', *News about Mahler Research*, 45 (Autumn 2001), pp. 13–27.
5 The essays are translated in Donald Mitchell, *Gustav Mahler: The Early Years*, revd and ed. Paul Banks and David Matthews (Woodbridge, 2003), pp. 288–90.
6 Natalie Bauer-Lechner, 'Mahleriana', unpublished manuscript; trans. in Henry-Louis de La Grange, *Gustav Mahler*, vol. I: *The Arduous Road to Vienna (1860–1897)*, revd edn (Turnhout, 2020), p. 17.
7 Martner, ed., *Selected Letters*, p. 153.
8 Norman Lebrecht, ed., *Mahler Remembered* (New York, 1998), pp. 16–17.
9 Guido Adler, 'Gustav Mahler' [1914], trans. in Edward R. Reilly, *Gustav Mahler and Guido Adler: Records of a Friendship* (Cambridge, 1982), p. 19.
10 Mitchell, *Mahler: The Early Years*, p. 49.
11 Recollection of Friedrich Eckstein; cited in Erich Wolfgang Partsch, 'Gustav Mahler's Intellectual Curiosity', *News about Mahler Research*, 67 (April 2014), pp. 7–8.
12 Bruno Walter, *Gustav Mahler*, trans. James Galston (New York, 1941), pp. 128–9.
13 Theodor W. Adorno, *Mahler: A Musical Physiognomy*, trans. Edmund Jephcott (Chicago, IL, 1992), p. 137.
14 Arthur Schopenhauer, *Parerga and Paralipomena*, vol. II, trans. E.F.J. Payne (Oxford, 1974), pp. 440–41.
15 Walter, *Gustav Mahler*, p. 138.
16 Peter Conrad, *Shandyism* (Oxford, 1978), p. 174.
17 Bauer-Lechner, *Recollections*, p. 85.
18 'Beethoven's Instrumental Music' (1814–15), in *E.T.A. Hoffmann's Musical Writings: Kreisleriana, The Poet and the Composer, Music Criticism*, ed. David Charlton (Cambridge, 1989), p. 96.
19 Letter of 5 December 1901; Gustav Mahler, *Letters to His Wife*, trans. Antony Beaumont, ed. Henry-Louis de La Grange and Günther Weiss in collaboration with Knud Martner (London, 2004), p. 50.

20 E.T.A. Hoffmann, review of Beethoven's Fifth Symphony, *Allegemeine musikalische Zeitung*, XII (1810), in *E.T.A. Hoffmann's Musical Writings*, ed. Charlton, p. 238.
21 Timothy J. Casey, ed., *Jean Paul: A Reader* (Baltimore, MD, 1992), pp. 246, 250–59.
22 Walter, *Gustav Mahler*, p. 136.
23 William J. McGrath, *Dionysian Art and Populist Politics in Austria* (New Haven, CT, 1974), p. 142.
24 Adler, 'Gustav Mahler', p. 37.
25 Constantin Floros, *Gustav Mahler's Mental World: A Systematic Representation*, trans. Ernest Bernhardt-Kabisch (Frankfurt, 2016), p. 69.
26 Walter, *Gustav Mahler*, p. 139.
27 Anton Seljak, 'Polyphony and Theodicy: Gustav Mahler's Reception of Russian Literature', *News about Mahler Research*, 63 (Spring 2012), pp. 1–26.
28 Adorno, *Mahler*, p. 69.
29 Henry-Louis de La Grange, *Gustav Mahler*, vol. IV: *A New Life Cut Short (1907–11)* (Oxford, 2008), p. 452.
30 Alma Mahler, *Gustav Mahler: Memories and Letters*, trans. Basil Creighton, ed. Donald Mitchell and Knud Martner, 4th edn with additional notes and commentaries (London, 1990), pp. 9, 20.
31 Letter of 28 June 1904; Mahler, *Letters to His Wife*, p. 165.
32 Martner, ed., *Selected Letters*, p. 236.
33 Floros, *Gustav Mahler's Mental World*, p. 86.
34 Martner, ed., *Selected Letters*, p. 329.
35 Walter, *Gustav Mahler*, p. 135.
36 See Jeremy Barham, 'Mahler's *Verkehrte Welt*: Fechner, "Learned Satire" and the Third Movement of Symphony No. 3', in *Mahler im Kontext/ Contextualizing Mahler*, ed. Erich Wolfgang Partsch and Morten Solvik (Vienna, 2011), pp. 177–206.
37 Bauer-Lechner, *Recollections*, p. 40.
38 For Franklin, Rott's movement must be declared Mahler's model: Peter Franklin, *Mahler: Symphony No. 3* (Cambridge, 1991), p. 75.
39 Alma Mahler, *Mahler: Memories and Letters*, p. 109.
40 Leah Batstone, 'A Dance from Iglau: Gustav Mahler, Bohemia, and the Complexities of Austrian Identity', *19th-Century Music*, XLIV/3 (2021), pp. 169–86.
41 Paul Banks, 'An Early Symphonic Prelude by Mahler?', *19th-Century Music*, III/2 (1979), pp. 141–9.

42 Reinhold Kubik, 'New Information about Mahler's Biography and about *Das klagende Lied*', *News about Mahler Research*, 66 (Autumn 2013), pp. 38–41.
43 Mitchell, *Mahler: The Early Years*, p. 135.
44 Martner, ed., *Selected Letters*, p. 75.
45 Stephen E. Hefling, 'The Road Not Taken: Mahler's *Rübezahl*', *Yale University Library Gazette*, 57 (1983), pp. 145–70.
46 Letter to Marschalk, 26 March 1896; Martner, ed., *Selected Letters*, p. 179.
47 Nietzsche, *The Birth of Tragedy*, trans. Shaun Whiteside (Harmondsworth, 1993), p. 33.
48 Bauer-Lechner, *Recollections*, p. 34.

3 Mahler the Maestro

1 Natalie Bauer-Lechner, *Recollections of Gustav Mahler*, trans. Dika Newlin, ed. and annotated Peter Franklin (London, 1980), p. 36.
2 Ernestine Schumann-Heink, in *Mahler Remembered*, ed. Norman Lebrecht (New York, 1998), p. 85.
3 Lebrecht, ed., *Mahler Remembered*, p. 30.
4 Letter to Friedrich Lohr on his return to Iglau, late July 1883; Knud Martner, ed., *Selected Letters of Gustav Mahler* (London, 1979), p. 73.
5 Lebrecht, ed., *Mahler Remembered*, p. 31.
6 Bauer-Lechner, *Recollections*, pp. 35–6.
7 Martner, ed., *Selected Letters*, pp. 74–5.
8 Peter Franklin, *The Life of Mahler* (Cambridge, 1997), p. 64.
9 Lebrecht, ed., *Mahler Remembered*, pp. 46–7.
10 Jens Malte Fischer, *Gustav Mahler*, trans. Stewart Spencer (New Haven, CT, 2011), p. 159.
11 Stephen McClatchie, trans. and ed., *The Mahler Family Letters* (Oxford, 2006), pp. 35, 39–41.
12 Zoltán Roman, 'Mahler and the Budapest Opera', *Studia musicologica Academiae Scientiarum Hungaricae*, XXXI/4 (1989), pp. 353–69.
13 James L. Zychowicz, 'Mahler's Mozart', in *Neue Mahleriana: Essays in Honour of Henry-Louis de La Grange*, ed. Günther Weiss (Berne, 1997), p. 387.
14 Bauer-Lechner, *Recollections*, pp. 42, 160–61.
15 Henry-Louis de La Grange, *Gustav Mahler*, vol. I: *The Arduous Road to Vienna (1860–1897)*, revd edn (Turnhout, 2020), pp. 381–90; Franklin, *The Life*, pp. 74–6.

16 The full review is reproduced and translated in Donald Mitchell, *Gustav Mahler: The Wunderhorn Years. Chronicles and Commentaries*, 2nd edn (Woodbridge, 2005), pp. 151–4.
17 Donald Mitchell, 'Mahler's Hungarian Glissando', in *Discovering Mahler: Writings on Mahler, 1955–2005* (Woodbridge, 2007), pp. 125–30.
18 Lóránt Péteri, 'Mahler: Music, Reception, Identity', *Studia musicologica*, LX/1 (2019), pp. 219–42 (p. 238).
19 Bauer-Lechner, *Recollections*, p. 27.
20 Fischer, *Gustav Mahler*, p. 213.
21 Ibid., p. 219.
22 *The World* (15 June 1892); Dan H. Laurence, ed., *Shaw's Music: The Complete Musical Criticism of Bernard Shaw*, vol. II, 2nd revd edn (London, 1989), p. 650.
23 K. M. Knittel, '"Ein hypermoderner Dirigent": Mahler and Anti-Semitism in Fin-de-Siècle Vienna', *19th-Century Music*, XVIII /3 (1995), pp. 257–76 (p. 273).
24 Anna's description of Mahler's character in her essay 'Aus Briefen Mahlers', *Moderne Welt*, III/7 (1921–2), pp. 13–14, is very interesting; trans. in Lebrecht, ed., *Mahler Remembered*, pp. 90–91.
25 Bruno Walter, *Gustav Mahler*, trans. James Galston (New York, 1941), pp. 86–7.
26 On Mahler's interest in Smetana (and possible compositional influences) see Donald Mitchell, 'Mahler and Smetana: Significant Influences or Accidental Parallels?', in *Discovering Mahler*, pp. 537–49.
27 See Chris Walton, *Richard Wagner's Essays on Conducting* (Rochester, NY, 2021).
28 David Pickett, 'Arrangements and *Retuschen*: Mahler and *Werktreue*', in *The Cambridge Companion to Mahler*, ed. Jeremy Barham (Cambridge, 2007), pp. 178–200 (p. 188).
29 Eduard Reeser, 'Cosima Wagner', in *Mahler's Unknown Letters*, ed. Herta Blaukopf (London, 1986), pp. 199–227.
30 Postcard of 3 August 1894; McClatchie, ed., *The Mahler Family Letters*, p. 283.
31 Reeser, 'Cosima Wagner', pp. 199–225.
32 Fischer, *Gustav Mahler*, p. 250.
33 Ernst Křenek, 'Biographical Sketch', in Walter, *Gustav Mahler*, pp. 200–201.
34 Fischer, *Gustav Mahler*, p. 289.
35 Ibid., p. 290.
36 La Grange, *Mahler: The Arduous Road to Vienna*, p. 739.

37 Kurt Blaukopf, *Mahler: A Documentary Study* (London, 1976), p. 210.

38 Sandra McColl, *Music Criticism in Vienna, 1896–1897: Critically Moving Forms* (Oxford, 1996), pp. 101–2.

39 *Reichspost* (14 April 1897); Blaukopf, *Mahler: A Documentary Study*, p. 211.

40 See Christian Glanz, 'Contested Vienna – Mahler versus Lueger', *News about Mahler Research*, 74 (December 2021), pp. 49–74.

41 Bauer-Lechner, *Recollections*, p. 89.

42 *Fremden-Blatt* (12 May 1897); Blaukopf, *Mahler: A Documentary Study*, p. 174.

43 McColl, *Music Criticism in Vienna*, pp. 77, 103.

44 Herta Blaukopf, 'Mahler's First Season as Director at the k.k. Hofoperntheater: The Composer Waits in the Wings', in *Perspectives on Gustav Mahler*, ed. Jeremy Barham (Aldershot, 2005), pp. 327–43.

45 McColl, *Music Criticism in Vienna*, pp. 73–6.

46 Franklin, *The Life*, pp. 106–7.

47 McColl, *Music Criticism in Vienna*, p. 94.

48 See David Brodbeck, *Defining 'Deutschtum': Political Ideology, German Identity, and Music-Critical Discourse in Liberal Vienna* (New York, 2014).

49 Bauer-Lechner, *Recollections*, pp. 101–2.

50 Ibid., p. 180.

51 Natalie Bauer-Lechner, 'Mahleriana', unpublished manuscript; trans. in La Grange, *Mahler: The Arduous Road to Vienna*, p. 178.

52 La Grange, *Mahler: The Arduous Road to Vienna*, p. 390.

53 Henry-Louis de La Grange, *Gustav Mahler*, vol. II: *Vienna: The Years of Challenge (1897–1904)* (Oxford, 1995), pp. 550–52.

54 *Neue Musikalische Press* (31 October 1897).

55 Stephen McClatchie, 'Mahler's Wagner', in *Mahler im Kontext/ Contextualizing Mahler*, ed. Erich Wolfgang Partsch and Morten Solvik (Vienna, 2011), pp. 407–36 (p. 423).

56 David Kasunic, 'On "Jewishness" and Genre: Hanslick's reception of Gustav Mahler', in *Rethinking Hanslick*, ed. Nicole Grimes, Siobhan Donovan and Wolfgang Marx (Rochester, NY, 2013), pp. 311–38.

57 Bauer-Lechner, *Recollections*, p. 142.

58 Stephen E. Hefling and Morten Solvik, 'Natalie Bauer-Lechner's "Mahleriana": A Review of the Sources and the Passages on Brahms', in *Naturlauf: Scholarly Journeys toward Gustav Mahler*, ed. Paul-André Bempéchat (New York, 2016), pp. 227–77.

59 K. M. Knittel, '"Polemik im Concertsaal": Mahler, Beethoven, and the Viennese Critics', *19th-Century Music*, XXIX/3 (2006), pp. 289–321.
60 Fischer, *Gustav Mahler*, p. 424.
61 Ibid., p. 427.
62 James L. Zychowicz, 'Mahler's Mozart', in *Neue Mahleriana*, ed. Weiss, p. 381.
63 Henry-Louis de La Grange, *Gustav Mahler*, vol. III: *Vienna: Triumph and Disillusion (1904–1907)* (Oxford, 1999), p. 597.
64 Ibid., p. 649.
65 Ibid., p. 660.
66 Ibid., p. 673.
67 The contract is reproduced in Zoltan Roman, *Gustav Mahler's American Years, 1907–11: A Documentary History* (New York, 1989), pp. 26–33.
68 Alma Mahler, *Gustav Mahler: Memories and Letters*, trans. Basil Creighton, ed. Donald Mitchell and Knud Martner, 4th edn with additional notes and commentaries (London, 1990), p. 128.
69 See the reviews collected in Roman, *Gustav Mahler's American Years*, pp. 51–7.
70 Martner, ed., *Selected Letters*, pp. 309–11.
71 Fischer, *Gustav Mahler*, p. 576.
72 Martner, ed., *Selected Letters*, p. 316; Mahler's italics.
73 Fischer, *Gustav Mahler*, p. 581.
74 Roman, *Gustav Mahler's American Years*, p. 17.
75 Letter to Countess Wydenbruck, 17 April 1908; Martner, ed., *Selected Letters*, p. 319.
76 Letter of 8 December; Blaukopf, ed., *Mahler's Unknown Letters*, p. 146.
77 *New York Sun* (7 April 1909); Roman, *Gustav Mahler's American Years*, p. 235.
78 Ibid., p. 330.
79 Ibid., p. 314.
80 Fischer, *Gustav Mahler*, pp. 604–6.
81 Martner, ed., *Selected Letters*, p. 348.
82 Quoted in Fischer, *Gustav Mahler*, p. 658.
83 McClatchie, ed., *The Mahler Family Letters*, p. 397.
84 Martner, ed., *Selected Letters*, p. 354.
85 Walter, *Gustav Mahler*, p. 58.
86 Miriam Russell, *Cleveland Plain Dealer* (7 December 1910); Roman, *Gustav Mahler's American Years*, p. 418.
87 Ibid., p. 458.

88 Joseph Horowitz, review of Henry-Louis de La Grange, *Gustav Mahler: A New Life Cut Short*, *Journal of the Society for American Music*, III/1 (2009), pp. 110–13.

89 Joseph Horowitz, 'A Perfect Storm: Mahler's New York', in *Mahler im Kontext*, ed. Partsch and Solvik, pp. 81–90 (p. 90).

90 Letter of 16 February 1908; Roman, *Gustav Mahler's American Years*, p. 82.

91 Ibid., p. xxiv.

92 Fischer, *Gustav Mahler*, p. 572.

93 Stuart Feder, *Gustav Mahler: A Life in Crisis* (New Haven, CT, 2004), pp. 170–71.

94 Krehbiel sustained his low opinion of Mahler as a composer: he sided with the more traditional, integrative use of American 'folk' materials in Dvořák's 'New World' Symphony (1893), in contrast to Mahler's 'extravagant' treatment of his own 'indigenous' melodies.

95 Henry-Louis de La Grange, *Gustav Mahler*, vol. IV: *A New Life Cut Short (1907–11)* (Oxford, 2008), p. 75.

96 Horowitz, review, p. 107.

97 Fischer, *Gustav Mahler*, p. 679.

98 Alfred Roller, *Die Bildnisse von Gustav Mahler* [1922]; trans. in Lebrecht, ed., *Mahler Remembered*, pp. 154–5.

99 Ibid., p. 198.

100 Roman, *Gustav Mahler's American Years*, p. 377.

101 Knittel, '"Ein hypermoderner Dirigent"', pp. 268–9.

102 Roman, *Gustav Mahler's American Years*, p. 366.

103 Fischer, *Gustav Mahler*, p. 571.

4 Mahler Composing in the Country

1 Alma Mahler, *Gustav Mahler: Memories and Letters*, trans. Basil Creighton, ed. Donald Mitchell and Knud Martner, 4th edn with additional notes and commentaries (London, 1990), p. 184.

2 Knud Martner, ed., *Selected Letters of Gustav Mahler* (London, 1979), p. 56.

3 Thomas Peattie, *Gustav Mahler's Symphonic Landscapes* (Cambridge, 2015), p. 162.

4 Ibid., p. 9.

5 Theodor W. Adorno, *Mahler: A Musical Physiognomy*, trans. Edmund Jephcott (Chicago, IL, 1992), p. 71.

6 The different versions of the symphony are usefully summarized in a chart in Donald Mitchell, *Gustav Mahler: The Wunderhorn*

Years. Chronicles and Commentaries, 2nd edn (Woodbridge, 2005), pp. 158–9.

7 Peattie, *Gustav Mahler's Symphonic Landscapes*, pp. 9, 24.

8 David Charlton, ed., *E.T.A. Hoffmann's Musical Writings: Kreisleriana, The Poet and the Composer, Music Criticism* (Cambridge, 1989), pp. 76–7.

9 Martner, ed., *Selected Letters*, p. 201.

10 Henry-Louis de La Grange, *Gustav Mahler*, vol. I: *The Arduous Road to Vienna (1860–1897)*, revd edn (Turnhout, 2020), p. 525.

11 Natalie Bauer-Lechner, *Recollections of Gustav Mahler*, trans. Dika Newlin, ed. and annotated Peter Franklin (London, 1980), p. 32.

12 Webern's diary entry of 3 February 1905; Kurt Blaukopf, *Mahler: A Documentary Study* (London, 1976), p. 239.

13 Bauer-Lechner, *Recollections*, p. 38.

14 Ibid., p. 59.

15 Ibid., p. 67; the note and sketch is transcribed in Peter Franklin, *The Life of Mahler* (Cambridge, 1997), Appendix, pp. 100–103.

16 Ryan R. Kangas, 'Mahler's Early Summer Journeys through Vienna, or What Anthropomorphized Nature Tells Us', *Journal of the American Musicological Society*, LXVIII/2 (2015), pp. 375–428.

17 Bauer-Lechner, *Recollections*, p. 40.

18 Kangas, 'Mahler's Early Summer Journeys'.

19 Martner, ed., *Selected Letters*, pp. 197–8.

20 Julian Johnson, 'Mahler and the Idea of Nature', in *Perspectives on Gustav Mahler*, ed. Jeremy Barham (Aldershot, 2005), pp. 23–36.

21 Bauer-Lechner, *Recollections*, p. 96.

22 La Grange, *Mahler: The Arduous Road to Vienna*, p. 529.

23 Bauer-Lechner, *Recollections*, p. 36.

24 Henry-Louis de La Grange, *Gustav Mahler*, vol. II: *Vienna: The Years of Challenge (1897–1904)* (Oxford, 1995), p. 176.

25 Bauer-Lechner, *Recollections*, pp. 134, 148.

26 Ibid., p. 147.

27 Ibid., p. 152.

28 La Grange, *Vienna: The Years of Challenge*, p. 800.

29 See, for example, Edward F. Kravitt, 'Mahler's Dirges for His Death: February 24, 1901', *Musical Quarterly*, LXIV/3 (1978), pp. 329–53.

30 La Grange, *Vienna: The Years of Challenge*, p. 800.

31 Julian Johnson, 'The Sound of Nature? – Mahler, Klimt and the Changing Representation of Nature in Early Viennese Modernism', in *Wien, 1897: Kulturgeschichtliches Profil eines Epochenjahres*, ed. Christian Glanz (Frankfurt, 1999), pp. 189–204 (p. 203).

32 Peattie, *Gustav Mahler's Symphonic Landscapes*, p. 105.
33 Anna Stoll Knecht, *Mahler's Seventh Symphony* (Oxford, 2010), p. 167.
34 Ibid., p. 170.
35 Johnson, 'Mahler and the Idea of Nature', p. 27.
36 Deryck Cooke, *Gustav Mahler: An Introduction to His Music* (London, 1980), pp. 88–90.
37 Knecht, *Mahler's Seventh Symphony*, p. 168.
38 Peattie, *Gustav Mahler's Symphonic Landscapes*, p. 10.
39 Quoted in Knecht, *Mahler's Seventh Symphony*, p. 64.
40 Gustav Mahler, *Letters to His Wife*, trans. Antony Beaumont, ed. Henry-Louis de La Grange and Günther Weiss in collaboration with Knud Martner (London, 2004), pp. 356–7.
41 Knecht, *Mahler's Seventh Symphony*, p. 264.
42 Mahler, *Letters to His Wife*, p. 357.
43 Stephen Johnson, *The Eighth: Mahler and the World in 1910* (London, 2022), p. 31.
44 Joseph Leo Koerner, *Caspar David Friedrich and the Subject of Landscape*, 2nd edn (London, 2009), pp. 210–13, 225.
45 Fredric Jameson, *The Ancients and the Postmoderns* (London, 2015), p. 67.
46 Sigmund Freud, 'On Transience' [1916], in *The Pelican Freud Library*, vol. XIV: *Art and Literature: Jensen's 'Gradiva', Leonardo Da Vinci and other Works* (Harmondsworth, 1985), pp. 283–90.
47 J. H. Prynne, 'Huts', *Textual Practice*, XXII/4 (2008), pp. 613–33 (p. 624).
48 Eftychia Papanikolaou, 'Trauma as Memory in Ken Russell's *Mahler*', in *After Mahler's Death*, ed. Gerold Gruber, Morten Solvik and Jan Vičar (Olomouc, 2013), pp. 72–89 (p. 73).
49 Franz Willnauer, 'Mahler the House Builder', *News about Mahler Research*, 76 (June 2023), p. 45.
50 Theodor Reik, *The Haunting Melody: Psychoanalytic Experiences in Life and Music* (New York, 1953), pp. 325–6.
51 Kravitt, 'Mahler's Dirges for His Death', pp. 336–9.

5 Gustav and Alma

1 Letter of 5 September 1910; Gustav Mahler, *Letters to His Wife*, ed. Henry-Louis de La Grange and Günther Weiss in collaboration with Knud Martner, trans. Antony Beaumont (London, 2004), p. 386.
2 Joseph Horowitz, *The Marriage: The Mahlers in New York* (Charleston, SC, 2023).

3 Stuart Feder, 'Before Alma: Gustav Mahler and "Das Ewig-Weibliche"', in *Mahler Studies*, ed. Stephen Hefling (Cambridge, 1997), pp. 78–109 (p. 80).

4 Henry-Louis de La Grange, *Gustav Mahler*, vol. I: *The Arduous Road to Vienna (1860–1897)*, revd edn (Turnhout, 2020), p. 357.

5 Carl Niekerk, *Reading Mahler: German Culture and Jewish Identity in Fin-de-Siècle Vienna* (Rochester, NY, 2010), pp. 30–31, 48–52.

6 Jens Malte Fischer, *Gustav Mahler*, trans. Stewart Spencer (New Haven, CT, 2011), pp. 310–11.

7 Franz Willnauer, ed., *Gustav Mahler, 'In Eile – wie immer!': Neue unbekannte Briefe* (Vienna, 2016), p. 333.

8 Letter to Hans Riehl, February 1917; trans. with a commentary in Morten Solvik and Stephen E. Hefling, 'Natalie Bauer-Lechner on Mahler and Women: A Newly Discovered Document', *Musical Quarterly*, XCVII/1 (2014), pp. 12–65.

9 Alma Mahler, *Gustav Mahler: Memories and Letters*, trans. Basil Creighton, ed. Donald Mitchell and Knud Martner, 4th edn with additional notes and commentaries (London, 1990), p. 13.

10 Two new French biographies are worth noting: Évelyne Bloch-Dano, *L'Âme Sœur: Natalie Bauer-Lechner and Gustav Mahler* (Paris, 2021), with Natalie characterized as soulmate; and Maurice Dahan, *La Vie amoureuse de Gustav Mahler* (Paris, 2021), structured as a counterpoint between Natalie and Alma.

11 For an overview, see Stephen E. Hefling and Morten Solvik, 'Natalie Bauer-Lechner's "Mahleriana": A Review of the Sources and the Passages on Brahms', in *Naturlauf: Scholarly Journeys toward Gustav Mahler*, ed. Paul-André Bempéchat (New York, 2016), pp. 227–41.

12 Alma Mahler-Werfel, *Diaries, 1898–1902*, selected and trans. Antony Beaumont, ed. Beaumont and Susanne Rode-Breymann (London, 1998), pp. 77, 84, 96.

13 Ibid., pp. 163, 253.

14 Alma Mahler, *Mahler: Memories and Letters*, pp. 3–4.

15 Mahler-Werfel, *Diaries*, p. 443.

16 Ibid., pp. 446–8.

17 Ibid., p. 345.

18 Ibid., pp. 447–9.

19 Ibid., p. 461.

20 Stephen McClatchie, trans. and ed., *The Mahler Family Letters* (Oxford, 2006), pp. 361–6.

21 Alma Mahler, *Mahler: Memories and Letters*, p. 13.

22 Mahler, *Letters to His Wife*, pp. 78–84.
23 Mahler-Werfel, *Diaries*, p. 462.
24 Alma Mahler, *Mahler: Memories and Letters*, p. 23.
25 Oliver Hilmes, *Malevolent Muse: The Life of Alma Mahler*, trans. Donald Arthur (Boston, MA, 2015), p. 42.
26 Mahler-Werfel, *Diaries*, pp. xiii–xiv.
27 Alma Mahler-Werfel, *Tagebuch-Suiten, 1898–1902*, ed. Antony Beaumont and Susanne Rode-Breymann (Frankfurt am Main, 1997), p. 751; in the English translation, it is rendered as 'Bliss and Rapture'; and 'Rapture without End', which doesn't quite seem to catch Alma's original; Mahler-Werfel, *Diaries*, pp. 466–7.
28 Alma Mahler, *Mahler: Memories and Letters*, p. 26.
29 Mahler-Werfel, *Diaries*, p. 468.
30 Alma Mahler-Werfel, *And the Bridge Is Love* (London, 1959), p. 25.
31 Alma Mahler, *Mahler: Memories and Letters*, p. 53.
32 Ibid., pp. 33, 116.
33 Ibid., p. 120.
34 Hilmes, *Malevolent Muse*, p. 52.
35 Henry-Louis de La Grange, *Gustav Mahler*, vol. II: *Vienna: The Years of Challenge (1897–1904)* (Oxford, 1995), p. 816.
36 Alma Mahler, *Mahler: Memories and Letters*, p. 60.
37 Ibid., p. 75.
38 Mahler, *Letters to His Wife*, p. 129.
39 Alma Mahler, *Mahler: Memories and Letters*, p. 68.
40 Mahler-Werfel, *And the Bridge Is Love*, p. 32.
41 Edward F. Kravitt, 'Mahler's Dirges for His Death: February 24, 1901', *Musical Quarterly*, LXIV/3 (1978), p. 353.
42 Stuart Feder, 'Gustav Mahler, Dying', *International Review of Psycho-Analysis*, V/2 (1978), pp. 125–48.
43 Hilmes, *Malevolent Muse*, pp. 26–8.
44 Mahler-Werfel, *And the Bridge Is Love*, p. 18.
45 Mahler-Werfel, *Diaries*, p. 32, entry of 22 May 1898.
46 Ibid., p. 457.
47 Mahler-Werfel, *And the Bridge Is Love*, p. 27.
48 Steven E. Aschheim, 'Reflection, Projection, Distortion: The "Eastern Jew" in German-Jewish Culture', *Osteuropa*, LVIII/8–10 (2008), pp. 61–74.
49 Mahler-Werfel, *And the Bridge Is Love*, p. 27.
50 Mahler, *Letters to His Wife*, pp. 117–18.
51 Ibid., p. 284.

52 Stephen McClatchie, 'Mahler's Wagner', in *Mahler im Kontext/ Contextualizing Mahler*, ed. Erich Wolfgang Partsch and Morten Solvik (Vienna, 2011), p. 423.
53 Cited in Donald Mitchell, *Gustav Mahler: The Early Years*, revd and ed. Paul Banks and David Matthews (Woodbridge, 2003), p. 4.
54 Alma Mahler, *Mahler: Memories and Letters*, p. 127; Mahler-Werfel, *And the Bridge Is Love*, p. 38.
55 Hilmes, *Malevolent Muse*, pp. 62–3.
56 Alma Mahler, *Mahler: Memories and Letters*, p. 172.
57 Mahler-Werfel, *And the Bridge Is Love*, p. 52.
58 Henry-Louis de La Grange, *Gustav Mahler*, vol. IV: *A New Life Cut Short (1907–11)* (Oxford, 2008), p. 840.
59 Ibid.
60 Ibid., pp. 844–7.
61 Jonathan Carr, *The Real Mahler* (London, 1997), p. 107.
62 Alma Mahler, *Mahler: Memories and Letters*, p. 173.
63 La Grange, *A New Life Cut Short*, p. 862.
64 Hilmes, *Malevolent Muse*, p. 69.
65 Alma Mahler, *Mahler: Memories and Letters*, p. 176.
66 Mahler, *Letters to His Wife*, p. 384.
67 Peter Franklin, 'A Farewell, a Femme Fatale, and a Film: Three Awkward Moments in Twentieth-Century Music', in *Musical Meaning and Human Values*, ed. Keith Chapin and Lawrence Kramer (New York, 2009), pp. 150–69 (p. 153).
68 Stuart Feder, *Gustav Mahler: A Life in Crisis* (New Haven, CT, 2004), p. 197.
69 Ibid., pp. 204, 224.
70 La Grange, *Mahler: A New Life Cut Short*, p. 882.
71 Feder, *Gustav Mahler*, p. 206.
72 Ibid., pp. 227–9.
73 Ibid., p. 233.
74 Ibid., p. 238.
75 Mahler-Werfel, *And the Bridge Is Love*, p. 54.
76 Ibid., p. 55.
77 Ibid., pp. 12, 15.
78 Alma Mahler, *Mahler: Memories and Letters*, p. 175.
79 Feder, *Gustav Mahler*, pp. 81, 84, 237.
80 La Grange, *Mahler: A New Life Cut Short*, pp. 405, 835, 852, 864.
81 Joseph Horowitz, review of Henry-Louis de La Grange, *Gustav Mahler: A New Life Cut Short*, *Journal of the Society for American Music*, III/1 (2009), pp. 104–10.

82 Hilmes, *Malevolent Muse*, pp. 29–35.
83 Cate Haste, *Passionate Spirit: The Life of Alma Mahler* (New York, 2019).
84 Susanne Rode-Breymann, *Alma Mahler-Werfel: Muse, Gattin, Witwe* (Munich, 2014).
85 Nancy Newman, '#AlmaToo: The Art of Being Believed', *Journal of the American Musicological Society*, LXXV/1 (2022), pp. 39–79.
86 Eleonore Büning, 'Mahler und #MeToo', afterword to Franz Willnauer, *Frauen um Mahler* (Mainz, 2022), pp. 367–74.
87 La Grange, *Mahler: A New Life Cut Short*, pp. 854, 865.
88 Susan Filler, 'A Composer's Wife as Composer: The Songs of Alma Mahler', *Journal of Musicological Research*, IV/3–4 (1983), pp. 427–41 (p. 430).
89 Mahler-Werfel, *Diaries*, pp. 98–9, entry of 28 February 1899.
90 From the album *That Was the Year That Was* (1965), available at 'Tom Lehrer: Alma (concert live) (1965)', www.youtube.com, accessed 8 August 2024.
91 Diane Follet, 'Redeeming Alma: The Songs of Alma Mahler', *College Music Symposium*, XLIV (2004), pp. 28–42.
92 Hilmes, *Malevolent Muse*, p. 25.
93 *Frasier*, season 3, episode 8, 'The Last Time I Saw Maris', NBC, 28 November 1995. This would seem to be a quick change of taste by Frasier: two years earlier, in *Cheers*, series 11, he enthusiastically tells the barflies of his love for Mahler's Third Symphony.
94 Mahler, *Letters to His Wife*, p. 79.
95 Alma Mahler, *Mahler: Memories and Letters*, p. 91.
96 Ibid., p. 70.
97 Seth Monahan, '"I have tried to capture you . . .": Rethinking the "Alma" Theme from Mahler's Sixth Symphony', *Journal of the American Musicological Society*, LXIV/1 (2011), pp. 119–78.
98 Stephen Hefling, 'Aspects of Mahler's Late Style', in *Mahler and His World*, ed. Karen Painter (Princeton, NJ, 2002), pp. 199–224 (p. 215).
99 Mahler, *Letters to His Wife*, p. 346.
100 Feder, *Gustav Mahler*, p. 234.

6 The Late Gustav Mahler

1 Epigram for Alma Mahler-Werfel, *And the Bridge Is Love* (London, 1959).
2 Arthur Schopenhauer, *Parerga and Paralipomena*, vol. II, trans. E.F.J. Payne (Oxford, 1974), p. 279.

3 Pierre Boulez, 'La Biographie, pourquoi?', preface to Henry-Louis de La Grange, *Mahler* (Paris, 1979), pp. 2–3.
4 Richard Taruskin, *Oxford History of Western Music*, vol. IV: *The Early Twentieth Century* (Oxford, 2010).
5 Alma Mahler, *Gustav Mahler: Memories and Letters*, trans. Basil Creighton, ed. Donald Mitchell and Knud Martner, 4th edn with additional notes and commentaries (London, 1990).
6 Thomas Mann, *Pro and Contra Wagner*, trans. Allan Blunden (London, 1985), p. 92.
7 Stephen Johnson, *The Eighth: Mahler and the World in 1910* (London, 2022), p. 82. Webern's description comes in a letter written directly after the premiere. Two years later Webern played the celeste part in two performances of the Eighth in Vienna and Prague.
8 Bruno Walter, *Gustav Mahler*, trans. James Galston (New York, 1941), p. 58.
9 *Neue Freie Presse* (19 May 1911); Henry-Louis de La Grange, *Gustav Mahler*, vol. IV: *A New Life Cut Short (1907–11)* (Oxford, 2008), p. 1639.
10 Norman Lebrecht, ed., *Mahler Remembered* (New York, 1998), p. 306.
11 La Grange, *Mahler: A New Life Cut Short*, p. 1249.
12 Jens Malte Fischer, *Gustav Mahler*, trans. Stewart Spencer (New Haven, CT, 2011), p. 682.
13 Alma Mahler, *Mahler: Memories and Letters*, p. 201.
14 Ibid.
15 Theodor W. Adorno, 'Afterthoughts' (1961), in *Quasi una Fantasia*, trans. Rodney Livingstone (London, 1992), p. 110. Fischer says the sculptor Anton Sandig took the death mask; Fischer, *Gustav Mahler*, p. 684.
16 In 1912; Lebrecht, ed., *Mahler Remembered*, p. 314.
17 Knud Martner, ed., *Selected Letters of Gustav Mahler* (London, 1979), p. 25. No other source has been found for this remark.
18 'Gustav Mahler', *Der Merker* (March 1912); Lebrecht, ed., *Mahler Remembered*, pp. 315–16.
19 Julius Korngold, *Neue Freie Presse* (19 May 1911); trans. La Grange, *Mahler: A New Life Cut Short*, pp. 1638–9.
20 Natalie Bauer-Lechner, *Recollections of Gustav Mahler*, trans. Dika Newlin, ed. and annotated Peter Franklin (London, 1980), p. 76.
21 Robert Hirschfeld, *Wiener Zeitung* (20 May 1911); trans. in *Mahler and His World*, ed. Karen Painter (Princeton, NJ, 2002), pp. 344–7.
22 Paul Bekker, *Frankfurter Zeitung* (May 1911); trans. in *Mahler and His World*, ed. Painter, pp. 349–50.

23 Stephen Hefling, 'Aspects of Mahler's Late Style', in *Mahler and His World*, ed. Painter, p. 200.
24 La Grange, *A New Life Cut Short*, p. 1400.
25 Fischer, *Gustav Mahler*, p. 669.
26 La Grange, *Mahler: A New Life Cut Short*, p. 1232; my italics.
27 Donald Mitchell, *Gustav Mahler*, vol. III: *Songs and Symphonies of Life and Death* (Berkeley, CA, 1985), p. 430.
28 Martner, ed., *Selected Letters*, p. 329.
29 Karen Painter, 'On Creativity and Lateness' and Stanley Cavell, 'A Scale of Eternity: Gustav Mahler and the Autobiographical', in *Late Thoughts: Reflections on Artists and Composers at Work*, ed. Painter and Thomas Crow (Los Angeles, CA, 2006), pp. 1–11 (p. 1) and pp. 207–16 (p. 207).
30 Theodor W. Adorno, *Mahler: A Musical Physiognomy*, trans. Edmund Jephcott (Chicago, IL, 1992), p. 146.
31 Andrew Deruchie, 'Mahler's Farewell or The Earth's Song? Death, Orientalism and "Der Abschied"', *Austrian Studies*, XVII (2009), pp. 75–97.
32 Fischer, *Gustav Mahler*, p. 614.
33 Leonard Bernstein, *The Unanswered Question* (Cambridge, MA, 1976), p. 317.
34 La Grange, *Mahler: A New Life Cut Short*, p. 1411, n. 154.
35 Walter, *Gustav Mahler*, p. 124.
36 Vera Micznik, 'The Farewell Story of Mahler's Ninth Symphony', *19th-Century Music*, XX/2 (1996), pp. 144–66.
37 La Grange, *Mahler: A New Life Cut Short*, pp. 1400, 1449.
38 Adorno, *Mahler*, p. 147.
39 Richard Specht, *Gustav Mahler* (Berlin, 1913), trans. in Micznik, 'The Farewell Story', p. 146.
40 Joseph N. Straus, *Broken Beauty* (Oxford, 2018), p. 58.
41 Josef Bohuslav Foerster, *Der Pilger: Erinnerungen eines Musikers* (Prague, 1955), pp. 705–6; trans. in La Grange, *Mahler: A New Life Cut Short*, p. 1277.
42 Bauer-Lechner, *Recollections*, p. 44.
43 Foerster, *Der Pilger*, p. 706.
44 Jonathan Williams, *Mahler* (London, 1969), n.p.
45 Stephen Hefling, 'Siegfried Lipiner's "On the Elements of a Renewal of Religious Ideas in the Present"', in *Mahler im Kontext/Contextualizing Mahler*, ed. Erich Wolfgang Partsch and Morten Solvik (Vienna, 2011), pp. 91–114.
46 My translation.

Further Reading

Listed below are selected key English-language texts.

Adorno, Theodor W., *Mahler: A Musical Physiognomy*, trans. Edmund Jephcott (Chicago, IL, 1992)

Barham, Jeremy, ed., *The Cambridge Companion to Mahler* (Cambridge, 2007)

—, ed., *Perspectives on Gustav Mahler* (Aldershot, 2005)

Bauer-Lechner, Natalie, *Recollections of Gustav Mahler*, trans. Dika Newlin, ed. and annotated Peter Franklin (London, 1980)

Blaukopf, Herta, ed., *Mahler's Unknown Letters* (London, 1986)

Blaukopf, Kurt, ed., *Mahler: A Documentary Study* (London, 1976)

Cooke, Deryck, *Gustav Mahler: An Introduction to His Music* (London, 1980)

Feder, Stuart, *Gustav Mahler: A Life in Crisis* (New Haven, CT, 2004)

Fischer, Jens Malte, *Gustav Mahler*, trans. Stewart Spencer (New Haven, CT, 2011)

Franklin, Peter, *The Life of Mahler* (Cambridge, 1997)

Haste, Cate, *Passionate Spirit: The Life of Alma Mahler* (New York, 2019)

Hilmes, Oliver, *Malevolent Muse: The Life of Alma Mahler*, trans. Donald Arthur (Boston, MA, 2015)

Johnson, Julian, *Mahler's Voices* (Oxford, 2009)

Johnson, Stephen, *The Eighth: Mahler and the World in 1910* (London, 2022)

La Grange, Henry-Louis de, *Gustav Mahler*, vol. I: *The Arduous Road to Vienna (1860–1897)*, revd edn (Turnhout, 2020)

—, *Gustav Mahler. Vienna*, vol. II: *The Years of Challenge (1897–1904)* (Oxford, 1995)

—, *Gustav Mahler. Vienna*, vol. III: *Triumph and Disillusion (1904–1907)* (Oxford, 1999)

—, *Gustav Mahler*, vol. IV: *A New Life Cut Short (1907–11)* (Oxford, 2008)

Lebrecht, Norman, ed., *Mahler Remembered* (New York, 1998)

McClatchie, Stephen, trans. and ed., *The Mahler Family Letters* (Oxford, 2006)

Mahler, Alma, *Gustav Mahler: Memories and Letters*, trans. Basil Creighton, ed. Donald Mitchell and Knud Martner, 4th edn with additional notes and commentaries (London, 1990)
Mahler, Gustav, *Letters to His Wife*, trans. Antony Beaumont, ed. Henry-Louis de La Grange and Günther Weiss in collaboration with Knud Martner (London, 2004)
Mahler-Werfel, Alma, *And the Bridge Is Love* (London, 1959)
—, *Diaries, 1898–1902*, selected and trans. Antony Beaumont, ed. Beaumont and Susanne Rode-Breymann (London, 1998)
Martner, Knud, ed., *Selected Letters of Gustav Mahler* (London, 1979)
Mitchell, Donald, *Gustav Mahler*, vol. III: *Songs and Symphonies of Life and Death* (Berkeley, CA, 1985)
—, *Gustav Mahler: The Early Years*, revd and ed. Paul Banks and David Matthews (Woodbridge, 2003)
—, *Gustav Mahler: The Wunderhorn Years. Chronicles and Commentaries*, 2nd edn (Woodbridge, 2005)
Niekerk, Carl, *Reading Mahler: German Culture and Jewish Identity in Fin-de-Siècle Vienna* (Rochester, NY, 2010)
Painter, Karen, ed., *Mahler and His World* (Princeton, NJ, 2002)
Peattie, Thomas, *Gustav Mahler's Symphonic Landscapes* (Cambridge, 2015)
Reilly, Edward R., *Gustav Mahler and Guido Adler: Records of a Friendship* (Cambridge, 1982)
Roman, Zoltan, *Gustav Mahler's American Years, 1907–11: A Documentary History* (New York, 1989)
Stefan, Paul, *Gustav Mahler: A Study of His Personality and Work*, trans. T. E. Clark (New York, 1913)
Stoll Knecht, Anna, *Mahler's Seventh Symphony* (Oxford, 2010)
Walter, Bruno, *Gustav Mahler*, trans. James Galston (New York, 1941)

Acknowledgements

I will not attempt to name all my intellectual debts, but no serious biography of Mahler would be possible without the preceding, herculean work of Henry-Louis de La Grange and Donald Mitchell. And there are some to whom I owe more personal thanks, for the way their assistance, conversations and inspirations over many years have, sometimes in small yet significantly nuanced ways, other times in game-changing manner, influenced and informed my understanding of Mahler, his contexts and his music: Jeremy Barham, Leah Batstone, Seth Brodsky, Federico Celestini, Keith Chapin, John Deathridge, Petr Dvořák, (the late) Stuart Feder, Peter Franklin, Daniel Grimley, (the late) Hans Werner Henze, Julian Johnson, Matthew Mugmon, Eftychia Papanikolaou, Milijana Pavlovic, Thomas Peattie, Lóránt Péteri, Morten Solvik, Michael Spitzer, Peter Tregear and Philip Vaughan.

'Wide-ranging, richly detailed and deeply thoughtful, this is also a very readable and enjoyable book. Downes doesn't just relate the familiar stories, he questions them and asks what we should make today of the idea that Mahler's music tells the story of his life.'
– Julian Johnson, author of *Mahler's Voices*

'"Full of energy and subtle understanding", this is a Mahler biography for the twenty-first century. Stephen Downes weaves an intricate tapestry of the composer's life, loves, ideas and music that is as accessibly readable as it is intellectually and culturally stimulating.'
– Jeremy Barham, author of *Rethinking Mahler*

Gustav Mahler's status as an icon of *fin-de-siècle* Viennese music is assured, with his works now staples of the concert repertoire. His life story has been told in numerous biographies, films and novels, yet he remains an ambiguous, provocative figure. Mahler was a composer who challenged musical form and style but identified with German Enlightenment and Romantic culture, disliking many contemporary artistic trends. He was a Jewish conductor who reached the pinnacle of his profession in antisemitic Vienna. He was supposedly haunted by death, embroiled in a torrid marriage, and his brief meeting with Freud has spurred posthumous psychoanalytical speculations. This book, reflecting the latest research, constructs a fresh interpretation of Mahler's music in relation to his life.

Stephen Downes is Professor of Music at Royal Holloway, University of London. His books include *Music and Sentimentalism in the Nineteenth and Twentieth Centuries* (2021).

With 32 illustrations

ISBN 978-1-83639-030-5
9 781836 390305 >
BIOGRAPHY/MUSIC

Reaktion Books Ltd
www.reaktionbooks.co.uk

CRITICAL LIVES

Cover: Gustav Mahler, 1893. Album/Alamy Stock Photo.